The Hiker's Guide
to **COLORADO**

Caryn and Peter Boddie

The Hiker's Guide
to **COLORADO**

Library of Congress Catalog Card Number 84-80091

ISBN 0-934318-36-0

Falcon Press Publishing Co., Inc.
P.O. Box 1718
Helena, MT 59624

Edited by Vito Zdanys.
Maps drafted by Louis Coburn.
Photos by authors except as noted.
Cover Photo: Spencer Swanger/Tom Stack & Associates

First Printing: March 1984
Second Printing: August 1985
Third Printing: July 1986
Fourth Printing: February 1988
Fifth Printing: March 1989

Dedicated
to
Crystal Rose

Contents

The Plateaus

Afterword

Resources

Acknowledgments

We have a lot of people to thank. At the top of the list is our publisher, Bill Schneider. Next, special thanks go to *all* the writers and photographers—too numerous to mention here. You will find their names at the ends of their respective hike descriptions and beneath their photos throughout the book. If you run into these folks on the trail sometime, *you* might also thank them.

Thanks go as well to employees of the U.S. Forest Service, National Park Service, Bureau of Land Management, and the Divisions of Parks and Recreation in several cities along the Front Range.

The American Wilderness Alliance and Colorado Mountain Club are two organizations we would like to acknowledge. To Clif Merritt, Executive Director of the Alliance, goes our gratitude not only for his contribution of the informative afterword to this book, but for his unflagging work of some twenty years in wilderness conservation. Thanks also go to the members of the Colorado Mountain Club in various parts of the state who provided us with descriptions and photographs. These are two worthwhile organizations: contact their main offices for membership information (see Appendix I).

We would be remiss if we did not thank Tim and Janet Shangraw for the loan of their word processor and Grandmother Elizabeth Frye for the regular babysitting stints that provided us with time to write, edit, work in the darkroom, and think.

Finally, we would like to thank our families, the Boddies and the Fryes, for introducing us to our wilderness heritage—and to hiking. The times we spent in the backcountry as children—Caryn in the Colorado mountains, Peter in the woods of Connecticut—will always be remembered fondly and serve as inspiration for us to pass those good times on to our daughter, Crystal, the rest of her generation, and the generations to come.—*Caryn and Peter Boddie*

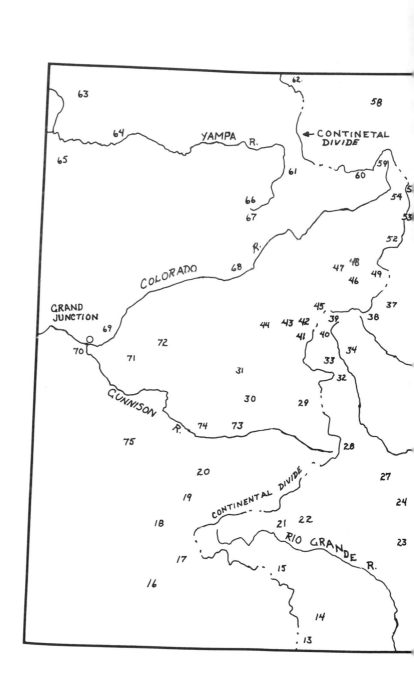

Hikes Throughout Colorado

Use this general map to locate the hikes—by
number—in the table of contents. More detailed
maps accompany the descriptions of the hikes.

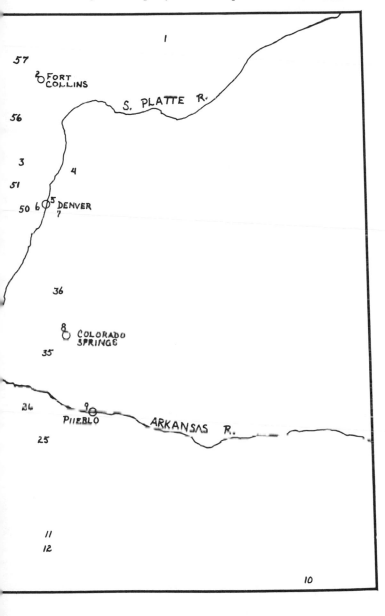

Hiking in Colorado: An Introduction

There's no experience quite like that of heading off on a new hiking adventure; nothing like discovering the beauty and character of country you've never seen before. That's what *The Hiker's Guide to Colorado* is all about.

In Colorado, the opportunities for opening your eyes on new country are unlimited—the regions and terrains of this state are that diverse. You may have climbed a fourteener or fished a high lake, but never watched a sunrise from the plains, taken advantage of the trail systems that run near and through our Front Range cities, or hiked along the bottom of a sandstone canyon. The purpose of this book is to aid you in discovering ALL of Colorado.

Of course we couldn't cover every trail in the state. However, we have gathered together information on 75 hikes representative of its different regions and terrains. If you fall in love with one area in particular, you can then turn to one of the many good regional guides available for a more indepth look—or simply go out and explore on your own.

In addition to taking you to a variety of places in Colorado, it is also our purpose to impart the importance of responsible use of those places. We believe strongly in minimal impact hiking and camping and have worked with federal and state agencies in selecting many of the trails included in this guide, not wanting to publicize those that are overused. But, no trail can sustain careless use. You will find information herein to help you touch the land lightly; to enjoy but not harm it.

We have also tried to include hiking experiences to suit the veteran hiker and beginner, backpacker and day hiker, and hope that our descriptions will provide a variety of information on flora, fauna, geology and history—whatever a particular writer found of interest on his or her trip through the area.

In reading these preliminary chapters, you will find information to help you

Early Hikers. Colorado Historical Society photo.

organize your trip, to make it a safe one, and to help you assist in preserving wilderness in Colorado.

Our resource section will direct you to hiking and conservation organizations, to books of interest to hikers, to sources for USGS topographic maps, and to the agencies that care for our trails and wild lands.

It's our hope that this book will help you discover and appreciate Colorado through hiking. Have fun!

Plains, Mountains and Plateaus: A Variety of Wild Places

From the eastern plains to the mountain ranges of central Colorado and on to the plateau and canyon country, the intricate workings of natural forces have combined to paint a landscape nearly infinite in its variety. An understanding of these workings and their resulting landforms and life zones will serve to enhance any hiker's enjoyment and appreciation of Colorado's wild places.

The following information is meant as a sort of primer to the natural history of Colorado with brief discussions of geology and ecology. Further information can be obtained through numerous field guides (birds, mammals, wildflowers, trees, geology, etc.). Additional information resources are available through libraries and museums. Many local conservation groups and government land agencies conduct guided hikes and have meetings where speakers may discuss a variety of natural history topics. The last chapter of this book, Resources, will direct you to many of these additional sources of information.

GEOLOGY

Colorado occupies portions of three physiographic provinces: the Great Plains, the Southern Rocky Mountains and the Colorado Plateaus. The landforms included in these large-scale divisons govern not only the topography of Colorado, but have largely determined the patterns of weather, plant and animal life, and human settlement in the state.

The Great Plains occupy approximately the eastern two-fifths of Colorado. They rise gently from about 3,500 feet at the eastern border of the state to about 5,000 feet at the foothills. The eastern plains are underlaid by nearly flat-lying sedimentary rocks which rise gently towards the west and are steeply upturned along the line of contact with the mountains. Most of the rocks exposed at the surface are young geologically, and contain many mammal fossils including those of ancestors of the horse and camel. The landscape of the Great Plains varies from featureless prairie to rolling hills over most of its area. In some sections, however, differential erosion of the sedimentary rocks has produced spectacular erosional remnants such as the Pawnee Buttes and deep canyons such as that of the Purgatoire River.

Butterfly on Rabbitbrush in the Transition—
Upper Sonoran Zone of western Colorado

The Rocky Mountains, for which Colorado is most well known, occupy the central and west central portions of the state. This lofty backbone of the continent, with numerous peaks reaching to more than 14,000 feet in elevation, is the source of four major rivers: the Colorado, the Rio Grande, the Arkansas, and the Platte.

The Colorado Rockies are composed of several (primarily north-south trending) ranges interrupted by broad open basins or "parks." The mountain ranges and parks are the result of complex folding and faulting which occurred as the entire region uplifted. This complexity combined with variations in the composition of the exposed rocks, makes each of Colorado's ranges unique. For example, the San Juan Mountains in the southwest are composed largely of volcanic breccias and lavas, while the Mosquito and Sangre de Cristo Ranges are composed primarily of Paleozoic sedimentary rocks. In contrast, along most of the Front Range sedimentary rocks have been removed by erosion, exposing the ancient metamorphic and igneous rocks of the mountain core. Acting upon this complex of geologic structure and composition, the forces of erosion have sculpted the mountains of Colorado into the myriad forms we see today. Most notable of these forces has been glaciation, which has been responsible for the impressive peaks and ridges, wide U-shaped valleys and numerous lakes which characterize the higher ranges of the state.

The Colorado Plateaus occupy the western portion of Colorado. This area is characterized by a series of uplifted plateaus and moderately dipping anticlines, synclines and monoclines. These structures are dissected by many canyons and broad valleys formed by tributaries to the Colorado River. The exposed rocks are predominately sedimentary, ranging in age from recent river deposits back to the Cambrian age. In a few places, such as the Black Canyon of the Gunnison, the underlying ancient Precambrian metamorphic rocks are exposed. This incredible range in the character of rock formations over western Colorado has provided an infinitely varied source of material upon which the forces of erosion have acted. These erosional forces have stripped away the less resistant rocks leaving the resistant layers to form alternating flat mesas and cliffs. Dissecting these uplands are numerous deep canyons and broad valleys. The result is a spectacular variation in scenery providing both far-reaching vistas and intricate erosional features throughout western Colorado.

ECOLOGY

Spread out across the framework of Colorado's landforms is an equally varied pattern of plant and animal life. Colorado displays ecological life zones ranging from the desert to the arctic, often over the space of only a few miles. These life zones are determined primarily by climatic factors, which in turn are governed largely by Colorado's topography. Two factors are dominant in this climatic-topographic relationship: elevation and the orientation to mountain barriers. Elevation of the land surface in Colorado varies by more than two miles from about 3,500 feet on the state's eastern boundary to more than 14,000 feet at the summits of several mountain peaks. The effects on temperature of this elevation range are similar to those associated with traveling a distance north from southern Colorado to above the Arctic Circle.

The relationship between precipitation and elevation is just the opposite—precipitation increases with elevation. The orientation of the mountains affects this pattern by creating a rain shadow on the leeward side. Because storm systems move predominantly from west to east across Colorado, the western slopes of the mountains generally receive greater precipitation than the eastern sides. This pattern may be observed for the length of the Continental Divide and, more locally, at individual ranges and high plateaus. In addition, there is a difference between north and south-facing slopes, with the latter receiving greater solar radiation, and being consequently drier.

In general, the types of plant and animal communities found in Colorado closely follow these large and small scale climatic patterns. Biologists and ecologists have categorized the plant and animal life of Colorado into several characteristic life zones. They are briefly described below, but you can obtain a far wider knowledge of them by visiting the Walter C. Mead Ecological Hall at the Denver Museum of Natural History (see Appendix IV).

Beginning at the eastern border of Colorado, we find the upper Sonoran Life Zone—the Colorado plains—from 3,500 to 5,500 feet in elevation. Characterized by short grass prairie, warm canyons, prairie ponds, marshes, sand hills and bluffs, this life zone features many species of grasses, as well as cactus, yucca, pinyon and juniper. It is home to many species of birds, including three of herons and Colorado's state bird, the lark bunting.

To the west at 5,500 to 8,000 feet is the Transistion-Upper Sonoran Zone, the Foothills, where ponderosa pine, Douglas fir, and Rocky Mountain juniper grow on rolling hills. Blue spruce, alder, narrow-leaf cottonwood, birch and willows grow along the streams. Animal and plant life here ranges from that of the plains to that of the higher coniferous forests—a true transition zone.

Further to the west and above the Transition Zone is the Boreal Region and within it three distinct life zones: the Canadian (8,000 to 11,000 feet), the Hudsonian (timberline—11,000 to 11,500 feet) and the Arctic-Alpine above timberline. These are the mountains of Colorado.

The Canadian Zone includes, at lower elevations lodgepole, pine, aspen, Douglas fir, and ponderosa. At higher elevations you will recognize Engelmann spruce, subalpine fir, white fir, and limber pine. A plethora of wildflowers bloom in this zone during the spring and summer, including Indian paintbrush, columbine, golden banner, fairy slipper, wild iris and many, many more species.

The Hudsonian Zone at timberline is a narrow zone, characterized by bristlecone pine, Englemann spruce, and subalpine fir, twisted into odd shapes by high winds and heavy snows.

The Arctic-Alpine Zone is like the life zones of the Far North: a delicate, yet harsh ecosystem of treeless alpine tundra and sparse vegetation, but with beautiful displays of wildflowers. Here small mammals and birds make their homes in the alpine meadows and boulder fields.

Beyond the mountains and on to the western border of Colorado, we come down to another Transition Zone at some 7,500 feet, characterized as typical sagebrush country: a cool shrub habitat.

Study of these life zones and the plant and animal life within them could last a lifetime. The average hiker just needs to know generally of their existence. If you find these subjects interesting, carry along field guides on some of your hikes, learn to know the names (scientific and common) of trees, birds, flowers and animals, as well as the geology of the areas you travel through. It's a lot of fun and is a good way to add to your knowledge of the State of Colorado.

Our Archaeological Resources

Colorado is a state rich not only for natural history, but in human history as well. The earliest people arrived on the eastern plains some 12,000 years ago as small hunting and gathering bands, probably migrating across the land bridge from Asia. These people hunted many now extinct large mammals in a boreal forest much cooler and moister than today's. Evidence of their lifestyle includes flakes of chert (remnants of the manufacturing of weapons and butchering tools) and fire hearths in old terrace arroyo walls, in sand dunes, and along the margins of ancient playa lakes.

Studies of soil and plant pollen indicate that the climate of Colorado gradually moderated until about 6,000 years ago. Archaeological evidence from caves and river terraces along the west slope indicates that the people responded to this climatic change by adjusting to more local ecological settings with a greater emphasis on gathering and collecting. The drier climate during this period was conducive to the preservation of more perishable materials such as sandals, wooden dart throwers and bone sewing implements. These types of artifacts have been found at habitation sites along the Gunnison, Colorado, and White Rivers.

By 2,000 years ago and until about A.D. 1300, the people inhabiting southwestern Colorado developed remarkably efficient capabilities for using regionally available resources. Agriculture and village life appeared on the highland plateau west of the San Juan and south of the LaPlata Mountains. Dwellings ranging from single room structures to multiple room pueblos have been identified at sites from Chimney Rock to Mancos Canyon, including the well known ruins at Mesa Verde. Evidence of irrigation, basket and pottery manufacturing, use of the bow and arrow and marked reliance on ceremonialism testify to the cultural sophistication achieved during this period.

Other areas of Colorado have provided a wide variety of natural resources to all prehistoric inhabitants, as well. Middle and South Parks were quarried for chert well prior to 6,000 years ago. Various mountain passes and subalpine pastures were seasonally exploited for game and edible plants. The San Luis Valley provided an opportunity for hunting waterfowl until modern agricultural needs affected the closed-basin water table.

The value of the archaeological evidence left by these peoples is enormous. Correct interpretation of the diverse Indian heritage of Colorado is dependent on evaluating remaining artifacts in their Plains, Great Basin, Plateau, and Intermontane contexts. Casual removal of this evidence by interested hikers and other backcountry visitors reduces the historic value of each site and gradually destroys a fragile cultural resource that is not renewable.

When you are hiking, remember that you are an essential part of a team including federal and state land management personnel working to conserve archaeological sites in Colorado. The Archaeological Resources Protection Act and State Antiquities Act encourage reporting of discovered sites to professional land managers. If you discover any prehistoric or historic sites on federal lands, report them to the appropriate land management personnel. Archaeological sites on land under state jurisdiction should be reported to the State Archaeologist in Denver. Leave the "souvenirs" for those who'll come after you to see and enjoy the intriguing archaeology of Colorado.

If you would like to read more about Colorado archaeology, *The Archaeology of Colorado* by E. Steve Cassells (Johnson Books) provides a good overview. A visit to the Denver Museum of Natural History and University of Colorado Museum would be of interest as well.—*Emerson Pearson*

Vandalized pictographs in southeastern Colorado.

Hiking Techniques and Equipment

Touching the Land Lightly

It's a special feeling to hike through pristine wilderness, imagining you're the first human being who's ever been there. It's also very disheartening to come upon evidence of other humans—unless that evidence is historic or prehistoric.

Colorado's backcountry has the capacity to handle the ever increasing number of users it will see in the coming years, but only if those users abandon the outdated ethics of past generations of hikers who left fire rings, dug trenches around tents, and set up camp near lakes and streams. As the size of our wilderness shrinks and the number of backcountry users multiplies, we must follow a new code of backcountry ethics based on one phrase: leave a minimum impact on any area you visit. The following tips will help you to develop good backcountry manners based on that idea.

When on the Trail:

● Stay on the trail. Cutting switchbacks and walking alongside trails causes erosion. On the tundra and in the desert, proceed with care to protect these fragile environments.

● Leave "souvenirs" for the next hiker to see, whether they be wildflowers or indian artifacts.

● Watch wildlife from a distance.

● If hiking with a dog, keep it under control at all times.

● Be considerate of other hikers when you meet them on the trail; be careful not to disturb the solitude and wilderness experience they may be seeking.

While camping:

● Choose a site well away from trails and lakes (at least 200 feet). This practice will both protect the water quality of high country lakes and streams, and give you and others seclusion, increasing everyone's enjoyment of the area.

● Try to camp below timberline. Alpine areas are delicate and require special care. Often, it's only a short hike to a good campsite below timberline.

● Do not build any structures at your campsite.

● Use a gas stove for cooking, if possible. But, if you do have a fire, keep it small. Dig out the native vegetation and topsoil and set it aside. *Don't build a fire ring with rocks.* When breaking camp, douse the fire thoroughly, scattering or burying the cold ashes. Replace with native soil and vegetation.

● Be careful with all waste. Bury human wastes at least six inches deep, 200 feet from water. Pack out all trash.

● Waste water from boiling foods should be poured around the perimeter of the fire: this keeps the fire from spreading and protects the natural vegetation as well. Wash dishes and clothing well away from streams and lakes and carefully discard dish water, perhaps in a sump hole to be covered with soil later. If you use soap, carry water at least 200 feet from a water source and wash there.

Strictly follow the pack-in, pack-out rule and leave your campsites and the backcountry, in general, as you found it. You will then be doing your part to protect wilderness for those who'll follow.

Dress and Equipment for Backcountry Travel

Nothing ruins a hiking or backpacking trip faster than improper clothing and equipment. Here are some time tested ideas on proper clothing and equipment for backcountry travel:

The most important thing to keep in mind is to dress in layers. Three layers of clothing, at least, will allow you to adapt to weather conditions as they change. The first layer, next to your skin, should provide some ventilation, the next—of wool or down—should insulate. The third should be wind and waterproof. How much money you spend on dressing for the outdoors is really up to you. You can buy the most expensive gear from your local sports store, or make do with military surplus. Just make sure the clothes you take with you will keep you comfortable, warm and dry, in any kind of weather.

Another essential item of clothing is a wool hat—if you'll be hiking in the high country. It is well known that a large percentage of body heat is lost during cold weather when a hat isn't worn so take one with you (and some mittens or gloves). It's good protection against hypothermia.

Probably the most important piece of equipment that you'll wear is your boots: pick them carefully. Be prepared to spend a few extra dollars. The old adage that you get what you pay for definitely applies. Spending extra time picking out your boots will pay off in the long run.

Shop in a reputable store and take the time to ask the sales people some questions. Ask about the "welt" of the boot; the manner in which the leather upper part of the boot is attached to the sole. Norwegian welting lends itself to a heavier boot; Littleway to a lighter boot (these are your best bets). Ask about seams, making sure your boots won't be causing pressure points on your feet. Look for quality boots made in one piece, with only one side or back seam. Look also for boots with a firm heel counter, box toe and arch for good support and protection and make sure you'll have proper ankle support for the kind of hiking you'll be doing. Inspect the backstay, which covers the seam on the back of the boot. It should be narrow. Finally, consider whether the boots are too heavy or too light for the type of hiking you plan to be doing and wear them around a bit. Make sure the fit is right!

After you've chosen your boots, take good care of them! Ask your sales person how.

Now that you're clothed and booted, let's take a look at the other equipment you'll want to take with you. If you're day hiking, you won't need too much. The essentials are a daypack for carrying your gear, a water bottle—with water, sunglasses, and sunscreen for protection from Colorado's high altitude ultraviolet radiation, a map and compass, and your emergency gear: matches and a small candle, a pocket knife, high energy food such as hard candy, dried fruits or nuts, a first aid kit and survival kit (see Chapter Three, Backcountry Safety).

If you are backpacking, you'll need to take all these things plus some others. To begin with you'll need a good sleeping bag—again take care to select the

Proper clothing is important for comfortable hiking.
Colorado Historical Society photo

All hikers should know how to use a topographic map.

bag that best fits your needs. Most backpackers prefer a bag that will take them through three seasons—all but winter—with a high loft and a shell of rip-stop nylon, which is durable and also "breathes" well. Check the stitching on the sleeping bag you plan to buy: stitches should be even and there should not be less than ten of them to an inch.

Next, you'll want a lightweight tent. There are so many new shapes and sizes of tents on the market these days that it shouldn't be hard for you to find one to suit your needs. Just decide whether you'll be using the tent in humid or arid environments—humid and you'll need room to store gear when it rains and good ventilation; arid and you'll need less room, but still want good ventilation. In any case, you'll want good mosquito netting and a tent that will withstand occasional downpours and heavy winds. Again, you have a wide variety of price ranges to choose from—and, once more, you get what you pay for. Just remember, when it's raining or blowing out there, you'll want a tent that will keep you dry and won't fall down in the middle of the night.

Packs are another item for backpackers. Once more, take the time to find one that fits and suits your anticipated needs. There are many types of packs on the market today with internal or external frames and a variety of pockets, straps, and other features. Get a good sales person to help you find the pack for you. Then wear it around for while with some weight in it, and make sure it's what you need.

One of the best ways to find the equipment you like best is to rent for an outing or two. You may save quite a bit of money by not buying before you really know what you want.

Beyond the clothing and equipment listed above, what you take on your hiking and backpacking outings is up to you. Just keep in mind your own comfort and safety in the wilderness and consult the checklist in Appendix VI before you go to make sure you have everything you need *and* want to take.

About the Maps

The maps which accompany each of the hikes have been prepared from United States Geological Survey (USGS) or National Forest maps. Each map is accompanied by a small map of Colorado indicating the location of the hike in the state. There is also a legend, a north-south directional indicator, and the scale.

While these maps are up-to-date, you should also take along the appropriate USGS topographic map(s) on more difficult hikes. (See Appendix V for outlets around the state.) The U.S. Forest Service maps are also helpful, offering an excellent overview of an entire national forest. The appropriate maps for each hike are listed in the introductory information prior to each hike description.

If you are not used to reading maps and not familiar with topographic maps, we would suggest that you set out on one of the easier hikes with a national forest map, topo map, compass and the book map and learn how to use all of them. Then when you really need a map you'll know how to use it. We also suggest consulting with the appropriate land management agency before your hike if you must drive to the trailhead on a low-grade road, particularly after bad weather.

Wild Rose

Making It A Safe Trip

Backcountry Safety

The history books are full of stories of men who ventured into the wilds of Colorado unprepared and overconfident only to meet with a less than pleasant end or, if they were lucky, to be rescued by wiser travelers. Safety advice can be never ending—we won't overdo it—but to make your hiking trips safe and enjoyable, follow these tips.

It's been said often enough, but it bears repeating: *be prepared:*
- Travel with the proper equipment to suit the climate, altitude and any weather you might encounter (see equipment).
- Dress in layers you can put on and take off with changes in the weather.
- Carry a first aid kit, topo map, and compass on more difficult hikes—and know how to use them. Also, take along matches and some high energy food. A space blanket is also a good thing to have in case of emergency (see checklist).

BE SMART:
- Don't underestimate the power of nature. Know how to read and interpret the weather and watch it carefully. You don't want to find yourself atop a high ridge in the middle of an electrical storm, in a gully during a flash flood, or at a high altitude during a snow storm.
- Know how to react to emergency situations. Take a first-aid course.
- Listen to your body. Learn the symptoms of hypothermia (see hypothermia) and guard against fatigue.

BE CAUTIOUS:
- In general, don't take unnecessary risks by glissading down steep snowfields with cliffs or boulders below, climbing rock faces without ropes, jumping ravines or canyons, or wading across swift mountain streams.
- Always file a "flight plan" with someone before you leave, telling them

where you're going and when you'll return.

• Do not drink the water unless you are positive it is safe to do so. Boil or chemically treat it. Become familiar with Giardia and the illness it causes—giardiasis (see Water).

• Avoid hiking alone.

• When hiking in a group, gear your pace to the slowest member and don't push on to a destination if a group member is really not up to do. Don't split up.

• Follow your topo map from the beginning of your hike and there is little chance you'll become lost.

• If you do become lost, don't panic. Sit down and relax, consult your map and compass. Thousands of hikers have spent unplanned nights in the wilderness and if you followed the rules and left word with someone of your whereabouts and expected return, they'll soon be searching for you. In the meantime, find shelter for yourself and stay put. (Children are taught these days to "hug a tree"—good advice for adults, too.)

SURVIVAL KIT

Compass, whistle, matches in waterproof container, candle, surgical tubing, emergency fishing gear, 60 feet of 6-pound line, 6 hooks, 6 lead shots, and 6 trout flies, safety pins, copper wire, signal mirror, fire starter, aluminum foil, water purification tables, space blanket and flare.

FIRST AID KIT

Sewing needle, snake bite kit, 12 aspirin, antibacterial ointment, 2 antiseptic swabs, 2 butterfly bandages, adhesive tape, 4 adhesive strips, 4 gauze pads, 2 triangular bandages, 12 codeine tablets, 2 inflatable splits, moleskin, 1 roll of 3-inch gauze and lightweight first aid instructions.

View from near the summit of Saint Vrain Mountain of Long's Peak and Pagoda Mountain. Norm Nielsen photo.

Hypothermia and Other Hazards

Be aware of the danger of hypothermia—subnormal temperature of the body. Lowering of internal temperature leads to mental and physical collapse.

Hypothermia is caused by exposure to cold, and it is aggravated by wetness, wind, and exhaustion. It is the number one killer of outdoor recreationists.

The first step is exposure and exhaustion. The moment you begin to lose heat faster than your body produces it, you are undergoing exposure. Two things happen:

You exercise to stay warm and your body makes involuntary adjustments to preserve normal temperature in the vital organs. Both responses drain your energy reserves. The only way to stop the drain is to reduce the degree of exposure.

The second step is hypothermia. If exposure continues until your energy reserves are exhausted, cold reaches the brain, depriving you of judgment and reasoning power. You will not be aware that this is happening. You will lose control of your hands. This is hypothermia. Your internal temperature is sliding downward. Without treatment, this slide leads to stupor, collapse, and death.

To defend against hypothermia, stay dry. When clothes get wet, they lose about 90 percent of their insulating value. Wool loses heat; cotton, down and some synthetics lose more.

Choose rainclothes that cover the head, neck, body and legs, and provide good protection against wind driven rain.

Understand cold. Most hypothermia cases develop in air temperature between 30 and 50 degrees Fahrenheit.

If your party is exposed to wind, cold, and wet, think hypothermia. Watch yourself and others for these symptoms: uncontrollable fits of shivering; vague, slow, slurred speech; memory lapses; incoherence; immobile, fumbling hands; frequent stumbling, lurching gait; drowsiness (to sleep is to die); apparent exhaustion; and inability to get up after a rest.

When a member of your party has hypothermia, he/she may deny any problem. Believe the symptoms, not the victim. Even mild symptoms demand treatment.

- Get the victim out of the wind and rain.
- Strip off all wet clothes.
- If the victim is only mildly impaired, give warm drinks. Get the person into warm clothes and a warm sleeping bag. Well-wrapped, warm (not hot) rocks or canteens will help.
- If the victim is badly impaired, attempt to keep him/her awake. Put the victim in a sleeping bag with another person—both stripped. If you have a double bag, put the victim between two warm people.
- Build a fire to warm the camp.—*U.S. Forest Service*

Water: To Drink or Not to Drink?

There are few backpacking pleasures that can top a cool drink from a high country lake or stream. Whether on a day hike close to a large metropolitan area or miles into the backcountry, the refreshing sip along the trail is a tradition.

Unfortunately, that cool sip of water from a cold mountain stream may be hazardous to your health.

The most common problem is a waterborne parasite called *Giardia Lamblia*, an invisible protozoan which, when ingested, can have results far from inconsequential. *Giardia* is now reported as being in epidemic proportions in Colorado.

The illness (called giardiasis, "beaver fever," or "backpacker's diarrhea") is caused by the ingestion of the dormant cyst form of the protozoan. These cysts can survive in cold (40F) streams for up to three months and can be spread by the droppings of dogs, cats, horses, cattle, beavers, rabbits, marmots, ground squirrels, elk, and especially people.

The cysts are activated in the small intestine of the host, changing into the reproductive trophozoite stage, which attaches to the wall of the intestine. Symptoms may appear from within several days to three weeks after ingestion of the cysts and are characterized by severe diarrhea, weight loss, "rotten egg" belches, fatigues, and cramps. Apparently some people are "carriers" of giardiasis and may have only very mild symptoms of the disease.

If you suspect you have the disease, see your doctor immediately. Giardiasis must be treated by a doctor. Quinacrine and metonidazole (Flagl) are most often used in treatment. Both have unpleasant side effects.

The only thing worse than coming down with giardiasis after a trip into the backcountry is coming down with it *during* a trip in the backcountry. There is little you can do, except try to get to a physician as best you can. You probably won't feel like eating anything, but you should avoid foods such as dairy products (milk, cheese, etc.) which may only worsen your discomfort. It is important to drink plenty of fluids, in order to lessen the dehydrating effects of the illness. Also, stomach coating medicines such as Peptobismol and Milk of Magnesia may calm (but not cure) the intestinal cramps and allow you to hike out to civilization.

How can you prevent the spread of this nasty protozoan? By practicing good sanitary habits in the wilderness. Studies done in Colorado indicate that backpackers may be the most common cause of the spread of *Giardia*, because of improper human waste disposal. Bury feces at least 200 feet away from any waterway and cover them with six inches of organic soil to aid in decomposition. If you travel with dogs or horses, keep them out of streams and lakes as much as possible.

The *Giardia* cyst is a hardy little bugger, difficult to kill in the water. Halazone and chlorine don't work against it, and iodine (besides being dangerous in itself) will kill only 90-95% of all cysts. Your best bet is to boil water for at least one minute—and longer, especially if above 6,000 since water's boiling temperature decreases with altitude. This may prove impractical on longer trips, where you just can't carry enough fuel. Look for springs which can supply fresh, uncontaminated ground water in some areas.

The ultimate solution appears to be water purifying kits just coming onto the market. Designed for travelling in foreign countries where contaminated water is a problem, these water purifying kits weigh between four ounces and two pounds. *Giardia* cysts are removed by a resin column or celluloid filter. The kits' major drawback appears to be the incredibly slow rate water passes through the filters, as slow as a quart every twelve minutes.

Improvements in these kits is sure to come as the seriousness of the *Giardia* problem becomes more widely known. Until some better solution is devised, boil your water, or take your chances, and remember to keep a clean camp.

River bottom flora.

Altitude or Mountain Sickness

It takes two to three days to acclimate to Colorado's high altitudes, particularly if you are coming from sea level. You may experience what is called altitude or mountain sickness while hiking if you do not allow time for acclimation. This condition is cause by a lack of oxygen at high altitude, resulting in a general "sick all over" feeling.

You may notice that you or someone in your party is experiencing nausea, dizziness, headache, and loss of appetite.

- Stop and rest.
- Go slower.
- Have the victim drink plenty of water (making sure he/she is also getting enough sodium, either in food or tablets).
- Have the victim eat high energy foods.

If these treatments don't help after a period of time, the only option is to go to a lower elevation where there is more oxygen.

Marmot. Colorado Division of Wildlife.

The Hikes

The Eastern Plains and Front Range Cities

The plains of Colorado are the state's forgotten country: wild and intricate, with a subtle beauty often lost on hikers used to mountain landscapes.

There's a lot to discover east of the Front Range, from wildflowers that bloom in a short, vibrant burst of color each spring to pictographs—Indian history recorded on the land itself—to a feeling of unlimited space the like of which you won't feel in many other places.

Colorado's Front Range cities—Fort Collins, Boulder, Denver, Colorado Springs, and Pueblo—also offer many unique hiking experiences. You won't find wilderness here, but you will discover some getaway places close to, or within these cities: good trails to take advantage of when you can't get away for the weekend.

We hope the following hikes will help you discover some of these overlooked places.

1 Pawnee Buttes

General Description: A short day hike or overnighter in the short-grass prairie to the Pawnee Buttes.

General location: 40 miles northeast of Greeley.

Maps: Grover SE and Pawnee Buttes USGS quads; Pawnee National Grassland Map.

Degree of difficulty: Easy.

Length: 2 miles one way.

Elevations: 5,200 to 5,420 feet.

Special Attractions: A unique hike accessible year-round; spectacular erosional features; abundant wildflowers in the spring; good bird watching.

Best season: Anytime, but spring is most colorful.
For more information: Contact Pawnee National Grassland, 2009 9th Street, Greeley, CO 80631; (303) 353-5004.

The trip to Pawnee Buttes is an easy and popular one and can be hiked during any season, weather permitting. In a short distance (two miles one way), the trail covers a surprising variety of terrains, from sweeping expanses of grassland to intricately dissected badlands. It arrives at the base of the Pawnee Buttes, two imposing landmarks of the plains, made famous as Rattlesnake Buttes in James Michener's novel, *Centennial.*

This land of sun, wind and grass may pique your imagination so that you feel the presence of those creatures and humans that have come before: ancient ancestors of the camel and horse now fossilized in the rocks forming the buttes, herds of giant bison and the Paleo-Indians that followed them, and, most recently, the settlers who tried to tame this land with plows.

Depending on the season, you may observe a variety of wildlife, including many species of songbirds, prairie falcons, and other raptors, and the graceful pronghorn antelope. In the spring the prairie turns green in one short, but spectacular burst of growth, and if it is an unusually moist year, you will encounter a display of wildflowers which would rival that of any mountain meadow.

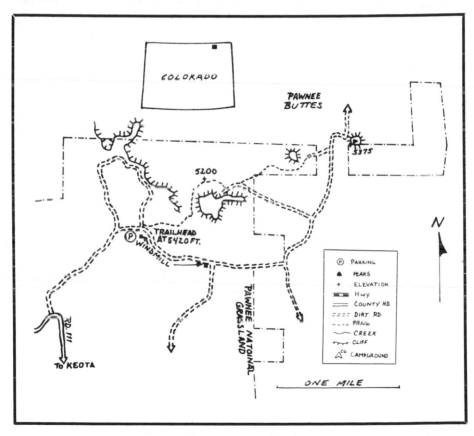

Pawnee Buttes

The eastern Pawnee Butte.

To reach the Pawnee Buttes trail, take State Highway 14 either 13 miles east from Briggsdale or 10 miles west from New Raymer and look for the sign to Keota. Follow the gravel road for approximately five miles until you reach Keota, now nearly a ghost town. From the northeast corner of town, follow County Road 105 for about three miles, to right on County Road 104 another three miles, and then turn left onto County Road 111. Follow 111 north about 4.5 miles until the road makes a sharp bend to the west. Look for a small dirt road which heads north from this curve.

This road climbs a short steep hill which is fairly rough. You may want to park at its base. If you choose to park here, you will only add about one mile to your hike in each direction.

Follow the dirt road about one mile to a fork. Take the right fork and park near the windmill a short distance ahead. Across from the windmill, there is another road leading northeast and a couple hundred feet along this road you will see the sign for the Pawnee Buttes Trail. From here you have an excellent view of the surrounding landscape with the Pawnee Buttes visible to the northeast.

From the sign, the trail descends a small draw and goes out onto the prairie again. After crossing a wide gully it passes through a gate and arrives at a saddle separating two bluffs. From here it descends into a badlands area where, in places, it becomes indistinct. Watch for it on the flat ground below where it emerges again and crosses a deep gully.

After crossing the gully a second time, the trail climbs onto a gently sloping grassland at the base of the bluff. From here you get your first good view of the western of the two Pawnee Buttes. Following the trail towards the buttes, you will reach a jeep road. Follow this for a short distance until you again see the trail heading left in the direction of the buttes. As you near the first of the two buttes, the trail becomes indistinct, but you should be able to see the trail posts circling the south side of the butte where the trail merges with jeep roads which lead to the second butte. Do not be surprised if you encounter company when you arrive at the Pawnee Buttes, as the jeep roads provided motorized access to the area.

You should allow about 2.5 hours for the roundtrip to the Pawnee Buttes, plus plenty of time for exploring. The buttes themselves are impressive landmarks and a hike around them will reveal a great deal about the geology of these erosional remnants. Climbing on the buttes is not recommended, however, due to loose rocks.

You will hear the cries of prairie falcons as you approach the buttes. They nest in the cliffs above and can be seen with the aid of binoculars. Please avoid disturbing any nests you may encounter, as these and many other prairie species are particularly sensitive to intrusion.

Because of the openness of the area, you can easily leave the trail to explore on your return trip. You may want to follow one of the gullies into the badlands area where hours can be spent discovering the infinite ways that water has been at work sculpting the land. If you should become disoriented while exploring, the Pawnee Buttes, the fence line, and the windmill near your car are all good landmarks.

Camping is permitted anywhere on the National Grassland property, but because of the concentrated use in the immediate vicinity of the Pawnee Buttes, camping here is not recommended. Likewise, you should avoid camping too near the trail and in gully bottoms where there is a danger of flash floods.

As you may have guessed, firewood and water are not in abundance on the prairie, so you should come prepared with plenty of water and a stove if you are going to camp. Any water you encounter while hiking should be considered unfit for drinking.

If you do spend a night out under the stars, you'll find a unique experience; an opportunity to feel what it must have been like to cross this vast prairie by covered wagon. The sense of unlimited space is impressive. The prairie sunrise, with grasses rustling in the wind, and birds singing in accompaniment, is an event not soon to be forgotten. —*Peter Boddie*

2 Poudre River Trail

General Description: An easily accessible day hike in the city of Fort Collins.
General location: The north end of Fort Collins.
Maps: City of Fort Collins Department of Parks and Recreation Map.
Degree of difficulty: Easy.
Length: 6.75 miles 1 way.
Elevations: No elevation gain.
Special attractions: An easily accessible hike along the Poudre River in undeveloped portions of Fort Collins; a wide, level and paved trail highly suitable to wheelchair travel, featuring river bottom flora.
Best season: Year 'round.
For more information: Fort Collins Parks and Recreation Department, 145 E. Mountain, Fort Collins, CO 80521, (303) 484-4220.

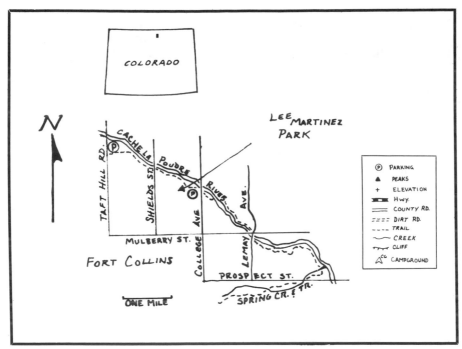

Poudre River Trail

The Poudre River Trail, located near the northern and northeastern city limits of Fort Collins, is ideally suited for all types of hikers, from the youngest to the eldest members of any family to wheelchair-bound people who enjoy the outdoors. The wide, paved trail paralleling the Cache la Poudre River has multiple purposes, multiple accesses, and is hikeable during any season of the year.

You may reach the trail at four different access points: Taft Hill Road, north of Vine Drive; Lee Martinez Park at College Avenue and Cherry Street; Lemay Avenue and Mulberry Street; or Prospect Avenue east of Timberline Road. The two parking lots for the trail, however, are located at the Taft Hill and Lee Martinez Park access points. To reach the Taft Hill access point, simply drive west on any major road to Taft Hill Road, and go north past Vine Drive to the Cache la Poudre River. The parking lot is just south of the river. To reach Lee Martinez Park, drive north on Fort Collins' main drag, College Avenue to Cherry Street.

The Poudre River Trail is 6.75 miles measured from Taft Hill Road to Prospect Street where it connects to another trail heading southwest, the Spring Creek Trail, five miles long. Beyond that, the trail also connects to Fort Collins' extensive bicycle trail network.

Beginning at Taft Hill Road, you will first travel through the only "open" portion of the trail between your starting point and Shields Street. Here you will have a panoramic view of the foothills to the west. This is a beautiful spot for a stroll during autumn's change of color; a perfect stretch for grandma to take her new grandchild to see the golds, reds and browns of the season. At Shields Street you may exit the trail or continue on via an underpass (there is a horse rental establishment here).

The one-mile stretch of trail between Shields Street and Lee Martinez Park at College Avenue is the most diversified and heavily-used portion of the trail. You're likely to encounter people traveling by every mode of transportaton imaginable—except those modes that are motorized. You will also find numerous benches to relax on or—if you're energetic—the mile-long "Wells Fargo Physical Fitness Trail".

From Lee Martinez Park you'll have to cross College Avenue and then you'll continue over the .75-mile section to Lemay Avenue, a section less traveled and without the man-made convenience of the last section, but surrounded by the same lush river-bottom flora.

When you reach Lemay Avenue, follow the trail along the street for .25 miles, across the overpass, then back to the river. It is still quite well marked. This final 3.5-mile stretch is used by fishermen and the occasional jogger and it is here that you are most likely to see birdlife such as herons, kingfishers, ducks and geese.

At Prospect Street you have the option of continuing southwest on the Spring Creek Trail, catching a ride back in whatever way you've arranged, or hiking back the way you came. Whatever you decide to do, I'm sure you'll agree that the Poudre River Trail offers limitless possibilities for relaxation and recreation not far from the busy center of this northern Front Range city.
—*Kevin, Leslie & Jesse Conrad*

3 Mesa Trail

General Description: An easy, accessible, and scenic day hike along the base of the Flatirons.

General location: West edge of Boulder.

The Mesa Trail along the Flatirons.

Maps: Boulder and Eldorado Springs USGS quads; Arapaho National Forest
   Map.
Length: Approximately 6 miles 1 way.
Degree of difficulty: Easy.
Elevations: 5,600 to 6,500 feet.
Special attractions: Good views of Boulder, the Flatirons, and the eastern
   plains; wildflowers and a good example of the contact between the plains
   and the Rocky Mountains.

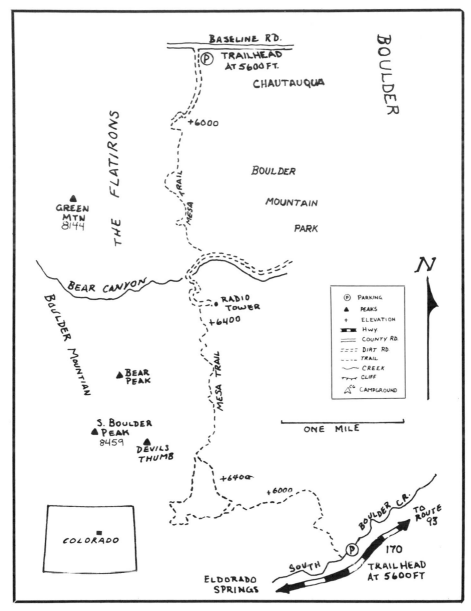

Mesa Trail

Best season: Year 'round.

For more information: Boulder Mountain Parks and Open Space Department, 2045 13th St., P.O. Box 471, Boulder, CO 80306, (303) 441-3950.

The Mesa Trail offers an easy hike along the base of the Flatirons near Boulder, taking you through forest, meadows and grasslands, and offering many great views. It traverses the contact line between the eastern plains and the Rocky Mountains where the underlying Precambrian rocks have been uplifted and the overlying sedimentary rocks upturned. Nowhere along the Front Range is this geological phenomenon more spectacular than here in the Flatirons. Great slabs of Pennsylvanian-age rocks of the Fountain Formation rise nearly vertically at the western edge of Boulder. Similarly, this area is the contact point where the grassland vegetation of the eastern plains merges with the mountain brush and ponderosa pine forests of the foothills. The trail is about six miles long and takes you from Boulder's Chatauqua Park south to South Boulder Creek near the town of Eldorado Springs.

To reach the north end of the Mesa trail, take Baseline Road west in Boulder to Chautauqua Park. From there hike south on the paved road near the park entrance about .5 miles to where the road begins to switchback and look for the Mesa Trail to the left.

To reach the south end of the trail, go south from Boulder on State Highway 93 (Broadway) to State Highway 170 and the sign for Eldorado Springs. Head west on 170 about 1.5 miles and look for the trailhead parking area down and to the right next to South Boulder Creek. If you decide to hike the entire length of the Mesa Trail, you will need to shuttle cars between these two points.

Starting at the north end of the trail, you quickly enter a beautiful forest of ponderosa pines, alternating with many small meadows and offering views of the Flatirons and Boulder to the northeast. At one point, the trail swings around to the base of one of the cliffs, giving you an appreciation of the steepness of the Flatirons. As you hike along, you may notice that other hikers have cut switchbacks. This is a heavily used area and, for that reason, it is important that you not cut switchbacks.

About two miles into your hike, the trail drops down and connects with a road along Bear Canyon. Follow this road upstream to where it crosses the creek and then climbs steeply uphill. Near the top of the hill, and before you reach the radio tower, look for the Mesa Trail taking off to the right. This stretch of the trail, leading through many meadows with spectacular views of the Flatirons, is beautiful and only lightly used.

About two miles farther, you are rewarded by a view of the Devil's Thumb, a spectacular rock outcrop of the Flatirons. Shortly past this point, there is a fork in the trail. The left fork follows an old road for about 1.5 miles to the south trailhead. As you descend, the vegetation changes from ponderosa pine forest to open grassland. The right fork takes you to a beautiful meadow at the base of Shadow Canyon. From here you can climb a low saddle and drop down into Eldorado Springs where you can sooth your tired muscles at the hot springs or follow the trail down the valley where it connects with the other fork.

The Mesa Trail can be hiked during any season and offers access to many side trails along its length. You could easily spend many hours exploring all the hiking possibilities they provide. —*Caryn, Peter and Crystal Boddie*

4 Barr Lake State Park Trail

General description: A pleasant day hike around a prairie reservoir with excellent opportunities to observe wildlife and birdlife.

General location: 18 miles northeast of Denver.

Maps: Park brochure map available at park office.

Degree of difficulty: Easy.

Length: Approximately 9 miles one way.

Elevation: Remains at about 5,000 feet.

Special attractions: Easily accessible from Denver Metro area; lots of wildlife and birdlife to observe; a boardwalk takes you out into the lake for a good view of a heron rookery; the trail is accessible to wheelchairs, though parts of it are steep.

Best season: Spring or fall.

For more information: Contact Barr Lake State Park, 13401 Picadilly Rd., Brighton, CO 80601, (303) 649-6005.

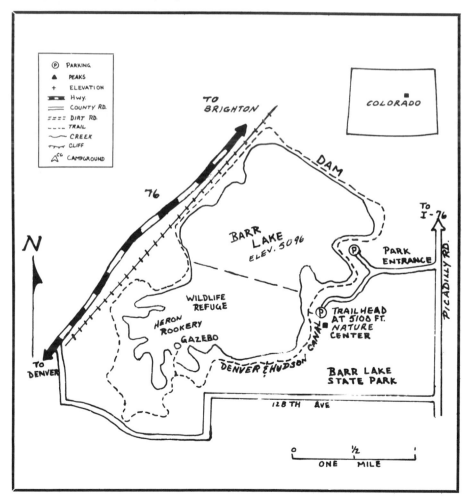

Barr Lake State Park Trail

Boardwalk and gazebo at Barr Lake State Park.

In the middle of the plains east of Denver, Barr Lake State Park, with its towering cottonwoods and accompanying wildlife, is a veritable oasis in a dry and spacious land.

To reach it, take Interstate 76 east to Bromley Lane, continue east on Bromley Lane to Picadilly, and head south on Picadilly to the park entrance. There is a park pass fee for all motorized vehicles.

Barr Lake is an irrigation reservoir surrounded by the old ditchrider's road. You will be hiking a trail which follows this road closely—an easy hike, maintaining a fairly constant elevation of approximately 5,000 feet. Keep in mind that the trail and canal road become quite muddy after a rain.

Begin your hike at the Nature Center located within view of the parking area. The center, operated through the Nongame Program of the Division of Wildlife, offers informational displays and a naturalist who will inform you of recent and/or unusual bird sightings.

From the center, cross the bridge over the Denver-Hudson Canal. Immediately to the left of the bridge is the Niedrach Nature Trail, named for Robert Niedrach, an ornithologist who did much fieldwork in the Barr Lake area. This trail includes a boardwalk with a beautiful view of the lake.

Here, as you pass under the tall cottonwoods and by the willows that form their understory, you may observe smaller birds that frequent the lakeshore. In the spring, you may see waterfowl such as coots or the elusive western grebe (a species that seems to spend more time under the water than above it).

From the nature trail, you will rejoin the main canal trail, passing a treeless section of the shoreline. When the water level is high in the lake, this area is a shallow bay where you may see mallards, pintails, and teal. Beyond the bay is a side trail which leads onto a spur of land extending into the lake. From the end of the trail, hikers can rest on wooden benches and observe the old heron rookery that exists nearby. All that remains of the old rookery are toppled cottonwoods, but their branches still provide a resting place for large birds like double-crested cormorants and great blue herons.

After returning to the canal trail, you will approach a meadow that lies between the canal road and the lakeshore. Here you can remain on the main trail or follow a side trail along the shore under the cottonwoods. This trail leads to a photoblind built along the shore. If you are a photographer, set your camera up here and wait for the white pelicans, grebes, and other waterfowl that may float within range of your camera lens.

Back again on the main canal trail, proceed to the highlight of your hike: the boardwalk which extends about .25 miles out over the lake to a large gazebo from which you can focus your binoculars and spotting scopes—or just your eyes—on an active rookery to observe great blue herons, double-crested cormorants, black-crowned night herons, and snowy egrets. Geese, coots, and grebes will dot the water surrounding you, especially in the spring when the water is highest.

If you can tear yourself away from the gazebo, you may choose to hike back to the nature center, making a round trip of about three miles. If you choose to proceed around the lake, you will discover some cattail marshes, alive with yellow-headed blackbirds in the spring. A second photoblind is located just a short distance off the main canal trail in this area.

Just beyond the two-mile marker on the trail are the headgates which control the water entering the lake from the South Platte River. At this point, you will leave the park and hike along the gravel road in order to cross the canal. Turn to your right to cross the bridge on the road. Follow the trail marker telling you how to re-enter the park. The southern end of the lake has many shallow bays which become isolated pools as the water recedes during the summer. These are prime feeding areas for great blue herons. In this area you will come upon the old headgates and canal which fed the lake prior to 1906, when the size of the dam was increased.

As you continue hiking, notice that the trees in this area form a dense screen along the lake, and be alert for flocks of pelicans, geese, grebes, coots, and other waterfowl.

From the south end, the canal trail continues along the west side of the lake. As you pass the middle of the west side, you will be in an open field where a variety of hawks are frequently seen. From here, the trail follows the railroad tracks for a short way. The trail continues to the west end of the dam. A stone house, constructed in 1888, is situated here. Although the house has not been restored, steps have been taken to stabilize its condition for possible future restoration.

At this point, cross the top of the dam, an earthen structure faced with concrete, from which you are offered an expansive view of the nearly 2,000-acre reservoir. Then follow the eastern side of the lake past the boat ramp and back to the nature center. Here you have a last opportunity to observe many small birds, as well as an occasional hawk or owl.

Be sure to take plenty of water with you, to not take pets into the southern end of the park (which is a wildlife refuge), and to enjoy this unique hike.
—*Carol Leasure*

5 Historic Denver

General description: Guided walking tours through Denver.
General location: Denver.
Maps: None.
Degree of difficulty: Easy.
Length: Varies with tour.
Elevations: A mile high.
Special attractions: Historic mansions of Denver; tour of business district; tour of lower downtown, Union Station and restoration projects.
Best season: Anytime.
For more information: Historic Denver, Inc., Denver Union Station, 1701 Wynkoop, Suite 200, Denver, CO 80202; (303) 534-1858.

If you're new to Denver or an old timer who's just never taken the time to get to know the city, Historic Denver Tours' walking tours are for you. Says their brochure, "Historic Denver Tours can show you the city while bringing to life the people and places that make Denver special." Several different tours are available year round from this non-profit Colorado corporation, but reservations are required and a fee is charged.

Several tours are available. The Quality Hill/Capital Hill Walking Tour explores the homes along Denver's Millionaire Row, one of the city's oldest and most prestigious residential neighborhoods. You'll come to understand why Denver was known as the "City of Mansions" in the 1880s and 1890s as you tour these Victorian mansions, including that of the "Unsinkable" Molly Brown and other notables. You'll also see the early 1900s Grant Humphreys Mansion and Governor's Mansion.

The Larimer Square Lower Downtown Walking Tour takes you from historic Union Station, which is much quieter than it was some 50 years ago, through Denver's oldest business district, which is enjoying a wonderful rebirth. As you walk you will hear stories of life in the early settlements that became Denver and of fortunes won and lost. You will visit Larimer Square, a restored area containing many Victorian buildings, you will see historic luxury hotels such as the Brown Palace.

If your interest is more modern than historic, you will enjoy the 16th Street Mall Tour, which takes you along Denver's pedestrian mall and introduces you to Denver's business world.

Of course, you could just find a way to see the important historic sites of the "Queen City of the Plains" on your own. But these organized tours help you to hit all the right places with a minimum amount of difficuty and you'll hear some pretty good tales about the places you'll be seeing. Contact Historic Denver Tours at the number listed above.—*Caryn Boddie*

6 John Hayden Trail

General description: An easy and easily accessible day hike through a relatively undisturbed foothills ecosystem.
General location: About 4 miles north of Morrison.
Maps: Jefferson County Open Space Hayden's Green Mountain Park Map.
Degree of difficulty: Easy.
Length: 3.5 miles 1 way; 7.25 miles round trip.
Elevations: 6,200 to 6,185 feet.

Special attractions: An easily accessible area with beautiful wildflowers in spring.

Best season: Anytime, but spring is most colorful.

For more information: Jefferson County Open Space Department, 1801 19th St., Golden, CO 80401; (303) 277-8332.

The John Hayden Trail offers an easily accessible day hike through a foothills environment close to Denver.

To reach the trailhead follow State Highway 6 west to its junction with State Highway 40. Take 40 south for .5 miles and turn south (left) on Rooney Road. Take Rooney Road south for .9 miles and look for a small parking area on your left at the John Hayden Trail trailhead.

Begin your hike by entering Hayden's Green Mountain Park and noting the regulations posted by the Jefferson Open Space Department. Then start off to your right up Green Mountain.

This park was dedicated to the memory of William Frederick Hayden, a pioneer and rancher whose family donated property on the mountain as a memorial.

In the spring and early summer you will see why this area is called Green Mountain. Its wide variety of grasses and other plants makes it a green oasis in the rapidly developing area surrounding it. It is one of the few undisturbed foothills ecosystems close to the metro area.

If you are hiking in the spring, you might try to identify all the wildflowers you'll see along your hike. In spring, the first flowers are pasque flowers and sand lilies, and there is an ever larger array of species into the summer season.

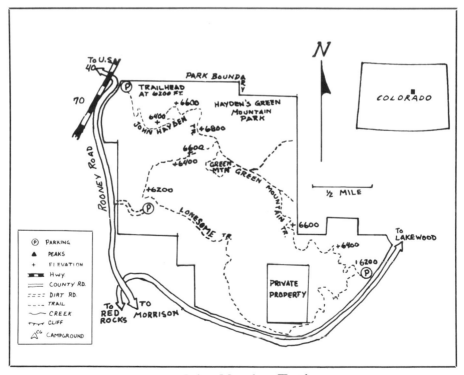

John Hayden Trail

The undisturbed foothills environment of Green Mountain.

The trail climbs up and away from the highway below and follows a ravine toward the summit of Green Mountain. The bulk of the mountain is formed by the Denver Formation, which is overlain by a more resistant cap of coarse sedimentary rock called the Green Mountain Conglomerate. At the lower levels of the mountain you may pass outcroppings of older rocks deposited during the Upper Cretaceous period. These geological formations are covered by a mid-grass type of prairie, representing the higher amount of precipitation here at the edge of the mountains.

At about one mile you will encounter a fork in the trail where the Green Mountain Trail meets the Hayden Trail. This is the loop trail that you will meet again near the end of your hike. Keep going straight. In another .16 miles you will encounter another fork in the trail. Go to your right and you will loop around the summit of the mountain for a good view on all sides. Then you'll come back to the main trail.

Be sure to keep your eyes open for mule deer as you hike. Look also for prairie chickens, which may be hard to spot in the long grass.

Continue on down to the Alameda Parkway, going straight on at the next fork in the trail and right at the one following that. You can end your hike at the Alameda Parkway, in which case you will have had to shuttle cars. This is a 3.3 mile hike. You can also take the Lonesome Trail, which meets the Hayden Trail .12 miles from the Alameda Parkway and loops back to the Green Mountain Trail, which winds back to meet with the Hayden Trail about one mile from its trailhead and your beginning.

Don't expect your hike along the John Hayden Trail to be a wilderness experience, and you will find it a pleasant break from the busy metropolitan area.—*Caryn Boddie*

7 Highline Canal

General description: A day hike in the southern portion of the Denver Metropolitan area.

General location: Beginning one mile southwest of Waterton near Chatfield Reservoir and ending near the Rocky Mountain Arsenal.

Maps: USGS Front Range Corridor Map, Sheet 2 of 3.

Degree of difficulty: Easy.

Length: Can be hiked in easily accessible sections for 58 of its 71 total miles.

Elevations: Follows a "highline of gravity," dropping only 300 feet for its entire length.

Special attractions; A beautiful strip of open space winding its way through residential, urban and country settings; used by a variety of people; features lush prairie pond vegetation and wildlife; accessible to the wheelchair-bound; beautiful views of the Front Range.

Best season: Year 'round.

For more information: The Denver Water Department, Office of Community Affairs, (303) 623-2500.

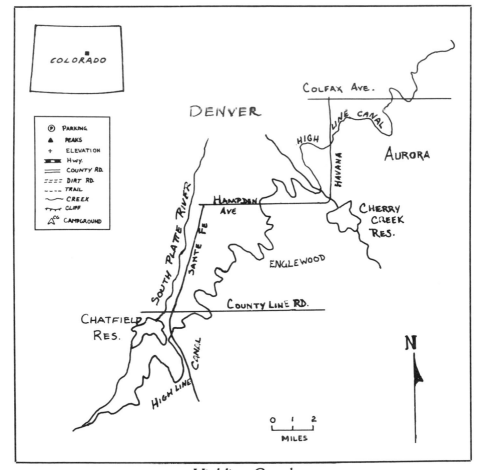

Highline Canal

Hikers on the High Line Canal Trail.

When James Duff, a hardy Scotman, introduced the idea of irrigating the dry plains of Colorado back in 1870, he met with the overwhelming skepticism of early Denver residents. But he completed his 71-mile irrigation ditch anyway and opened it in 1883. Little did he realize that, with this "High Line Canal," he was not only providing Denver and the eastern plains with a water source but with a narrow oasis that Denverites of the next century would value more for its recreational opportunities than for its original purpose of irrigation.

The High Line Canal today is used by people on horseback, by joggers, bikers, the wheelchair-bound, roller skaters, mothers with babies in strollers, and by hikers. It is a refreshing strip of nature in the midst of a very busy city.

To reach the High Line Canal, which winds its way through the southern portion of the Denver Metro area, take a look at the map portion of the Denver Metro area listed above and find the street nearest to you which meets the canal. Or, if you are ambitious and want to see a variety of country, begin at the canal's southern end near Waterton and Chatfield Reservoir and hike its length in sections.

For the 58 miles that is hikeable (it is unhikeable in Waterton Canyon and near the Arsenal), the canal is paralleled by a 12-foot-wide road along which you'll be hiking, and which is lined with tall cottonwoods, providing shade in summer and beautiful colors in fall.

As you follow the canal, you will hike through open plains where you will feel far away from the hustle and bustle of the city, through beautiful open areas where you'll have views of both the Front Range and the skyline of downtown Denver, and through urban areas where the canal is paved and used mostly by joggers and bikers. For its length, you will be seeing the lush vegetation typical of a prairie pond: cottonwoods, Queen Anne's lace, and wild asparagus. You will also see geese and a variety of species of ducks, as well as magpies, meadowlarks, prairie dogs, and even foxes and pheasants in open areas.

You will also hike through or around several parks, residential areas, and golf courses, and the flowers that some residents grow in their backyards during the summer months will highlight your walk.

The wonderful gift of an ambitious man who thought he was providing just an irrigation ditch, the High Line Canal is a narrow strip of country Denverites can enjoy year 'round without having to leave town: a place to see the changing leaves in autumn, walk in the snow in wintertime, first notice the appearance of the greenery of spring, and enjoy the cool shade of the cottonwoods in summer.—*Caryn Boddie*

8 Monument Valley Trail

General description: A day hike through the City of Colorado Springs along Monument Creek.

General location: Colorado Springs.

Maps: Colorado Springs Parks and Recreation Department Map.

Length: Several options exist for day hikes of varying lengths. Eventually, the trail may go from Rampart Reservoir on the north to North Cheyenne Canyon on the south and connect with several side trails.

Elevations: Little elevation gain.

Special attractions: An exceptional finger of open space extending into the city of Colorado Springs; excellent views.

Best season: Year 'round.

For more information: Colorado Springs Parks and Recreation Department, 1400 Glen Avenue; Colorado Springs, CO 80905; (303) 578-6640.

The Monument Valley Trail takes you along Monument Creek from Bijou Street at its southern end to Monroe Street at its northern end (soon to extend farther in both directions). You'll pass parks and residential areas and have scenic views in all directions on this exceptional strip of open space.

At this writing, you should begin your hike at Bijou Street. Take Interstate I-25 to the Bijou Street exit and head east to Cascade. Park along the street near a small park and walk down the hill to the trail following Monument Creek (it goes along both banks), the headwaters of which are in the rolling country north of Colorado Springs and which join Fountain Creek farther south—the route Zebulon Pike once followed from Pueblo.

As you start walking, look up to the west. You will have an excellent view of Pikes Peak, rising massive above the city. The peak has inspired people for centuries, including the Ute Indians who believed that the Great Spirit was restless one day so he took a large stone, gouged out a hole in the sky and poured ice and snow into the hole until he had made a great peak.

To the north as you hike along, you will have views of the foothills and mesas; to the east you will be able to see Pulpit Rock, a unique geologic formation; to the south is the skyline of downtown. As you walk away from the city, at South Circle Drive and Fillmore Street, you will be able to experience a

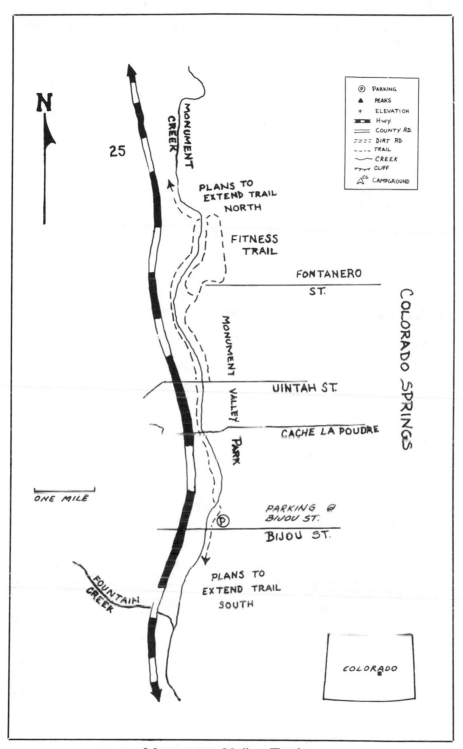

Monument Valley Trail

more natural streamway environment that supports a host of plant, animal and bird life, ranging from mallard ducks to beaver and deer.

Between Bijou and Cache La Poudre Streets, on the west side of the creek, you will see a softball/baseball field, volleyball courts, a large group picnic shelter and other public recreation facilities. Farther along, near Uintah Street, there is a duck lake on the west side, as well as an historical sundial and a pinetum (an arboretum of pine trees) and some tennis courts on the east side of the creek. The Colorado College campus is nearby to the east, as well.

The Monument Valley Trail with downtown Colorado Springs in the background.

Continue on into Monument Valley Park. Beyond the baseball field is the Monument Valley Fitness Trail, which circles around the north end of the park and past a scenic overlook and a geologic column. This was a gift from William Jackson Palmer, founder of Colorado Springs and a wise man who banned horses and vehicles from this park in its early days, sensing that people needed open space and parks to walk in.

The Colorado Springs Parks and Recreation Department has great plans for this trail and others in this city. For an up-to-date description of future revisions and additions to the trail system, contact their office as listed above.—*Caryn Boddie*

9 *Pueblo River Trails*

General description: A wide, paved trail along the Arkansas and Fountain Rivers in Pueblo.

General location: The City of Pueblo.

Maps: City of Pueblo Trail System Map.

Degree of difficulty: Easy.

Length: Will be approximately 20 miles long when completed; offers opportunities for several shorter day hikes.

Elevations: Little elevation gain from the confluence of the Arkansas and Fountain Rivers at 4,650 feet.

Special attractions: A scenic and easily accessible trail along the river bottoms of the Arkansas and Fountain Rivers; many species of birds and waterfowl; accessible to the wheelchair-bound.

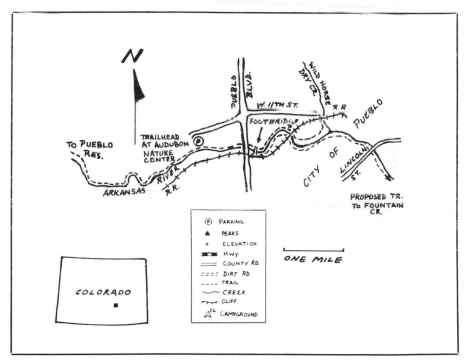

Pueblo River Trails

Best season: Year 'round.

For more information: The City of Pueblo, Parks Department, City Park & 860 Goodnight Ave., Pueblo, CO 81005; (303) 566-1745.

This river trail system through the southern Front Range City of Pueblo will be, when completed, an extensive system taking you from the El Paso County Line and Colorado Springs on the northeast to Pueblo Reservoir at the trail's southwest end.

At this point of development, probably the best place to begin your hike is at the Audubon Nature Center west of Pueblo Boulevard on West 11th Street. To reach it, take State Highway 50 (Canon City Highway) west to Pueblo Boulevard. Go south on the boulevard for about three miles to the Arkansas River Valley. Pass over a railroad on a high bridge and turn right (west) at the foot of the grade on 11th Street. Follow 11th Street west for one mile and park at the Nature Center at the foot of the hill beside the river. You can hike either way on the trail, but we recommend going west toward Pueblo Reservoir, a hike of about 3.5 miles one way.

As you hike west from the Nature Center, you will be hiking along the cottonwood-lined river bottom of the Arkansas River. There you may see birds and wildlife, including beavers, whose mud paths cross the trail as they fell trees and build their dams. Deer and an occasional bear may be seen on the western end of the trail.

The Pueblo Reservoir at the end of your 3.5-mile hike is a typical reservoir, but with limestone cliffs and flat-top buttes rimming its irregular 17-mile-shoreline and the Greenhorn and Sangre de Cristo Mountains forming an alpine backdrop to the west. Prickly pear cactus are found there, along with cottonwoods and willows. There are red-tailed hawks in the area, too, as well as the occasional rattlesnake.

From the Reservoir, return to your starting point and, if you like, head the other direction to Pueblo's City Park.—*Frances C. Carter*

10 North Canyon

General description: A day hike in a prairie canyon in the Commanche National Grassland.

General location: 30 miles southwest of Springfield.

Maps: Tubs Springs and Campo SW USGS quads; Comanche National Grassland Map.

Degree of difficulty: Easy.

Length: 4 miles one way.

Elevations: 4,200 to 4,450 feet.

Special attractions: Short-grass prairie; many species of birds and wildlife; wildflowers in spring; many small canyons to explore; Indian pictographs.

Best season: Spring.

For more information: Carrizo Ranger District, Comanche National Grassland, 212 E. 10th St., P.O. Box 127, Springfield, CO 81073; (303) 523-6591.

Perhaps writer Willa Cather said it best when she compared the plains to a wild horse that couldn't be tamed; that ran wild and kicked things to pieces. The country that makes up the Comanche National Grasslands is like that. Though there are many successful farms in the area, there is also evidence of the many other people who tried to tame this land and failed. Old equipment and battered structures that used to be homesteads dot the land.

Rock window in North Canyon.

The beauty of the Comanche National Grasslands is subtle and you must get out on the land to appreciate it. North Canyon is located in the southernmost portion of the area where the rolling short-grass prairie has been dissected by erosion to form a series of small canyons. There is a variety of wildlife and vegetation to be discovered here, as well as evidence of the Indian peoples who left their history in the form of pictographs.

To reach North Canyon, take U.S. Highway 287 south from Springfield about 17 miles. At the point where the highway bends to the east, turn right on County Road M. You will also see a sign for the Carrizo Picnic Area. Follow this gravel road west for about eight miles and turn left on County Road 18. Follow Road 18 south for about seven miles to where it bends to the left, and you come to a ranch house. Take the small dirt road that is across from the ranch house south into Picture Canyon for .5 miles. Park just inside the fence

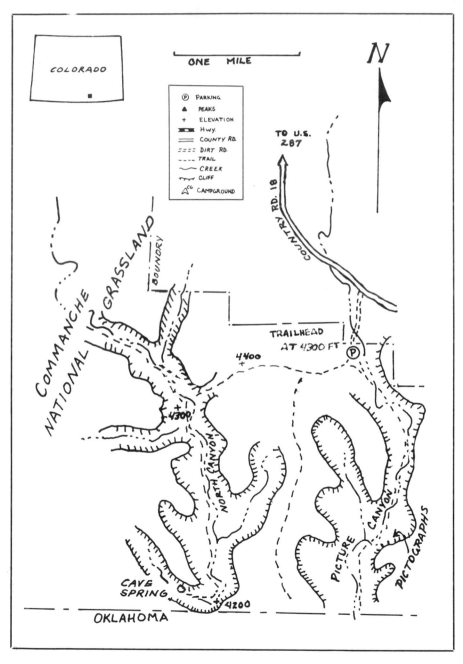

North Canyon

Old homesteader's cabin in North Canyon.

and cattle guard, which marks the national grassland boundary.

Begin hiking on the jeep road and bear right at the fork. (The left fork takes you about 2.5 miles into Picture Canyon—a once interesting canyon where the original Indian pictographs have been carved and painted over with graffiti. A real disappointment.)

As you hike away from Picture Canyon and towards North Canyon, think of all the people who have come before you to this wild land. In fact, recorded history of the inhabitants of this area begins about 1535 A.D. At that time, the Mescalero Apache were known to live here. However, recent investigations in the canyons of southern Baca County indicate that this area was inhabited as early as 385 A.D. From 1540 to 1727 the Spanish explored and occupied the area. Around 1700 the Ute Indians came from west of the Rockies and were followed by the Comanches. It was not until the 1800s that white man came into the area to trade with the Indians. They were followed by the cattlemen in the late 1800s and the farmers in the early 1900s.

Follow the jeep road up and over a small saddle to the west. Go straight at another fork in the road and drop down into a small canyon, which will connect you with North Canyon (Holt Canyon on USGS map). From here you can explore in any direction you like, but a good destination would be Cave Spring. From the intersection with North Canyon, hike south about 1.5 miles until you come to an old homestead. The fenceline, a few hundred feet to the south marks the Oklahoma border, while the side canyon to the east contains Cave Spring. Drink at your own risk.

Prairie flora on the grasslands consists mainly of short-grass on the hard land (buffalo grass and blue grama are the primary species) and mid-grass, occuring mostly in sandy areas (sand drop seed, side oats grama, little blue stem, western wheat grass, sand sage, and yucca are common).

Wildlife on the grasslands includes 275 different species of birds including quail, pheasant, dove, bald eagle, golden eagle, ducks, geese, hawks, and road runners. Mountain lion, bear, deer, antelope, fox, coyote, and bobcat are among the mammals found in the area.

Be sure to take plenty of water with you and wear good stout boots. Keep an eye out for rattlesnakes as you're hiking. You can return the way you came or explore some of the other canyons before heading back to your car.—*Caryn, Peter and Crystal Boddie*

The Mountains

"With all their infinite variations, the mountains comprise not only heaving waves of forest, but jutting cliffs, abysmal gorges, and deep sunless canyons, vast open parks and tiny arctic meadows, small blue lakes, gushing warm geysers, mineral springs, cold trout pools, lacy falls, heavy cataracts and great soggy marshes, cones and craters of extinct volcanoes, bristling hogbacks, rolling hills of sage and cedar, high groves of aspen, immense flat-topped mesas, solitary bluffs and weirdly eroded buttes."

This passage by writer Frank Waters really says it all. The following hikes, grouped not by range but by region, are meant to show you Colorado's mountains "with all their infinite variations."

The Spanish Peaks. U.S. Forest Service photo.

44

11 *Wahatoya Trail*

General description: A day hike or overnighter to a saddle separating the Spanish Peaks and an additional longer route around the West Peak.

General location: Approximately 20 miles southwest of Walsenburg.

Maps: Spanish Peaks, Cuchara, Cucharas Pass, and Herlick Canyon USGS quads; San Isabel National Forest Map.

Degree of difficulty: Moderate to difficult.

Length: From 5 to 15 miles one way.

Elevations: 8,500 to 11,500 feet.

Special attractions: The Spanish Peaks; unique geologic features.

Best season: Summer and fall.

For more information: San Isabel National Forest, San Carlos Ranger District, 248 Dozier St., Canon City, CO 81212; (303) 275-1626.

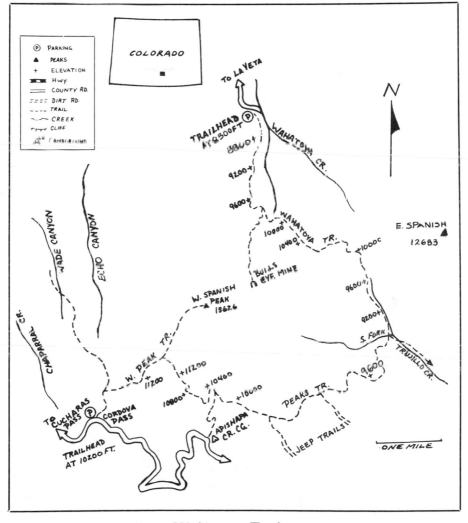

Wahatoya Trail

This hike takes you to the saddle between two important landmarks of south-central Colorado: the Spanish Peaks. You also have the option of circling the peaks to the south and west.

Located east of the Sangre de Cristo Range, the Spanish Peaks have been of importance to Indians, Spanish explorers and settlers at various times in history, and are also known worldwide for their unique volcanic geology. The Indian tribes of southern Colorado believe that all life gets its nourishment from the "Huatollas," these mountains they call the "Breasts of the World." They say that all clouds are born here and hence the life-giving moisture that feeds us all. Indeed, these two peaks rise spectacularly above the plains like some gigantic cleavage. The East Peak is 12,683 feet high. The West Peak, more famous, is 13,626 feet.

To reach the trailhead for the Wayatoya Trail, drive into the quaint town of La Veta. Stay on State Highway 12 and take the dirt road to the left (east) just south of town, before you cross the Cucharas River. This is Wahatoya Road, but isn't marked as such. (Anyone in town can direct you if you get lost.) The road winds through the countryside for about two miles, past Town Lakes on the right and around a sharp turn to the left. Turn right after approximately .5 miles. From here to the trailhead it is about 10 miles. Park your car near the San Isabel Forest sign at the top of the long hill before you go down into the canyon. Be sure and walk over to the edge of Lover's Leap and look down into Wahatoya Canyon before you start out.

From the Forest Service sign you climb to the saddle between East and West Spanish Peaks. The sign at the beginning of your hike indicates that Trujillo Creek, located on the other side of the saddle, is a three-mile-hike. This is wrong. It is about five miles to the saddle and 1.5 miles to Trujillo Creek.

As you begin your hike, you will follow a four-wheel-drive road which ends at the Bulls Eye Mine. About 1.5 miles up the road, turn to your left. There is a Forest Service sign marking the trail turnoff.

If you go straight ahead you will come to the mine, once a thriving, active, working mine, containing no small amount of gold and silver. As you ascend this old jeep trail you will appreciate the tenacity of those old miners who hauled equipment, food, and the various necessities of life up this grade on a regular basis. The mine is privately owned, so if you detour to see it, please respect it.

From here to the saddle, the trail climbs much more gradually and crosses several small tributaries to Wahatoya Creek. If you are making a short overnight trip, there are some good camping spots along this stretch of the trail, but you should select one a good distance from both the streams and the trail.

As you wind your way up and over the saddle, you will come across an avalanche chute and a large rock slide. You should have good views of the peaks from here.

Soon you will head down to the South Fork of Trujillo Creek and a small meadow where there is a cabin. This is a good place to turn around if you are making a day hike. If you plan to continue on, around the south and west sides of West Spanish Peak, follow the trail to the left past the cabin. This is the Peaks Trail, which will take you west towards Apishapa Pass (Cordova Pass) and a side trail to Apishapa Campgrounds. You could car shuttle to either of these points for a long one-way hike of between 11 and 13 miles from the Wahatoya trailhead.

At Apishapa (Cordova) Pass you will intersect the West Peak Trail taking you to the summit of West Spanish Peak (see the West Spanish Peak hike description).

If you are ambitious, you can hike down along the west slope of the peak into Echo, Wade, and Chapparal Canyons where there are many interesting rock formations and Chapparal Falls. This is a beautiful and little-used area. However, you cannot get out of the bottom of these canyons which end in private land. You will have to retrace your steps to Apishapa Pass and/or all the way back to the Wayatoya trailhead. Be sure to have a topo map if you continue on into this area.

The Spanish Peaks and surrounding area have been proposed as a wilderness area. After visiting the area, you may want to encourage your congresspersons to support it as such.—*Leslie Hicks*

12 *West Spanish Peak*

General description: A day hike taking you to the summit of West Spanish Peak and/or the circuitous Apishapa Trail at the base of the mountain.

General location: 20 miles southwest of Walsenburg.

Maps: Cuchara, Cucharas Pass, Herlick Canyon and Spanish Peaks USGS quads; San Isabel National Forest Map.

Degree of difficulty: Moderate.

Length: 5 miles round trip to West Spanish Peak summit; 8.5 miles on Apishapa Trail.

Elevations: 9,700 to 13,626 feet.

Special Attractions: Solitude; beautiful views; interesting geology.

Best season: Spring, summer or fall.

For more information: San Isabel National Forest, San Carlos Ranger District, 248 Dozier St., Canon City, CO 81212; (303) 275-1626.

The Devils Stairway, one of the volcanic dikes radiating from West Spanish Peak. U.S. Forest Service photo.

A hike up the western of the two Spanish Peaks or "Breasts of the World," as they were called by the Indians who so revered them, is a hike up a very distinctive landmark, culminating with beautiful views of surrounding country and the unique volcanic geology of the area.

To reach the trailhead, drive west on State Highway 160 from Walsenburg and turn south on State Highway 12 through La Veta and Cuchara. The highway continues over 9,941 foot Cucharas Pass.

At the summit of the pass, turn left on the good gravel road. Follow it through the beautiful forest of spruce and fir for six miles to Cordova Pass at 11,248 feet (formerly called Apishapa Pass and still noted that way on the USGS quad.) Park beneath the trees in the large parking area provided and look for the gate and sign on the north side of the road. The sign reads, "West

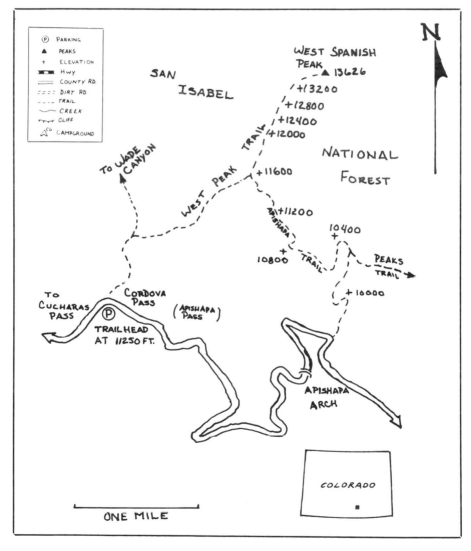

West Spanish Peak

Peak Trail" and the gate is there to keep motorbikes out.

You begin your hike as the trail winds along an almost-level ridge offering good views for 1.5 miles until you come to a sign pointing to the right (east) and downhill and labeled "Apishapa Trail." (The Apishapa trail marked on the Cucharas Pass quad is wrong. The trail really begins 1.5 miles from Cordova Pass, at elevation 11,600 feet.) At this point, you can either continue on to climb the West Spanish Peak by continuing on the West Peak Trail, or you can follow the Apishapa Trail in a circle of 8.5 miles, which will lead you back to your parking spot.

The latter is an excellent trail and well-marked. It takes you down four miles, almost 2,000 feet, through forest cut by some streams, where wildflowers grow. It takes you past several volcanic dikes and ends at the gravel road which you followed over Cordova Pass. From there you will need to hike about 4.5 miles back up the road to your car. On your way up, you will pass Apishapa Arch, a hole in a dike through which a road passes. The road is closed and blocked to motorized vehicles.

The West Peak Trail takes you to the edge of timberline where you will see West Spanish Peak to the east. The trail becomes indistinct as it enters the boulder field on the west side of the peak, but any route you choose from here to the summit is safe. You will probably tend to follow the distinct east-west ridge to the top. The rock is safe and stable, but stout hiking boots are advisable.

Once atop West Spanish Peak, be sure to sign the register and mark the date you arrived at the summit of this amazing 13,626 foot peak, rising so sharply from the flatlands below. Spend some time taking in the views. East Spanish Peak is only 3.5 miles away and beyond it are the Great Plains. To the west is the Sangre de Cristo Range and to the north are the Wet Mountains and the Wet Mountain Valley.

At the base of the mountain you will see volcanic dikes (vertical rock walls) radiating out like spokes from the hub of a wheel. These walls, formed by extrusions of moten lava forced through crevices beneath the earth's surface and left standing when the surrounding rock eroded away, are hundreds of feet high and many miles long. They are very uncommon and known to geologists the world over. The Spanish Peaks, themselves, are intrusives, having been forced up from beneath the earth. Enjoy these fantastic views and then return as you came.—*Janina and Don Janes*

13 West Chama Trail

General description: A day hike or overnighter along the Chama River into the upper Chama Basin.

General location: Approximately 7 miles north of Chama, New Mexico; about 35 miles southwest of Antonito, Colorado.

Maps: Chama Peak 15 minute USGS quad; Rio Grande National Forest Map.

Degree of difficulty: Moderate.

Length: 8 miles one way.

Elevations: 8,800 to 10,800 feet.

Special attractions: Access to the upper Chama Basin with its steep and colorful volcanic cliffs; waterfalls; beautiful colors in fall.

For more information: Rio Grande National Forest, Conejos Ranger District,

Highway 285 North, Rt. 1, P.O. Box 520 G, La Jara, CO 81140; (303) 274-5193.

The West Chama Trail leads you along the Chama River up into the beautiful Chama Basin, one of the most scenic areas in the Rio Grand National Forest and in the San Juan Mountain Range.

To reach the trailhead, take State Highway 17 southwest from Antonito into New Mexico or drive seven miles north from Chama, New Mexico, on 17 to the Chama River Road (Forest Route 121). The Lobo Ranch is a good landmark at the intersection. Take this road north through private property for six miles to the Rio Grande National Forest boundary. At the forest boundary, take the left fork of the road to the campground beside the river. The road is closed on the east bank of the river. It may reopen eventually. Ford on foot and go about two miles to West Chama Trail, which begins at the road closure.

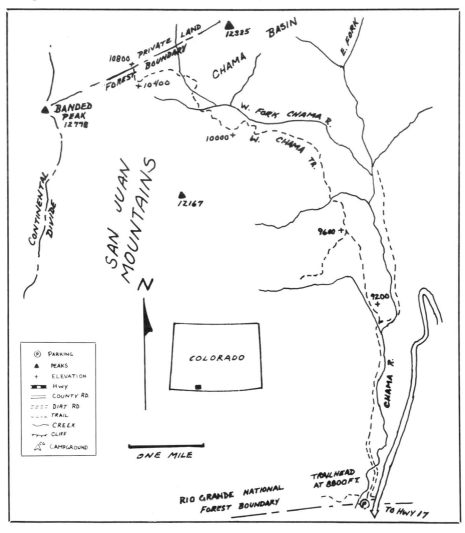

West Chama Trail

The trail climbs steeply away from the Chama River along a small tributary stream bordered by stands of aspen that are spectacular in the fall. As the trail leaves this tributary and follows the Chama River to the confluence of the East and West forks, it stays high above the river and passes through dry subalpine meadows and more stands of aspen and then through virgin spruce-fir forests. A spectacular view of the entire valley is afforded from the trail above the confluence.

While the glacial valleys of the Conejos Plateau Area are steep and narrow, the Chama River Valley is wide and spacious. Steep cliffs of colorful volcanic and sedimentary rock intricately eroded, surround the valley. Waterfalls cascade over the cliffs from the plateau above.

The gentle slopes which descend from the foot of the cliffs to the river below are covered by forests of aspen, interspersed with spruce and fir. Fingers of forest creep up the ravines dissecting the cliffs. Willows and cottonwoods follow the river as it meanders through the grasslands of the lower valley. At the trailhead of the West Chama Trail, the valley narrows and narrowleaf alder and willow dominate the streamside vegetation.

Massive Banded Peak, a local landmark, rises to your left as you continue the strenuous climb up the trail to the Forest Boundary and the Continental Divide. Here, at the trail's end, you have superb views of the Chama Basin and south into New Mexico.

This is not only a very scenic area, but a historic one as well. To the west is the Tierra Amarilla Land Grant and to the south is the route of the Cumbres and Toltec Railroad, a narrow gauge steam route which runs from Antonito, Colorado, to Chama, New Mexico.

Water and camping sites are abundant along the entire length of the trail, but drinking water should be treated before consumption. Fishing is good for rainbow and cutthroat trout in the Chama River. Be extremely careful in fording the river during spring runoff both on foot and at the start in your vehicle.

After enjoying the view from this, the headwaters of the West Fork, return as you came.—*U.S. Forest Service*

14 Ruybalid Lake

General description: A good overnight backpack or strenuous day hike to a high lake overlooking the Conejos River Canyon.
General location: 35 miles southwest of Alamosa.
Maps: Spectacle Lake USGS quad; Rio Grande National Forest Map.
Degree of difficulty: Moderate.
Length: 7 miles roundtrip.
Elevations: 8,800 to 11,200 feet.
Special attractions: Beautiful lake and excellent views of the Conejos River Canyon, the San Luis Valley, and the Sangre de Cristo Mountains.
Best season: Early summer through late fall.
For more information: Rio Grande National Forest, Conejos Ranger District, Highway 285 North, Rt. 1, P.O. Box 520 G, La Jara, CO 81140; (303) 274-5193.

This hike takes you into the beautiful South San Juan Wilderness in an area of high, forested plateaus, lakes and deep canyons on the southeastern edge of the San Juan Mountains. Ruybalid Lake is perched on the edge of one of these

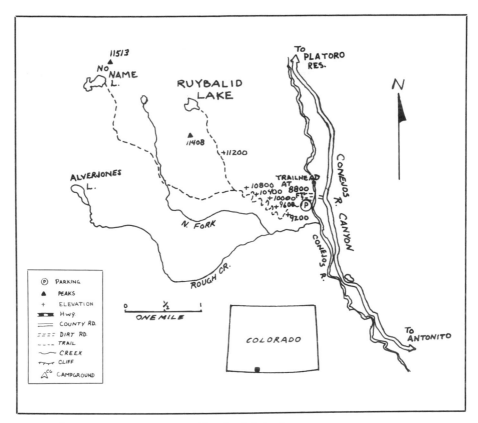

Legend:
- (P) PARKING
- ▲ PEAKS
- + ELEVATION
- ▅▅ HWY.
- = COUNTY RD.
- ==== DIRT RD.
- ---- TRAIL
- ⌇ CREEK
- ┬┬┬ CLIFF
- ⌂CG CAMPGROUND

Ruybalid Lake

plateaus overlooking the deep glaciated Conejos River Canyon.

To reach the trailhead, take U.S. Highway 285 south from Alamosa for about 25 miles. At Antonito, go west on State Highway 17 along the Conejos River. After approximately 15 miles, turn right onto the gravel road which follows the Conejos River to its headwaters near Platoro reservoir (the turn is well marked). After eight miles, you will pass through a small settlement and see a sign reading, "Ruybalid Lake and No Name Lake." Turn left at this sign, cross the Conejos River and park in the area provided. The trail leaves from the south end of the parking area, goes downstream for a hundred yards or so, then leave the river bottom area and climbs the steep canyon wall.

The Conejos River Canyon is a deep, U-shaped, glacial valley incised about 2,000 feet into the relatively flat-topped basalt plateau which extends eastward from the Continental Divide. You will have some nice views of the Conejos River, winding its way through the lush meadows in the canyon bottom as you climb the switchbacks to the top of the plateau. The climb up this slope looks short on the maps, but is actually about two miles. There are 12 long switch-backs, a short break, then 18 more short, steep switchbacks to the top. There isn't much water along the way, and if it weren't for the occasional views, this portion of the hike would have to be considered just a necessary evil on the road to your destination.

Once you reach the top, the trail breaks into some openings and levels off. Several hundred yards along, there is a sign where the trails to No Name and

Ruybalid Lakes diverge. (The sign looks as though it may not be there for long, however.) The trail to the left goes to No Name Lake, while the Ruybalid Lake trail goes straight across the meadow. The Forest Service map and USGS maps both show this intersection rather far up the North Fork of Rough Creek, with the trail to Ruybalid Lake traversing a saddle in a low divide. This is incorrect. Actually, the trails diverge shortly after you reach the top of the plateau and the Ruybalid Lake trail travels along the east side of the low divide. Once you take the fork to Ruybalid Lake, it's easy to lose the trail as it crosses the meadow, but you should be able to pick it up again on the opposite side. Ruybalid Lake is reached about 1.5 miles after the trails diverge. The lake is deep and rimmed on three sides by rocky cliffs. A rise in the ground surface of only 10 feet or so separates the lake from the Conejos River canyon, so you are able to look out to the east toward the historic San Luis Valley, through which Ute Indians, Spaniards, trappers, explorers, miners, and settlers have all passed at one time or another. This is a good campsite—away from the lake edge and with this beautiful view. There are few other sites between the lake and the canyon. Fishing is fair at the lake for brook trout.

The cliff area behind the lake makes for some good exploring. A good "cross country" route to No Name Lake leads up a small valley north of the lake onto the cliffs and then west-northwest through the woods. The woods are relatively thin here and it's difficult to get lost because you will intercept either the trail to No Name Lake or the edge of the canyon. There are several small, but scenic, ponds along the way.

Extended hikes may be taken west along the top of the plateau from the No Name Lake trail. The plateau rises in elevation to the west some 12,000 feet to where the Continental Divide crosses it. There are many other fine lakes in this backcountry and hiking is easy between them, but the trails are unreliable because they are so infrequently used by hikers that they are difficult to discern from cattle and game trails. For this reason, a topo map is a must if you plan any extensive trips into the South San Juan Wilderness.—*Bill Bath*

15   *Wolf Creek Pass Divide Trail*

General description: An easy day hike or the starting point for an extended backpack along the Continental Divide in the San Juan Mountains.

General location: About 45 miles west of Alamosa and 50 miles east of Durango.

Maps: Wolf Creek Pass and Spar City 15 minute USGS quads

Degree of difficulty: Easy.

Length: As long as you want.

Elevations: Follows the Continental Divide at between 11,000 and 12,000 feet.

Special attractions: Easy access to the Continental Divide; spectacular views; beautiful wildflowers; good opportunities to see wildlife.

Best season: Summer.

For more information: Rio Grande National Forest, Del Norte Ranger District, 810 Grande Ave., P.O. Box 40, Del Norte, CO 81132; (303) 657-3321.

This hike takes you west and northwest along a portion of the Continental Divide Trail from the top of Wolf Creek Pass. The trail is easily accessible and takes you immediately into the beautiful timberline country along the Continental Divide. You will have spectacular views of the surrounding mountain

The San Juan Mountains.

ranges as you hike into the Weminuche Wilderness Area.

To reach the trail, take U.S. Highway 160 west from Alamosa or southwest from Del Norte to the summit of Wolf Creek Pass. Just on the east side of the pass, look for a gravel road, which climbs up the north side of the mountain. This road climbs to the Lobo Overlook at an elevation of about 11,700 feet and overlooks Wolf Creek Pass. The road is steep but accessible to passenger cars once the snow has been cleared in late spring or early summer.

Park in the area provided at the end of the road. Begin your hike by walking down past and to the west of the microwave tower, staying on the ridgetop through timber until you encounter the trail where it leads out across an alpine meadow. From here the trail is easy to follow, except where it may disappear into snow drifts if you are hiking early in the summer season.

Within the first .5 miles, you may come across as many as three separate sign posts which have been vandalized. These may have been signs for the Continental Divide Trail and/or side trails which descend both north and south from the Divide. These side trails are indicated differently on both the USGS and Forest Service Maps and are difficult to follow.

About .75 miles along, the trail drops down on the south side of the Divide to avoid the steep ridgetop. The trail then traverses a beautiful bowl above Wolf Creek. At this point you may notice some timber cuts across the valley on the slopes of Treasure Mountain. They are clearcuts, but have been made in irregular shapes to approximate natural openings in the forest. These are a far cry from the square blocks so commonly associated with clearcutting in the past.

As you climb back toward the ridgetop and pass several outcroppings of rock, look for indications of the volcanic geology of this area. Extensive deposits of volcanic breccia and lava cover most of the San Juan Mountains.

After you reach the ridgetop, you will descend by way of a long meadow to a saddle along the Divide. This would make a good destination for a short day hike or provide a good camping spot if you plan on going farther. The

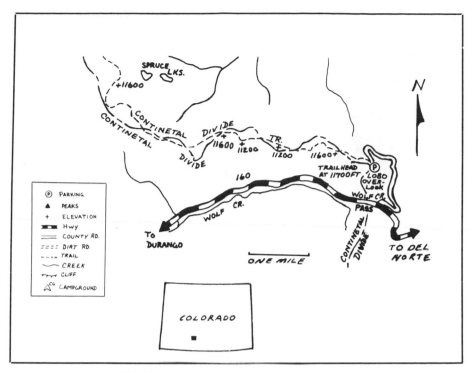

Wolf Creek Pass Divide Trail

possibilities for longer hikes are unlimited along this trail, which takes you through meadows of unsurpassed beauty, full of wildflowers, and provides you with spectacular views through its length. The trail will eventually extend all the way from the New Mexico border to the Wyoming border, following both existing trails and trail sections yet to be built as it traces the Continental Divide through the state. You may continue as far as Silverton, some 60 miles away, or just to Archuleta Lake, eight miles farther. There are side trails to be explored, too. Or you can always simply return as you came.—*Peter, Caryn and Crystal Boddie.*

16 Hermosa Trail

General description: A day hike or backpack taking you along the canyon of Hermosa Creek in the San Juan Mountains.

General location: Fourteen miles north of Durango.

Maps: Hermosa, Monument Hill, Elk Creek, Electra Lake, and Hermosa Peak USGS quads; San Juan National Forest Map.

Length: Up to 20 miles one way.

Degree of difficulty: Easy.

Elevations: 7,600 to 8,800 feet.

Special attractions: A completely roadless area; the trail follows a long canyon from which you will have ever-varying vistas; provides access to many side trails in the area.

Best season: Spring, fall, and early winter (when not snow covered).

For more information: San Juan National Forest, Animas Ranger District,

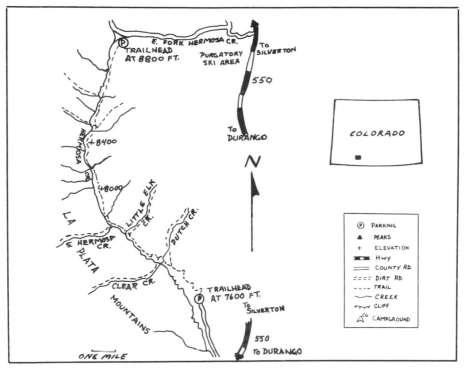

Hermosa Trail

Federal Building, 701 Camino del Rio, Room 100, Durango, CO 81301; (303) 259-0195.

The Hermosa Trail is at once one of the best and one of the most heavily used trails in southwestern Colorado. However, since it is 20 miles long, it has room to absorb many people.

You'll find the hiking good on the Hermosa Trail any time of the year when the snow is off, but hunting season is the poorest time to hike it. (This is great elk and deer country and during October and the first half of November the area is taken over by the hunters. Hikers should wear blaze orange during these months.)

Day hikes can be done from either end of the trail with the hiker returning the way he came. Backpackers should count on being out at least one night; two or more are necessary to traverse the entire canyon. There are also many side trails out of the canyon which can be explored, making a whole week in the area worthwhile for those who want a longer stay.

The south end of the trail is most-used and easiest to get to. To find it, go 10 miles north of Durango (or 40 miles south of Silverton) on U.S. Highway 550 to the unincorporated settlement of Hermosa. At the north end of the town the narrow gauge railroad crosses the highway. Just south of the crossing several yards, a road turns west off the highway. Take this road for about 30 yards until it dead-ends into a road paralleling the highway. Turn right (north) on this road and follow it to its end in four miles. The first half of the road is paved, the last half gravel. At the end of the road, park off to the side and begin your hike.

The trail starts directly at the end of the road and dips steeply for about 20 yards, then meets the main trail, which you take to the right. This point should be carefully noted for the sake of return, because you can easily miss this exit and find yourself not only bypassing your car, but entering private property.

Once on the main trail, you will find hiking quite easy for the first five miles, with only small ups and downs. It takes you through heavy stands of timber and along the side of the mountain, giving you a view far down below into the Hermosa Creek Canyon and up on both sides to the high mountains. You can see the La Plata Mountains to the west and south with several summits above 13,000 feet.

After five miles, the Dutch Creek Trail takes off to the right, joining Dutch Creek a mile up and eventually winding its way in a northerly direction to the top of the ridge at an altitude above 10,000 feet. One can hike the ridge trail several miles in either direction.

When the Dutch Creek Trail turns north, the Hermosa Trail swings left and down a long hill, some of it steep. After a mile, there is a fine Forest Service bridge across Dutch Creek. There is good camping nearby. Also at this point, you are back down to the level of Hermosa Creek where fishing is fair, mainly for rainbow trout. The Clear Creek Trail leads to it and up the other side into the La Platas. The main trail continues on without crossing Hermosa Creek and climbs high above the creek again. Several miles farther along it returns to stream level.

The canyon changes as you continue. At times, it is narrow with low cliffs on each side. At other times, there are grassy spots near the creek. Near the north end, it widens out into a large, open park. Most of the way, the trail is quite clear, but a few miles from the north end, it is sometimes grassy enough to be lost temporarily.

At one point, near an old cabin, there is a grassy spot obscuring the trail for a short distance. At this same point there is a side trail crossing the creek west over a dilapidated log bridge and going up a side canyon. If you find this spot, resist the temptation to cross the bridge and continue south on the east side of the canyon. You should pick up the trail again.

The north end of the trail can also be taken in and out a suitable distance for day hikes. Actually, if you want to hike the full length of the Hermosa Trail, the north to south route is easier since there is a net loss of 1,000 feet in elevation in that direction. For easy day hikes, however, the south end is slightly better since the north end drops steadily for several miles, making the return uphill. In spite of the favorable drop for a southbound full-length trip, it is not all downhill. The long Dutch Creek hill mentioned above will have to be climbed. Also, there are a couple of other long climbs before that.

To find the north entrance, take U.S. Highway 550, 28 miles north of Durango and 22 miles south of Silverton to the Purgatory Ski Area Road. It goes steeply west up to the ski headquarters in .5 miles. At the east end of the ski parking area, a small road turns right (north) uphill. Follow it as it winds 2.5 miles to the top of a ridge in a mostly westerly direction. At the top, a left turn will take you to the Purgatory Powder House. Follow the main road to the right. Half a mile later, a road runs downhill. Follow it down into Hermosa Park for five miles where a little road turns left (south) off the main road and crosses the East Fork of Hermosa Creek. In .25 mile, the road ends. Park here out of the way and begin hiking on the trail through a small gate. Late September or early October, just before the main hunting season starts, is an especially nice time for this end of the route since there are many aspen on the north side of Hermosa Park and at various points along the trail. The aspens are a brilliant gold at this time, set against a dark green background of conifers.

There are many side trails off the main trail, some of which may not be well maintained, but are worth the exploring time; each of them with their own fascinations.—*Paul Pixler*

(Paul Pixler is the author of *Hiking Trails of Southwestern Colorado,* published by Pruett Publishing.)

17 Chicago Basin

General Description: An overnight hike into the Chicago Basin and Needle Mountains with the added excitement of a ride on the Durango and Silverton Narrow Gauge Railway to reach the trailhead.

General location: About 30 miles north of Durango, 20 miles south of Silverton.

Maps: Columbine Pass and Mountain View Crest USGS quads; San Juan National Forest map.

Degree of Difficulty: Moderate to more difficult.

Length: 8 miles one way, not including access by rail.

Elevations: 8,100 to 11,000 feet.

Special attractions: Spectacular views of the rugged Needle Mountains and three fourteen-thousand-foot peaks: Elous, Windom and Sunlight; and a fun train ride.

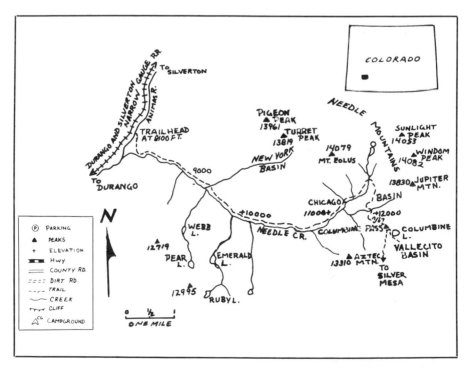

Chicago Basin

Best season: Summer.

For more information: San Juan National Forest, Animas Ranger District, Federal Building, 701 Camino del Rio, Room 100, Durango, CO 81301; (303) 259-0195.

This hike into the spectacular Needles Mountains and Chicago Basin in the San Juan Range north of Durango, combines the unique opportunity to ride one of the West's classic railways and to climb into some pretty rugged country.

The Needle Creek trail is reached via the Durango and Silverton Narrow Gauge Railway. The train departs from Durango, usually by eight A.M. After a ride of about an hour the train makes a stop at Needleton Bridge. This is one of two points at which the train stops for hikers, and Chicago Basin hikers should disembark here. Be sure the conductor knows you are hiking from Needleton when you board the train. As of this writing, the cost of a round-trip ticket to Needleton and back to Durango is $22.50.

After watching the old coalfire steam engine head on its way to Silverton, proceed across the Needleton Bridge which crosses the Animas River here, and find a trail that passes to the right of the remains of an old log cabin and heads to the south. Within about one-half mile, the trail comes to a junction. The right fork continues along the Animas River to the south, after crossing Needle Creek. The fork to the left is the trail to Chicago Basin, and follows the north bank of Needle Creek all the way to timberline. Within two miles the trail crosses a major drainage from New York Basin which descends from the north. Though there are side trails which cross Needle Creek at several points along the seven-mile route to Chicago Basin, the easiest and most direct route is the trail along the creek's northern (lefthand) bank.

As the trail climbs the narrow valley of Needle Creek through thick stands of pine, spruce and fir, the sharp, knife edge ridges of the Needle mountains begin to reveal themselves. The vista becomes superb as the trail approaches the upper basin near timberline. From any of the numerous campsites in the grassy, sparsely wooded meadows in the basin, three of Colorado's fourteen-thousand-foot peaks dominate the skyline. To the northwest is Mount Elous at 14,083, beyond and to the north lies Sunlight, 14,059, and Windom, at 14,087.

Because Chicago Basin gets moderate to heavy use, campers should be particularly careful to use low impact camping methods. And you should purify the water you find, which is plentiful. Avoid fires where stoves will do and be sure to pack out all trash.

Return as you came, making sure to give yourself plenty of time to reach the rail stop at Needleton. Be sure to find out what time the train will be returning when you buy your tickets. Also be prepared to flag the train as it approaches. *Chris Frye*

18 Lizard Head Trail

General description: A steep day hike or backpack into the heart of the San Juan Mountains.

General location: Approximately 60 miles north of Cortez; 14 miles south of Telluride.

Maps: Mount Wilson USGS quad; Uncompahgre and San Juan National Forest maps.

Hiking in the San Juans.

Degree of difficulty: Moderate.
Length: Approximately 3.5 miles one way, but offering the possibility for a longer backpack.
Elevations: 10,280 to 12,080 feet.
Special attractions: Spectacular view of the San Juans with their intriguing geology; interesting and beautiful hiking through conifer forest and aspen groves, beautiful wildflowers and many species of mushrooms.
Best season: Summer through early fall.
For more information: Uncompahgre National Forest, Norwood Ranger District, East Grande Ave., P.O. Box 388, Norwood, CO 81423; (303) 327-4261.

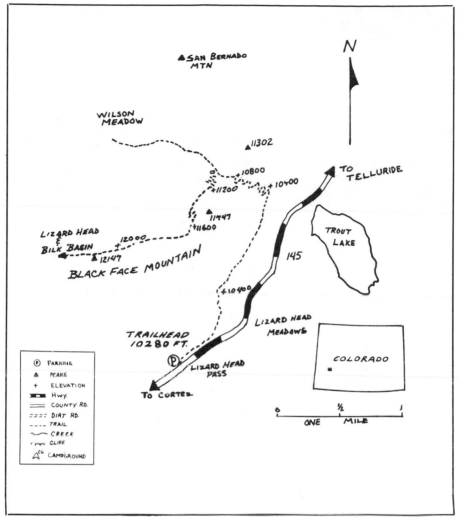

Lizard Head Trail

A hike along the Lizard Head Trail in the heart of the San Juans is a hike into some of Colorado's most rugged and beautiful country. You will travel through meadows alive with wildflowers, through thick conifer forests where mushrooms, moss and lichens grow profusely, and through beautiful aspen groves. When you reach the ridgetop that is your destination, you will be more than glad you made the trip. The scenery is fantastic; the famed Lizard Head juts into the sky to the west.

To reach the trailhead, drive south on State Highway 789 from Montrose to Ridgeway. Turn west at Ridgeway on Highway 62 and follow it until you reach the junction with State Highway 145. Turn south on 145 and follow it to the summit of Lizard Head Pass. You can also drive north from Cortez on 145 to the summit of the pass. Park in the area provided at the Lizard Head Pass sign on the west side of the highway.

Begin your hike by following the dirt road to the northeast about .12 miles.

The spectacular Lizard Head in the San Juan Range.

Look for the trail marker and the trail itself taking off to the left.

The first mile of the trail is fairly level (you even lose some elevation) as you contour the east side of Black Face Mountain. You will be hiking through beautiful aspen groves and open parks where you can look down into the valley eastward.

Soon you will enter the Lizard Head Wilderness Area, where you will begin to ascend steeply through heavy stands of spruce and fir, and then intercept the old trail coming up from the highway below. It is still indicated this way on the topo map. You will cross the old trail several times on your climb. Please do not use it, as the Forest Service is trying to revegetate it.

Try to pick out the different species of wildflowers as you make your way along the switchbacks that take you steeply up the mountainside: there are mountain asters, Indian paintbrush, larkspur, chiming bells, as well as a variety of mushrooms, lichens and moss.

Once up this steep pitch, you will reach a small clearing and a fork in the trail. A sign directs you straight ahead to Wilson Meadows or left to the Lizard Head Trail. Go left and you will again begin to climb, switching back many times until you reach the ridgetop. Watch for glimpses of the Lizard Head to your right as you climb through the trees.

Once on the ridgetop, the trail becomes indistinct. Look to your right and you'll see it emerge on the far side of a small meadow. Watch for the posts ahead of you as you continue on to your destination, as the trail disappears and reappears several times as you walk across the tundra.

The views you'll have as you climb this ridge leading to the summit of Black Face Mountain (12,147 feet) will have been well worth your effort. To the west is the unmistakeable Lizard Head, volcanic rock rising some 500 feet from the mountaintop as a lone pinnacle; beyond it are rugged Gladstone Peak and

Mount Wilson; to the northwest is Wilson Peak and to the northeast is Sunshine Mountain. Below you to the north is Wilson Meadows, an area inviting to elk and backpackers alike.

Should you want to continue on backpacking, you can follow the Lizard Head Trail along the ridge south of the Lizard Head and then northward down Bilk Basin along Bilk Creek to State Highway 145, where you will have had to shuttle a car before you started out. Otherwise, return as you came.—*Caryn, Peter and Crystal Boddie*

19 Bear Creek National Recreation Trail

General description: A full day hike or backpack through a wonderland of varied geological formations and diverse vegetation.

General location: 2 miles south of Ouray.

Maps: Ouray, Ironton, Handies Peak, and Wetterhorn Peak USGS quads; Uncompahgre National Forest map.

Degree of difficulty: Moderate.

Length: 4.2 miles one way with the possibility of a longer backpack.

Elevations: 8,440 to 11,200 feet.

Special attractions: Interesting geology; beautiful wildflowers.

Best season: Late spring, summer and fall.

For more information: Uncompahgre National Forest, Ouray Ranger District, 101 N. Uncompahgre Ave., P.O. Box 1047, Montrose, CO 81401; (303) 249-3711.

The Bear Creek National Recreation Trail takes you through country that has been referred to as "the little Switzerland of America," leading you over a variety of geologic formations to the Yellow Jacket Mine near timberline and on to Engineer Mountain Pass. It is only one in a system of trails in this part of the Uncompahgre National Forest. You can extend your hike by taking other, connecting trails to expand your experience of these verdant mountains.

You begin your hike near the nestled burg of Ouray, once a mining town with a population of several thousands. Drive south from the town on U.S. Highway 550 for two miles. Trail parking for the Bear Creek National Recreation Trail is on the east side of the highway and was once marked by a trail sign (gone in July of 1983 and probably in someone's living room). The trail itself begins on the west side of the highway and leads you over a tunnel and then, after a short walk, starts to switchback through a forest of white fir and Douglas fir, interspersed with stands of aspen that are glorious in the fall. It was once the site of intensive mining activity. There are many abandoned mines throughout the area, including the Grizzly Bear and Yellow Jacket mines you will come upon on this hike.

Still switching back on the trail, you will hike into the open and over quartzite and slate. This is the Uncompahgre formation, which is only exposed in this area south of Ouray. It is the oldest Pre-cambrian formation in Colorado and displays ripple marks and striations of graded bedding, reflecting its sedimentary origins. Climbing away from the Uncompahgre formation, you come upon the San Juan formation, composed of volcanic tuff cut by veins of pyrite and containing rich deposits of silver, lead, and zinc sulfide.

At the top of the switchbacks, you will see a sign for those descending, which reads, "Do not cut the switchbacks or throw rocks." Approximately 300 feet from the sign there is a small boulder slide to cross. The trail then

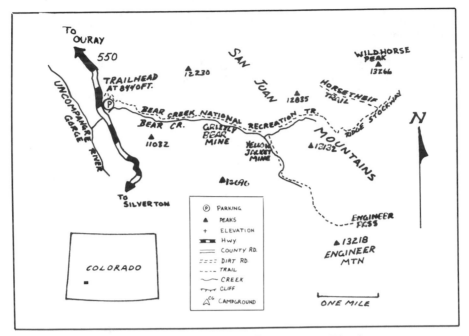

Bear Creek National Recreation Trail

levels and takes you under an overhang that runs with water at times and is lush with wildflowers such as mountain aster, yarrow, and wild geranium. Then it winds along a ledge high above Bear Creek.

When the Bear Creek Trail was built in the late 1800s by miners as access to claims along Bear Creek and an alternate route over Engineer Mountain, it was a substantial, well-built route hewn into the rock ledges and supported by log and rock cribbing. It is not unsafe today, either, though deterioration has occurred in some of the original cribbing and pinning. New supports have been added, replacing portions that were hazardous.

Soon the trail crosses two stream beds that may be flowing in spring and early summer and you can cross small patches of snow, depending on the previous winter's snowfall. After the trail levels out and takes you through open green meadows and cool green stands of aspen, you will come to a small steel shack on the left side of the trail and discarded mining equipment on the right. After another minute on the trail, you will see the Grizzly Bear Mine on the right, along Bear Creek.

After carefully poking around the mine, return to the trail and continue through more woods to the first major stream crossing. The trail is marked on both sides of the stream by wooden posts topped with orange metallic diamonds. After you carefully cross the stream, hike up through more lush green meadows and over a portion of the trail that is narrow (watch your step), then cross another stream and continue to an avalanche area with a lot of deadfall. Do not head up to your left along the bank where a worn area on the hill appears as a trail. Cross the avalanche area and continue on the trail through intermittent forest and meadow until you arrive at the Yellow Jacket Mine where you will find evidence of mining history in the form of buildings, equipment, shafts, and adits still remaining.

Bear Creek Trail in 1916. U.S. Forest Service.

At the mine, the trail forks. A turn to the left will take you along the Ridge Stock Driveway to a fork on the Continental Divide. A left turn there will take you onto the Horsethief Trail, which winds northeast to Dexter Creek. This makes a good backpack loop provided you shuttled vehicles to Dexter Creek before you left. (To do so, drive north from Ouray on U.S. Highway 550 to Forest Route 871, taking you to Lenore Lake. Drive past the lake to the trailhead.)

A turn to the right at the Yellow Jacket Mine will take you southeast to the Continental Divide and Engineer Mountain Pass. The trail becomes vague above timberline, but you will not become lost. Follow the switchbacks above the mining debris. A double-track jeep trail becomes evident above timberline; follow that to the Divide. As you go ever higher, look for the large rock glacier on the north-facing slope, and notice the grasses, sedges and forbs typical of this alpine tundra. Also keep an eye open for marmots, the ever-elusive pika, grouse, and ptarmigan at this high altitude. Once at the summit of Engineer Mountain Pass, take time to look around. You have a spectacular 360-degree view of the mountain summits and lakes of the San Juans. And there is time to rest, as time stands still.—*Jeanne Vallez*

20 Cimarron River Loop

General description: A 2 to 3 day backpack on an extended loop route through the Big Blue Wilderness.

General location: Approximately 25 miles southeast of Montrose.

Maps: Courthouse Mountain, Wetterhorn Peak, Uncompahgre Peak and Sheep Mountain USGS quads; Uncompahgre National Forest Map.

Degree of difficulty: Moderate.

Length: About 22 miles one way.

Elevations: 9,275 to 12,400 feet.

Special attractions: Long, scenic backpack through the Big Blue Wilderness; interesting geology; old mine; opportunities to see elk and deer; great views of fourteeners, Uncompahgre and Wetterhorn Peaks.

For more information: Uncompahgre National Forest, Ouray Ranger District, 101 N. Uncompahgre Ave., P.O. Box 1047, Montrose, CO 81401; (303) 249-3711.

The Middle Fork Trail along the Middle Fork of the Cimarron River, combined with the East Fork Trail along the river's East Fork, forms an excellent two to three day backpack loop in the Big Blue Wilderness in the San Juan Mountains.

To reach the trailhead, drive east from Montrose on State Highway 50 for about 20 miles or about 65 miles west from Gunnison to the Owl Creek-Cimarron Road going south (Forest Route 861). Follow this road south past

Wetterhorn, Matterhorn and Coxcomb Peaks. U.S. Forest Service photo.

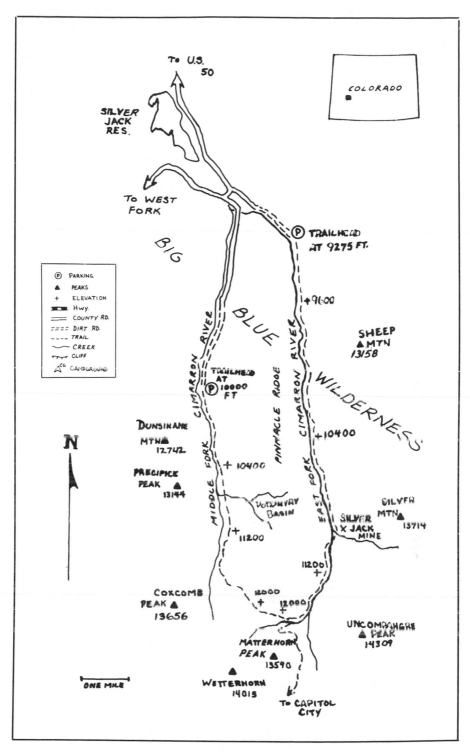

Cimarron River Loop

Silver Jack Reservoir until the road makes a big turn west. About .25 miles past the junction with the West Fork Road (Forest Route 860), turn left on Middle Fork Road (still Forest Route 861) and follow it 6.4 miles to the parking area at the end of the road. Since you will be doing a loop trip, you will need to shuttle cars to the trailhead of the East Fork Trail or plan on hiking an extra eight miles or so to your car. To shuttle, follow 861 back to the East Fork Road and follow it for two miles to the trailhead or park .5 miles before the trailhead in the open meadows—the last .5 miles is pretty rough and narrow.

The Middle Fork Trail begins on the right side of the parking area near the river. For the first six miles it parallels the Middle Fork of the Cimarron River and walking is easy. In early summer, a few bogs must be crossed within the first .5 miles of the trail, but they are usually dried up by mid-July. Two miles from the trailhead, you'll cross a stream where water from the Porphyry Basin to the east joins the Middle Fork. The old foot bridge is no longer useable and the trail is routed to an easy crossing. An old mining trail to Porphyry Basin takes off near the crossing.

You are hiking into the Big Blue Wilderness, beautiful and wild, and surrounded by mines. It includes two fourteeners—Wetterhorn and Uncompahgre Peaks—the latter being the highest mountain the San Juan Range. Throughout this area, you will find examples of the complex volcanic geology typical of the San Juans. Pinnacle Ridge, which separates the Middle and East Forks of the Cimarron River, is an especially interesting and spectacularly eroded ridge formed of volcanic breccia.

About two miles past the Porphyry Basin you will begin the steep climb to the pass between Wetterhorn and Uncompahgre Peaks, from which you will descend into the valley of the East Fork of the Cimarron River. As you make the top of the pass, stop and take in the panorama. To the west you will see Redcliff, Coxcomb, and Precipice peaks. To the south is Matterhorn Peak; to the southwest, Wetterhorn Peak; and to the southeast, Uncompahgre Peak.

At the top of the pass the trail is indistinct. Follow the drainage downhill towards the basin below Uncompahgre Peak and you will easily locate the East Fork Trail.

The East Fork follows an old mining road for much of its length and is one route for domestic sheep grazing the alpine country. Bands of sheep are driven by herders along the trail beginning in July. Water, though plentiful, must be considered unsafe to drink unless treated. As you make your way from the tundra down into the spruce and fir forests beginning at 11,600 feet elevation, watch for elk and deer.

At the base of Silver Mountain you will come upon the remains of the Silver Jack Mine, along with other evidence of past mining activity. The mining of metallic ores such as gold, silver, copper, lead and zinc has been an important industry in and around this area since 1875. The mining camps of Lake City, Telluride and Ouray once had populations of several thousand people.

The last portion of the East Fork Trail is easy walking along the river to your destination and, if you shuttled cars, to your vehicle. Otherwise, you'll have to walk the two miles down to Forest Route 861 and then hike to up the Middle Creek trailhead.

Please be careful to camp below timberline and use your backpacking stove instead of building fires, if possible. Also remember to camp at least 200 feet away from trails and water and enjoy this beautiful backpack through high mountain country.—U.S. Forest Service

21 East Bellows Trail

General description: A long day hike or overnighter taking you to Wheeler Geologic Area, Halfmoon Pass and the LaGarita Wilderness.

General location: Approximately 10 miles southeast of Creede.

Maps: Pooltable, Halfmoon Pass and Wagon Wheel Gap USGS quads; Rio Grande National Forest   Map.

Degree of difficulty: Moderate.

Length: About 8.5 miles one way.

Elevations: 10,800 to 12,700 feet.

Special attractions: Beautiful views; unique geologic features; good fishing for small brook trout.

Best season: Summer and fall.

For more information: Rio Grande National Forest, Creede Ranger District, Creede Ave., P.O. Box 270, Creede, CO 81130; (303) 658-2556.

Visitors to Wheeler National Monument in the 1930s. U.S. Forest Service photo.

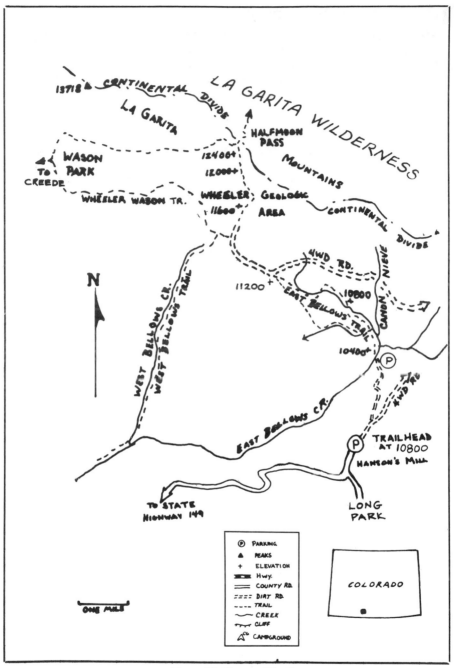

East Bellows Trail

The East Bellows Trail takes you up the East Fork of Bellows Creek to spectacular Wheeler Geologic Area and on up the Halfmoon Pass with its beautiful views and beyond to the LaGarita Wilderness.

To reach the trailhead, drive southeast from Creede for 7.3 miles or 14.4 miles northwest of South Fork on State Highway 149 and Forest Route 600 (Pool Table Road), located on the north side of the highway, then approximately 9.5 miles northwest on Pool Table Road to the Hanson's Mill camping area.

Begin your hike by following the old jeep road in a northeasterly direction. After about .25 miles, the road will fork. Follow the left (west) fork of the road for about one mile down into the East Bellows Creek drainage. The foot trail will begin just before this road crosses the creek. After crossing the creek (you'll have to wade it as the bridge is gone, so be very careful, particularly in early summer), the trail heads up the west fork of East Bellows Creek (Canon Nieve). In about .5 miles, there is a fork in the trail which is signed. Take the fork heading west, which will make a gradual climb of about four miles through open parks and scattered timber before joining the 4-wheel drive access road to Wheeler Geologic Area. Follow the road west for about one mile to its end at a pole fence in a small meadow below the area.

The unique, picturesque features of the geologic area are about .25 to .5 miles north from the end of the road. The foot trail to Wheeler will quickly meet the West Bellows Creek Trail. Follow the sign directions and continue up West Bellows Creek Trail. Just before reaching the lower base of the geologic formations, you will come to the junction of this trail with the Wheeler-Wason Trail. Take the fork heading north and in 150 yards you will arrive at the base of the beautiful Wheeler Geologic Area formations.

Named for Captain George M. Wheeler, who in 1874, was in charge of the surveying and exploration work being done in this part of Colorado by the War Department, the Wheeler Geologic Area was proclaimed a National Monument by President "Teddy" Roosevelt in 1908. The scenic geologic area occupies 640 acres, about 60 acres of which consist of formations of volcanic tuff, crumbled and eroded by wind and water into fantastic shapes.

The Ute Indians called the area "The Sand Stones," and tribal renegades are said to have used the strange place as a hideout. Others have called it, "The City of Gnomes," "The White Shrouded Ghosts," "Dante's Lost Souls," "Beehives," "Temples," and "Phantom Ships." Whatever you choose to call them, you'll be amazed at this conglomeration of pinnacles, domes, and spires of rock surrounded and hidden by mountains.

The rock itself is a moderately coarse volcanic tuff (debris blown into the air from volcanic vents), which settled here. Individual particles of this debris may range in size from dust flakes to blocks two or three feet across. They have not been cemented together or firmly compacted.

As the rains have fallen upon the easily eroded material, the water has carried away much of the finer debris. Larger blocks have remained as capstones for sharp spires or pinnacles, which stand alone when the surrounding unproteced material has been washed away. Slight differences in texture or in the amount of compaction results in the development of the different shapes and forms. Also, vertical joint cracks weaken the beds at intervals and these can form what appear to be hooded ghosts.

After enjoying the formations, follow the trail past a shelter house (be sure to stop and sign your name to the guest register), through a stand of timber, and climb above the formations. Some magnificent views are available before you conquer the crest of the LaGarita Mountains at Halfmoon Pass, about one mile way, and arrive finally at the LaGarita Wilderness Area, beautiful and rugged, beckoning you to spend some time. Then return as you came.—*U.S. Forest Service.*

22 Fremont's Camps

General description: A day hike or short overnighter in the LaGarita mountains.

General location: About 20 miles northwest of Del Norte.

Maps: From Cathedral Campground: USGS Pine Cone Knob and Pool Table Mountain quads.

From Groundhog Park: Pine Cone Knob, Pool Table Mountain, Bowers Peak, and Mesa Mountain USGS quads.

Rio Grande National Forest Map.

Degree of difficulty: Moderate.

Length: From Cathedral Campground, 3.5 miles; from Groundhog Park, 8 miles one way.

Elevations: 9,400 to 12,400 feet.

Special attractions: Historic site of John C. Fremont's winter camps.

Best season: Summer.

For more information: Rio Grande National Forest, Del Norte Ranger District, P.O. Box 40, Del Norte, CO 81132; (303) 657-3321.

In the winter of 1848, General John Charles Fremont made a disastrous attempt to cross the mountains of southern Colorado in the dead of winter. These two trails—one long and one short—lead to the historic site of his Christmas camp and to the December 27 camp nearby. The first trail is 3.5 miles and the second is eight miles one way.

From Cathedral Campground: To reach this trailhead, drive west of Del Norte on State Highway 160 to Embargo Creek Road (Forest Route 650). Go right (north) and cross the Embargo (Granger) bridge, then continue north on the Embargo Road, following the signs to Cathedral Campground.

Earlier visitors to Fremont's camps. U.S. Forest Service photo.

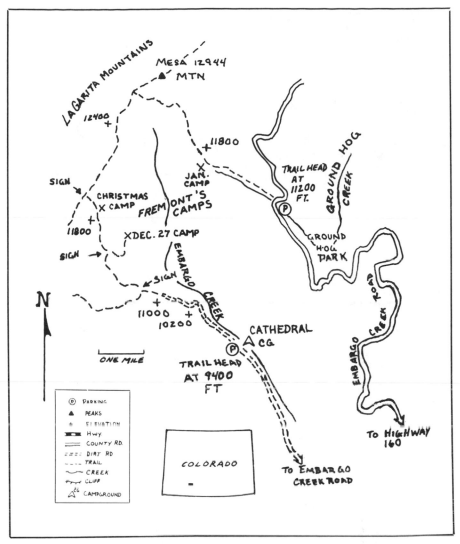

Fremont's Camps

Beginning at the campground, you will hike on jeep road #640 for about 2.5 miles. Approximately .5 miles of the road is on private land; please respect it. Approximately .5 miles after the end of the jeep road is the junction of the Big City Trail and the Fremont Trail. The sign directs you to the right and to Fremont's camp.

The trail passes through aspen stands, offering a view of the cliffs and rocks for which Cathedral Campground is named. It then climbs fairly steeply through stands of Douglas fir, then up into spruce and fir stands, and finally, into alpine meadows. During July, many wildflowers appear in the meadows. About 1.5 miles after the trail junction is another sign giving directions to the Fremont camps. The December 27 camp is to the right .5 miles and the Christmas camp is .5 miles past the sign on the same drainage, in the last string of trees.

The LaGarita Mountains around Mesa Mountain. U.S. Forest Service photo.

From Groundhog Park: To reach this trailhead, follow the same directions as to Cathedral Campground, except once on the Embargo Creek Road, you should follow the signs to Groundhog Park. The hike begins where the road crosses Groundhog Creek. Follow the trail up the creek to Mesa Mountain. In one of the fingers of timber on the left side of the draw, below timberline, lies another of Fremont's camps, where his party apparently stayed on its way out of the area in January. From the ridge of Mesa Mountain, the view is extensive in all directions. Travel southwest along the ridge, until you reach the sign to Fremont's Christmas camp. The camp is about .25 miles off the ridge towards the creek.

When the "Pathfinder," as Fremont was called, left St. Louis to find a railroad route through the Central Rockies, to California, he was certain that he could make it through the mountains during the height of winter and that this accomplishment would prove that a railroad could make it through in winter, as well. He headed west from Pueblo in November 1848 with 36 men and 120 mules into particularly harsh weather that made the LaGarita Mountains even more impassable than they would have been during a normal winter. There was even heavy snow cover on the floor of the usually dry San Luis Valley.

Although the exact route Fremont took into the mountains isn't clear, several camps around Mesa Mountain are known. There you'll see stumps of trees cut by the expedition at the snow level—at a depth of four to six feet—and the remains of one of the party's sleds. Diaries from several expedition members described the camps, including the Christmas camp where, after managing to cross the summit of the LaGaritas, Fremont decided to turn back, recross the mountains, and head down to the Rio Grande River.

The diaries tell a sad but fascinating tale. The party became stranded in the high country. For several weeks the only food was mule, while Fremont, with ponies secured from the Indians, was able to reach Taos and the famous Kit Carson, who went back with a rescue party to find a few men making their way across the San Luis Valley. Eleven of them had died of hunger and exposure. The rest made it to Taos and safety, and, although Fremont continued on to California in 1849, he never found the hoped for route across the southern Colorado Rockies.

The diaries can be read at the Del Norte Ranger District office or the museum in Del Norte where relics of the equipment used by the expedition are housed.—*Curtis Bates*

23 East Side Dune Trail

General description: A pleasant day hike along the eastern edge of the Great Sand Dunes or a longer hike into the Sangre de Cristo Mountains.

General location: Approximately 30 miles northeast of Alamosa.

Maps: Medano Pass and Mosca Pass USGS quads; Great Sand Dunes, National Monument; Rio Grande National Forest Map.

Degree of difficulty: Moderate to difficult.

Length: From 3 to 10 miles one way.

Elevations: 8,300 to 13,297 feet.

Special attractions: Great Sand Dunes; good views of surrounding mountain ranges; disappearing creeks.

Best season: Spring and fall.

For more information: Great Sand Dunes National Monument, Mosca, CO 81146; Rio Grande National Forest, Alamosa Ranger District, Highway 285 North, Rt. 1, P.O. Box 520 G, La Jara, CO 81140; (303) 274-5193.

This hike takes you into an intriguing and unique area in southern Colorado, long the focus of many legends and superstitions: the Great Sand Dunes. The trail follows a jeep road but offers you a good chance to disappear for awhile like the creek that runs through the shifting sands.

To reach the trailhead, drive east from Alamosa about 14 miles on U.S. Highway 160. Then go north on State Highway 150 about 20 miles to the Great Sand Dunes National Monument Visitors' Center. From the parking lot area proceed northwest on the Medano Pass Road on foot. It is easy hiking along this four-wheel drive road, which follows Medano Creek at the eastern edge of the sand dunes. You can also follow the creekbed.

Legend, mystery and superstition have long surrounded these shifting hills of sand. Some say there are huge, web-footed horses that race over the dunes at night. On a moonlit night, they say, you can see them. Bands of wild horses may actually roam the edges of the dunes, but web-footed they're not, just broad-hooved. They were probably brought here by the Spaniards in the 1500s.

When the wind blows over the dunes, it is said you can hear voices. The Indians who came often to the dunes called them the "singing sands" for this reason.

Medano Creek follows the eastern edge of the dunes for many miles. Then it diappears. Like the creek, many humans are rumored to have disappeared into the sands, as well as whole flocks of sheep and whole wagon trains, mules and all.

Whatever you think of the legends surrounding the dunes, you will, no doubt, be very impressed by the mountain ranges that surround them. To the

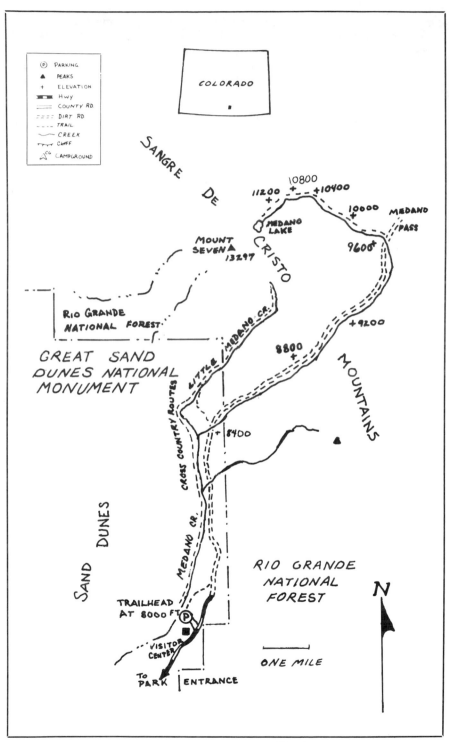

East Side Dune Trail

north and east is the Sangre de Cristo Range. To the west across the San Luis Valley are the San Juans. It was once believed that the sand dunes were formed from deposits from Medano Creek and other creeks flowing out of the Sangre de Cristos. Now it is believed that the sand came originally from the rocks that make up the San Juans. Streams brought them down to the San Luis Valley, the only true desert in the Southern Rockies. The winds—prevailing westerlies—picked up the sands and carried them eastward and when the winds rose to funnel through Medano and Mosca passes in the Sangre de Cristos, the sand was dropped in the dune area. Sometimes violent winds rage out of the mountain canyons to the east, too, creating strange shapes out of the sand.

Following the jeep trail (or creekbed) along the edge of the dunes, you will observe the constant battle between the shifting sands, the flowing water and the forest vegetation for control of this area. The sand is dropped here by the wind and in the spring, Medano Creek carries it away. But late in the year, the creek becomes lost in the sand. In places, new trees take root, stablizing the dunes and in other places are covered and die, leaving only their eerie skeletons behind, half-covered with sand.

Near the junction of Medano and Little Medano Creeks (about four miles along), the jeep road turns eastward and climbs to Medano Pass. At this point, you can continue on the road to Medano Pass and eventually intercept a trail to Medano Lake, located on the northeast side of Mt. Seven. This hike would necessitate a backpack. Or you can go left along Little Medano Creek and further explore the dunes on their northeastern edge or make an ascent of Mt. Seven along one of the creeks that begin on the peak.

Camping is good in the trees, but not allowed in the dunes. A campground is provided at the dune headquarters. Be sure to take water with you.

Enjoy your exploration of the dunes (you can climb atop them more easily when it has rained a bit) and then return as you came.—*Brian Dempsey*

24 Horn Lakes

General description: An overnighter to alpine lakes in the heart of the rugged Sangre de Cristo Range.
General location: About 60 miles southeast of Salida.
Maps: Horn Peak USGS quad; San Isabel National Forest Map.
Degree of difficulty: Moderate.
Length: 5 miles one way.
Elevations: 9,000 to 11,800 feet.
Special attractions: Deep glacial valley and cirque lakes; thick forests and abundant wildflowers at lower elevations.
Best season: Summer.
For more information: San Isabel National Forest, San Carlos Ranger District, 248 Dozier St., Canon City, CO 81212; (303) 275-1626.

The Sangre de Cristo Range, which extends some 150 miles from Salida southeast into New Mexico, is visible from much of the southeastern Colorado as a jagged, unbroken ridge. This hike takes you into the heart of this range and into the San Isabel National Forest.

To reach the trailhead, drive south from Salida or north from Walsenburg on State Highway 69 to the town of Westcliffe. From Westcliffe, go south approximately three miles on Highway 69, turning right onto Schoolfield Road, a paved road with signs to Alpine Lodge and Alavarado Campground. Follow

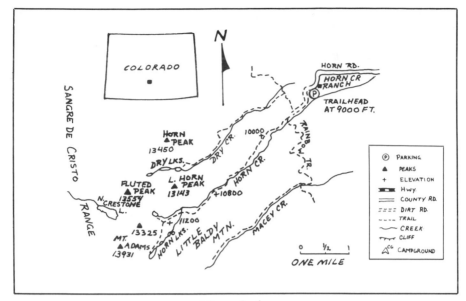

Horn Lakes

this road for .9 miles and turn left onto Colony Lane, another paved road. After two miles, turn right onto Horn Road for about 4.5 miles to its end near the Horn Creek Ranch. Bear right at the entrance to the ranch and continue about a hundred yards to the trailhead and a parking area.

There is a four-wheel drive road leaving the parking area to the left and a footpath going off to the right. The easiest route is along the four-wheel drive road, which is windy and stony, but not steep. The road terminates after about .75 miles at the Rainbow Trail, which parallels the eastern side of the mountain range at lower elevations for much of its length and offers access to the Dry Lakes Valley to the north and the Macey Lakes Valley to the south.

this point. It climbs at a moderate rate for the first 1.75 miles up the right (north) side of the Horn Creek Valley. The trail is generally within a few hundred yards of Horn Creek as it passes through dense forests of aspen, ponderosa pine and Douglas fir. The forest is interrupted occasionally by open, grassy meadows which offer some superb views back towards the Wet Mountains to the east. During mid-July, these meadows are brimming with many kinds of wildflowers, including several varieties of penstemon, wall flower, yellow pea, wild rose, and columbine. All in all, this lower stretch of the trail is quite enjoyable as you gain about a thousand vertical feet.

From the Rainbow Trail, the Horn Lakes Trail continues straight uphill on the old four-wheel-drive road, which is blocked off to motor vehicles beyond

After the trail crosses to the left (south) side of Horn Creek (no bridge), it climbs steeply for about 1.25 miles. The forest is rather dense here and you can't see far up or down the valley. The trail is rough and several muddy areas may be encountered along this section.

This steep stretch ends rather abruptly when you cross Horn Creek. (Again, there is no bridge, but the creek is much smaller here than downstream.) From here, you leave the dense forest and pass through gently rolling, high alpine meadows and two valleys become visible. The main Horn Lake is at the end of the valley straight ahead. The trail becomes rather rugged, but not too steep, and in places, passes through thick willows. In short, your progress along this stretch may be slower than you'd expect. As you go this slower pace, watch for occasional bristlecone pines and take in the views: they're awe-inspiring.

There are numerous small lakes and ponds below the main Horn Lake and some good camping spots. The lake itself is very scenic, edged by cliffs and with a small island in the middle. We do not recommend camping near the lake for a couple of reasons: first of all, like many other high alpine lakes in Colorado, this lake could be easily scarred by careless campers; secondly, being above timberline, there is very little firewood near the lake.

For those who like "top of the world" mountain views, a short day trip may be made by climbing the ridge to the north of Horn Lakes. The best route begins about .5 miles below the main lake. The climb is steep, but not dangerous. From the top of the ridge you get a good view of four "four-teeners": Crestone Needle, Crestone Peak, Humboldt, and Kit Carson Peak. This southern view is particularly impressive, but the views to the north along the backbone of the Sangre de Cristo Range and the views into the San Luis Valley to the west and the Wet Mountains to the east are equally impressive. This ridge also provides access to 13,931 foot Mt. Adams, which is about .5 miles to the southwest. This climb can be made without a rope, but it is not recommended.—*Bill Bath*

25 St. Charles Peak

General description: A day hike up the second highest peak in the Wet Mountains.

General location: Approximately 40 miles southwest of Pueblo.

Maps: St. Charles Peak USGS quad; San Isabel National Forest Map.

Degree of difficulty: Easy.

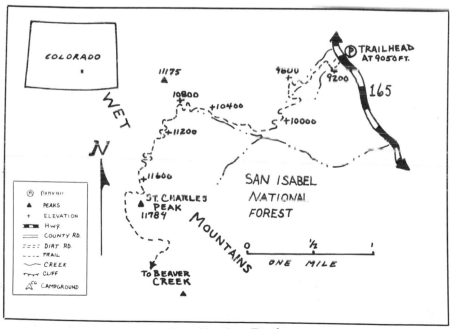

St. Charles Peak

Length: 10 miles round trip.

Elevations: 9,050 to 11,784 feet.

Special attractions: Pine, spruce and fir trees; small stream; excellent views from the summit.

Best season: Summer and fall.

For more information: San Isabel National Forest, Pikes Peak Ranger District, 320 West Fillmore, Colorado Springs, CO 80907 (303) 636-1602.

This hike takes you to the summit of St. Charles Peak, the second highest peak in the Wet Mountains, a southern continuation of the Front Range west of Pueblo.

To reach the trailhead, take State Highway 78 southwest to Beulah (26 miles). Instead of driving into Beulah, take the highway (now Pine Drive) southwest for 12 miles to its junction with State Highway 165. Turn north on 165 and in less than one mile park in the area provided on the right side of the road. The trailhead is directly across the road.

The trail leads you west and up onto a ridge, then drops a few feet and crosses a small stream. A series of switchbacks leads you to another stream crossing and through evergreen forests up to a pass at 10,050 feet. The trail then descends a bit, crosses a boggy place, then climbs again westward with more switchbacks to another pass at 10,800 feet.

Turning south-southwest (left), the trail now switchbacks to a small, rocky point with a good view of the summit. Beyond, at 11,480 feet, one climbs out of the thick woods to open tundra with timberline trees, wildflowers and rocks—and a good view.

Follow the ridge, go through more forest and then begin to follow the trail around the western side of the summit dome. At this point, leave the trail and hike carefully across the tundra to the obvious top of St. Charles Peak.

From here you could follow the trail generally southward down Beaver Creek to Lake Isabel Campground and a waiting vehicle, which you would have had to shuttle before your start.

You can also descend the western side of the mountain to a logging road leading to the Ophir Creek Road. A shuttle would be needed in that case as well.

The view from the summit is excellent. To the west is the Wet Mountain Valley—a structural valley—separating the Wet Mountain Range from the Sangre de Cristo Range that you can see in the distance. To the east are the Great Plains.

Enjoy the view and then return as you came.—*Frances C. Carter*

26 Tanner Trail

General description: A solitary day hike into the Wet Mountains, culminating in an alpine meadow with views of both the eastern plains and western Sangre de Cristo Mountains.

General location: 12 miles south of Canon City.

Maps: Curley Peak USGS quad; San Isabel National Forest Map.

Degree of difficulty: Moderate.

Length: 4 miles one way.

Elevations: 7,362 to 9,600 feet.

Special attractions: Terrific views both east and west; lush vegetation;

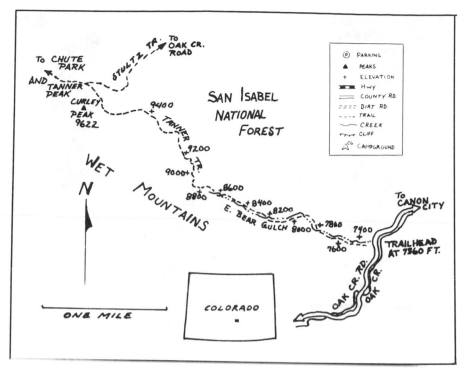

Tanner Trail

little-used.

Best season: Summer and fall.

For more information: San Isabel National Forest, San Carlos Ranger District, 248 Dozier St., Canon City, CO 81212; (303) 275-1626.

The Tanner Trail to Curley Peak in the San Isabel National Forest is a trail well worth hiking if you are seeking a short day hike featuring an abundance of mountain wildflowers, varied mountain terrain, and an escape from the heavily traveled trails in the northern mountain ranges.

To reach the trailhead, drive to Canon City and turn south from the city's main street onto 9th Street (Colorado 115). Turn right (west) at the Lakeside Cemetery and then left (south) onto Fremont County Road 143. Follow this road past a golf course and a large mill and continue going toward the Oak Creek Campground. The trailhead is reached before the campground. It is on your right and marked by a poorly-placed sign, which is somewhat overgrown by brush so look closely for it. There is no parking area, but it is not difficult to pull safely off the road.

The trail begins at 7,362 feet and climbs to 9,600 feet, mostly within the first 2.5 miles. It is sometimes covered with loose rock which makes for difficult walking.

The early part of the trail winds up East Bear Gulch through shady mountain forest. Scrub oak, aspen, blue spruce and other conifers are all along the route, as are a surprising variety of wildflowers and butterflies. Tall tansy asters, Indian paintbrush, wallflower, harebell, pinedrops, scarlet gilia, and an intriguing variety of mushrooms are easily identified.

The Sangre de Cristo Mountains from the Tanner Trail. Chuck Kall photo.

After an ascent of about two miles, you will begin to have a view of the eastern plains. Continuing upward, this view will be complimented by a western view of the Sangre de Cristo Mountains and the intervening Wet Mountain Valley. At about three miles, the trail stretches out into a lovely mountain meadow providing an easy walk of another one mile or so to the high point of the trail. Curley Peak is a stony nob that is seen a few hundred feet from the Tanner Trail. The trail does not actually lead to its summit, but it is an easy side trip. The view here southwest to the Sangre de Cristos is nothing short of spectacular.

If you wish to continue on for a longer hike from here, you can follow the Tanner Trail to its intersection with the Tanner Peak Trail in 3.5 miles and in 4.5 miles, the Stultz Trail which returns to the Oak Creek Grade Road about four miles north of the Tanner Trail trailhead.

Be sure to carry a supply of drinking water with you; little is available along the way. And enjoy this opportunity to spend an entire day on a little-used mountain trail.—*Chuck and Babs Kall*

27 Garner Creek

General description: A day hike or overnighter to the crest of the Sangre de Cristo Range.

General location: About 35 miles southeast of Poncha Springs.

Maps: Valley View Hot Springs USGS quad; Rio Grande National Forest Map.

Degree of difficulty: Difficult.

Length: About 4.5 miles one way with opportunities for peak ascents and an extended backpack.

Elevations: 8,700 to 13,588 feet.
Special attractions: Great views; access to high peaks.
Best season: Summer.
For more information: Contact Rio Grande National Forest, Saguache Ranger District, 444 Christy Ave., P.O. Box 67, Saguache, CO 81149; (303) 655-2553.

This hike takes you up the western flank of the Sangre de Cristo Range and provides you with many great views, as well as access to several high peaks.

The trail begins as a jeep road, but quickly diminishes, becoming an obscure trail as it ascends the steep drainage of Garner Creek to the crest of the mountain range. A topographic map, a good sense of direction, and some sturdy hiking boots will be invaluable to you on this hike.

To reach the trailhead, take U.S. Highway 285 south past Poncha Springs, over Poncha Pass and into the San Luis Valley to the town of Villa Grove. Go four miles south of the town to the junction of 285 and State Highway 17. At the junction there is a dirt road running east (Forest Route 964). Follow it for 6.3 miles to the "Y," then go south about one mile to the first draw, which is Garner Creek. (A turn north at the "Y" will take you to Valley View Hot Springs.) Park somewhere along the short jeep road up the draw and begin your hike.

The San Luis Valley, which you will be hiking away from, is a flat-floored desert park where there are more than 7,000 flowing artesian wells. At one time a lake filled the valley and at the southern end there was a lava dam, now

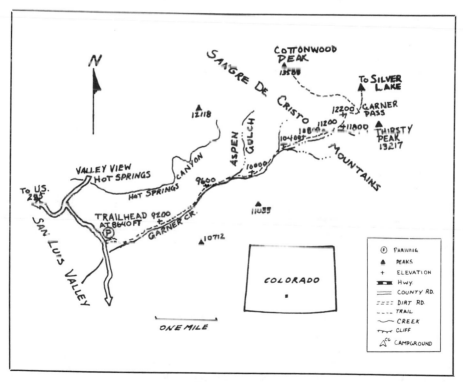

Garner Creek

known as the San Luis Hills. Today, badger, pronghorn antelope, deer and rattlesnakes make it their home.

As you hike up Garner Creek Draw, keep to the south on all tributaries. You will ascend from your parking spot at 8,700 feet to the crest at 12,650 in 4.5 miles. Keep an eye out for deer, elk and possibly bobcat as you climb. You may want to try your luck fishing Garner Creek. However, it is rated as only fair for small brook trout.

At the pass where small mammals like the marmot and pika make their homes, you can proceed northwest to the summit of Cottonwood Peak (13,588) about one mile away via an old mining road going nearly all the way to the summit, or turn southeast to Thirsty Peak (13,217 feet). Then you can continue south over Lakes Peak (13,382 feet) to Electric Peak (13,621 feet), which is directly above Banjo Lake to the east.

From the summits of these peaks your views will be of the Wet Mountains to the east, and the intervening Wet Mountain Valley; the San Juan Mountains to the west and the intervening San Luis Valley. Along the Sangre de Cristo Range (the name means "Blood of Christ" and refers to the red glow the mountains take on at sunrise and sunset) as you look to the southeast, you will see many fourteeners, including Kit Carson Peak (14,165), Crestone Peak (14,295 feet) and Humboldt Peak (14,064). Beyond them is the Crestone Needle (14,191 feet) and, at the western base of the range, the Great Sand Dunes. Far to the southeast are Little Bear and Blanca Peaks and Mt. Lindsey. Beyond that lies New Mexico.

Returning along the ridge to Garner Pass you could conceivably follow the Garner Trail east past Silver Lake (fair fishing for small natives) and Rainbow Lake (fair fishing for 10- to 14-inch rainbow trout) to Lake Creek Campground on San Isabel Forest Route 300, making a long backpack out of your trip. To do so, however, you would have to shuttle vehicles before you leave by driving southeast from Salida, taking U.S. Highway 50 east to State Highway 69 and then going south past the town of Hillside and bearing right when State Highway 69 turns southeast, to take Forest Route 300 to Lake Creek Campground.

Otherwise, return as you came, hiking down the Garner Creek Trail to your vehicle.—*Brian Dempsey*

28 *Mt. Ouray*

General description: A short, but steep, day hike to the summit of Mt. Ouray in the Sawatch Range.

General location: About 15 miles southwest of Poncha Springs.

Maps: Pahlone Peak and 15 minute Bonanza USGS quads; San Isabel National Forest Map.

Length: About 3.5 miles one way.

Degree of difficulty: Moderate.

Elevations: 10,800 to 13,971 feet.

Special attractions: A short climb to a peak near 14,000 feet; beautiful views; many wildflowers.

Best season: Summer.

For more information: San Isabel National Forest, Salida Ranger District, 230 W. 16th St., Salida, CO 81201; (303) 539-3591.

This hike takes you to the summit of a "near fourteener" in the Sawatch Range. Named after the great Ute Indian chief, Mt. Ouray stands at 13,971 feet and is reached with a short but steep climb, beginning near Marshall Pass. This could also be the starting point for a long hike along the Continental Divide to Monarch Pass, which would require a car shuttle.

To reach the trail to the peak, drive south from Poncha Springs on U.S. 285

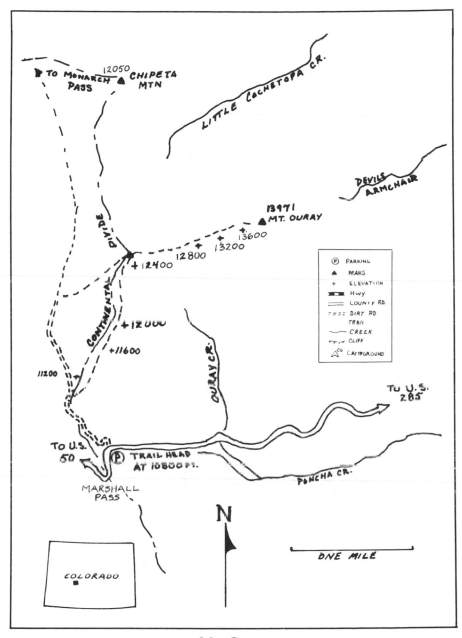

Mt. Ouray

for five miles and turn right (west) on Chaffee County Road 200 (Marshall Pass Road). After about .25 miles turn right towards O'Haver Lake on Forest Route 243, then turn right at the Marshall Pass Sign. From there it is about 10 miles to the top of the pass as you follow the scenic route of the old Denver & Rio Grande Railroad. About .25 miles before the summit of the pass is the sign for the Crest Trail at an old jeep road to the right. Park across the road from the trailhead.

Begin your hike by following the upper of the two jeep trails at the trailhead, away from the meadows and marshy area on the south side of the road where Poncha Creek has its headwaters and where wild iris grow. The trail switches back two times and heads into a forest of spruce-fir, then climbs at a moderate grade until it reaches a ridgetop. From this point the summit of Mt. Ouray looms above you to the northeast. To the west are the tributaries to the Gunnison River. You are straddling the Continental Divide. After you cross the cattle guard, continue along the road for about .25 miles paralleling the ridge.

The easiest route to the peak summit is to leave the road where it makes a sharp bend to the right, cross the fence and climb through intermittent meadow and forest up the broad ridge to the northeast. After a good steady climb, you will reach timberline and shortly after that, the terrain flattens out to a broad saddle, which connects to Mt. Ouray. This saddle with its many wildflowers would make a good destination in itself.

Once across the saddle, you will reach the summit after a steep, rocky climb of .75 miles, which may necessitate some scrambling, but is not dangerous.

From the summit you can see the peaks of the Sawatch Range to the north, the Elk and the West Elk Mountains to the northwest, the Gunnison Valley to the west, the Cochetopa Hills to the southwest and the San Juan Mountains beyond, the San Luis Valley to the south, the Sangre de Cristo Range to the southeast and the Arkansas Valley to the east with the summit of Pikes Peak in the distance. Truly a spectacular view! Directly below you on the east side of the peak is the fantastic Devil's Armchair.

After enjoying the view, return as you came. Should you decide to make the long 10 mile hike to Monarch Pass (U.S. Highway 50), continue north along the jeep road which you left to climb Mt. Ouray. The road ends about one mile farther along and becomes the Monarch Trail. This portion is included as part of both the Continental Divide National Scenic Trail and the Colorado Trail.—*Peter, Caryn and Crystal Boddie*

29 Henry Lake

General description: A backpack to Henry Lake, an alpine lake in the proposed Fossil Ridge Wilderness Area.

General location: Approximately 20 miles northeast of Gunnison.

Maps: Matchless Mountain, Taylor Park Reservoir and Fairview Peak USGS quads; Gunnison National Forest Map.

Degree of difficulty: Moderate.

Length: 12 miles round trip.

Elevations: 9,140 to 11,704 feet.

Special attractions: A beautiful alpine lake nestled right at the base of Henry Mountain and offering good fishing; numerous private campsites and spectacular views; good opportunities to see deer and elk.

Best season: Summer and fall.

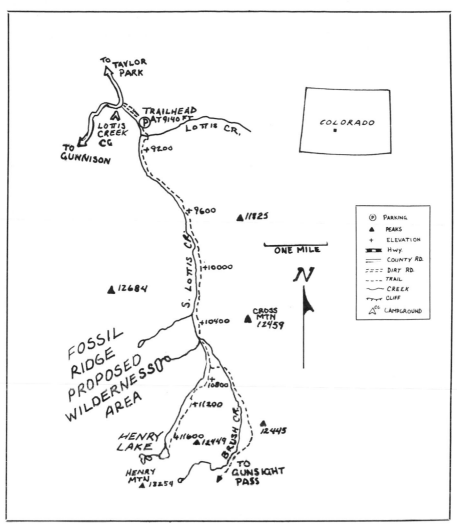

Henry Lake

For more information: Contact Gunnison National Forest, Taylor Ranger District, 216 N. Colorado, Gunnison, CO 81230; (303) 641-0471.

This hike beginning at Lottis Creek Campground, a Gunnison National Forest recreation site and ending at Henry Lake at the base of 13,254-foot Mt. Henry, offers scenic campsites, fair fishing for eight-to 12-inch cutthroat and some large rainbow trout, and access to the summits of mountain peaks.

To reach the trailhead, drive north from Gunnison on State Highway 135. At the town of Almont, turn right onto the Taylor Canyon Road and follow it 15 miles up the canyon to Lottis Creek Campground. (Watch for bighorn sheep on your drive up. They can sometimes be seen across the river to your left.) Once at the campground, take the second right entrance and follow the road through the overflow camping area for .25 miles to the signed trailhead. Lottis Creek Campground may also be reached by driving over Cottonwood Pass, through Taylor Park, and four miles down Taylor Canyon from the dam.

Once at the trailhead, be sure to sign the register before starting out. Then, rather than hiking up Lottis Creek into Union Canyon (a very nice day trip), cross over the creek on the log bridge and begin following the trail up South Lottis Creek.

The trail climbs south through the timber, along the east side of South Lottis Creek. It remains fairly level, with only an occasional steep section. A small, rocky clearing at 9,950 feet and about 2.5 miles up the trail makes for a nice resting or lunch spot. A bit over a mile above the clearing, the trail crosses a small creek coming from the left, down off the west side of 12,459 foot Cross Mountain. For those in no hurry to reach Henry Lake, camp may be set up here.

From the creek crossing, it is another .5 miles to the junction with the trail to Gunsight Pass. The pass is three miles up Brush Creek and makes for a nice day hike. It is little used, however, and may require a bit of route-finding ability.

Taking the right fork, continue up the last 1.5 steep miles to Henry Lake. The trail continues to climb along the east side of South Lottis Creek, directly below the northeast ridge of Henry Mountain. The final half-mile is the steepest, as is often the case when reaching an alpine lake in Colorado. But, as soon as you crest the top and view the lake, there is no doubt the pull was worth it.

Level campsites are abundant, both in clearings and in the timber. Please camp at least 200 feet away from the lake, as this is a very fragile environment and easily impacted. Areas near the small lakes directly west of Henry Lake also make for nice campsites.

Once settled, it is time to try the fishing, gaze at the views, or for the more energetic, climb to the broad summit of Henry Mountain. Whatever you choose to do once at the lake, you will certainly enjoy the scenic alpine setting and likely leave vowing to return for a more lengthy visit next time.—*Chris Gore*

30 Mill-Castle Trail

General description: A backpack into the West Elk Wilderness, culminating in a panoramic view from the top of Storm Pass.

General location: Approximately 15 miles northwest of Gunnison.

Maps: Squirrel Creek and West Elk Peak quads; Gunnison National Forest Map.

Degree of difficulty: Moderate.

Length: 9 miles one way.

Elevations: 9,000 to 12,450 feet.

Special attractions: Good views of The Castles and other rock formations, of the Baldys and of the Elk Range fourteeners; opportunities to see elk and deer.

Best season: Summer and fall (be especially careful during hunting season).

For more information: Gunnison National Forest, Taylor River District, 216 N. Colorado, Gunnison, CO 81230; (303) 641-0471.

The Mill-Castle Trail takes you into the heart of the West Elk Wilderness to Storm Pass where there is a spectacular view of the unique rock formations of the Castles. The trail also provides access to further backpacking opportunities.

To reach the trailhead, drive three miles north of Gunnison on State Highway 135. Turn left onto the Ohio Creek Road and drive nine miles to the Mill Creek Road, which turns off to the left just before the paved section of the Ohio Creek Road ends. Turn onto the Mill Creek Road and go four miles to its end where the Forest Service maintains a locked gate just before the wilderness boundary. With careful driving and dry conditions, passenger cars can make it this far. But, if you find the going too rough, park your car lower and begin your trip at that point.

The Castles. U.S. Forest Service photo.

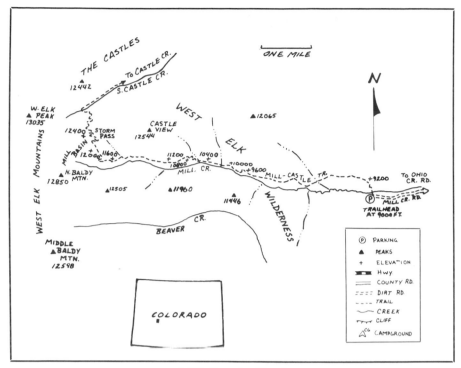

Mill-Castle Trail

As you start out, continue to follow the old road, now closed to motor vehicles. Be sure to have a member of your party sign the Forest Service register before you begin your hike.

You will pass the West Elk Wilderness boundary sign and the trail sign and soon the old road becomes a trail. Shortly above this point, you make the one and only crossing of Mill Creek. The trail then climbs a steep bank, continues above the creek, and then enters a stand of aspen. Keep alert for deer and elk.

Immediately, you will begin to see beautiful, serene campsites off towards Mill Creek to your left, but keep on going! It is still about six miles to Storm Pass.

Cattle make drinking untreated, unboiled water from Mill Creek a poor idea, but numerous little flows from the rocks to the north, some of which flow all season, provide dependable drinking water.

Once in the trees, it becomes obvious that the trail is gaining elevation. As it does, you will gain exciting glimpses of the rock formations to the north. The West Elk Mountains, like the San Juans to the south, are primarily of volcanic origin and the extensive deposits of ash and lava in them have been eroded into a spectacular array of cliffs and pinnacles. Before you know it, the trail has brought you up far enough to be at eye level with these interesting rock walls. Be sure to locate the rock figure there resembling an upright creature. It can be seen watching hikers near the western end of the formations.

By now, you have left enough miles behind you to make for a short, enjoyable trek up to Storm Pass tomorrow. You can begin searching for campsites or wait until you have reached the end of the trees and entered Mill Basin. When selecting a site, look away from the trail, water, and over-used areas.

The Castles from Mill-Castle Trail. Chris Gore photo.

And when you move on, leave your site as litter-free and undisturbed as when you found it.

As you leave the trees and begin climbing into Mill Basin, you will notice the trail becoming less distinct. At this point, you will find yourself relying on rock cairns to point out the route. Consulting the West Elk Peak quad map as you move upwards will help assure you of following the proper route. Keep looking for deer and elk in Mill Basin.

Soon the trail, marked by a large rock, heads to the north, and reaches the foot of Storm Pass. At this point, the trail again becomes distinct, as it switchbacks up the final steep pitch to the pass.

Even before reaching the top, as you travel the switchbacks and gain elevation, you will begin anticipating the view ahead. At the top, looking to the north, The Castles appear close enough to touch! No where else are you able to view The Castles from such a vantage point. Further north, the Elk Mountain fourteeners are clearly visible (most noticeably the Maroon Bells). For those wishing to continue, the trail drops steeply from the pass to join South Castle Creek, eventually reaching Castle Creek. From here, the Lowline Trail will take you north over Beckwith Pass to the Kebler Pass Road or south back to Mill Creek Road, where you can connect with your vehicle. The Lowline Trail also provides access east to the Ohio Pass Road, via the Swampy Pass Trail. Vehicle shuttles would be necessary for those hiking out to either Kebler Pass or Ohio Pass Roads.

Whether you choose to adventure further, visit only as far as Storm Pass, or simply day hike Mill Creek, the wildlife, rock formations, and scenic beauty and solitude of the West Elk Wilderness are sure to please in many ways.—*Chris Gore*

31 Dark Canyon Trail

General description: A backpack taking you through a spectacular canyon and into the high country of the Raggeds Wilderness Area.

General location: About 25 miles northeast of Paonia.

Maps: Paonia Reservoir and Marcellina Mountain USGS quads; Gunnison National Forest Map.

Degree of difficulty: Moderate.

Length: 19 miles one way.

Elevations: 6,920 to 8,920 feet.

Special attractions: Takes you into the beautiful Ruby Mountains and Raggeds Wilderness Area; beautiful wildflowers; ends at inviting Horse Ranch Park; provides access to Oh-be-joyful Pass.

Best season: Late spring, summer and fall.

For more information: Gunnison National Forest, Paonia Ranger District, North Rio Grande St., Paonia, CO 81428; (303) 527-4131.

Although it receives heavy use during the height of the summer season, the Dark Canyon Trail is worth hiking because it takes you into the beautiful Raggeds Wilderness Area and provides access to Oh-be-joyful Pass in the Ruby Mountains, an area which is under consideration for wilderness designation.

The Dark Canyon Trail in itself is 19 miles long one way, a good two- to three-day backpack which requires a car shuttle. You can extend your hike by following connecting trails.

To reach the trailhead, drive northeast from Paonia on State Highway 133 to the fork in the highway just south of Paonia Reservoir, some 14 miles. Take the right fork to Erickson Springs Campground.

The Ruby Range above the Dark Canyon Trail. U.S. Forest Service photo.

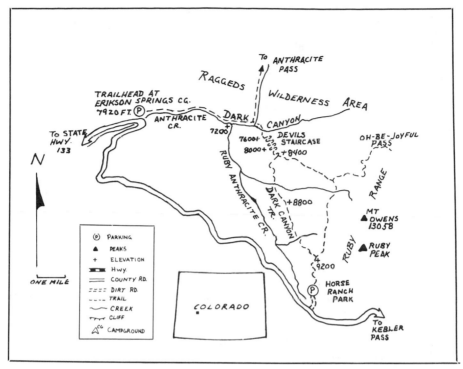

Dark Canyon Trail

From the campground the Dark Canyon Trail follows Anthracite Creek east into the steep-walled Dark Canyon. In the early summer season, waterfalls thunder down from cliffs and canyons high above and in the first six miles there is excellent fishing along the creek. The combined attractions of fishing opportunities and beautiful scenery mean this part of the trail receives the heaviest use.

As you reach the junction of Anthracite and North Anthracite Creeks, (the first good camping spots are here), the trail crosses two bridges—one over North Anthracite Creek, the other over Middle Anthracite Creek—and forks left and right. There is also an unmaintained trail up Middle Anthracite Creek. A hike north will take you over Anthracite Pass to an end point near Marble. A turn south follows the Dark Canyon Trail and will take you up the steep Devil's Stairway and on to Horse Ranch Park, a distance of about 13 miles. This southern fork also provides access to Oh-be-joyful Pass to the east.

Take the right fork and you will begin your ascent of the Devil's Stairway, as you head around Prospect Point to your right. The trail climbs a series of switchbacks gaining approximately 1,200 feet in .75 miles for a very steep ascent. Once you top the Devil's Stairway, you will begin a gradual climb along the bench which lies at the base of the Ruby Mountain Range to the east and is drained by tributaries to Ruby Anthracite Creek to the west. At its southern end is Horse Ranch Park, your destination.

You will reach another fork in the trail about one mile along. If you go left, you will head southeast for another three miles or so to another fork. There a left turn will take you northeast to the top of Oh-be-joyful Pass, a spot befitting its name, where you will have beautiful views of the surrounding mountains of the Ruby Range. A right turn will take you south to another fork from which you can head east to Lake Irwin Campground or straight ahead to meet with the Dark Canyon Trail as it heads into Horse Ranch Park.

The most direct route to the park is simply to hike straight southward from the top of the Devil's Stairway. You will cross three major creeks—Silver, Sardine and Gold—where camping spots and water are plentiful. Be sure to camp at least 200 feet away from the streams and trail and treat your water; sheep are run in this area during the summer.

At Dyke Creek, the fourth creek you'll meet atop the plateau (you will also come across some small tributaries to these creeks and pass a number of ponds), you will meet a fork in the trail. A left connects you with the trail doubling back to Oh-be-joyful Pass. Straight ahead past a number of ponds is Horse Ranch Park, a beautiful, open mountain park divided by Ruby Anthracite Creek.

From here you can return as you came, or meet a vehicle that you will have had to shuttle before your start. To shuttle cars to this end point at Forest Route 826, drive south from the Erickson Springs Campground on Forest Route 780 past the turn off to Lost Lake Campground to Horse Ranch Park and a road going to the north. Follow this road to the trailhead. For those who prefer a downhill hiking route you can travel the Dark Canyon Trail from Horse Ranch Park to Erickson Springs where you can meet a vehicle. However, by hiking in this direction you will miss the feeling of accomplishment and the reward of having made the ascent of the Devil's Staircase.

Whatever flight plan you set for hiking the Dark Canyon Trail, throughout your hike you will enjoy beautiful wildflowers, lush meadows of rushes, sedges, and grasses fringed by stands of aspen, forests of Douglas fir, ponderosa pine and ldogepole pine, and passes offering wide vistas of this gorgeous country. Be sure to keep your eyes peeled for deer, elk, and birds such as the brilliant mountain bluebird or gregarious gray and Steller's jays.—*Caryn Boddie*

32 *Kroenke Lake*

General description: A day hike along a roaring stream within a lush
    mountain forest, leading to a subalpine lake.
General location: 8 miles west of Buena Vista.
Maps: Mt. Harvard 15 minute USGS quad; San Isabel National Forest Map.
Degree of difficulty: Moderate.
Length: 8 miles round trip.
Elevations: 9,000 to 11,600 feet.
Special attractions: Beautiful subalpine lake; fourteener, Mt. Yale.
Best season: Summer and fall.
For more information: San Isabel National Forest, Leadville Ranger District,
    Post Office Building, 130 W. 5th St., P.O. Box 970, Leadville, CO 80461;
    (303) 486-0749.

This hike takes you into the beautiful Collegiate Mountain Range to Kroenke Lake in a subalpine setting surrounded by evergreens and vast mountain meadows.

To reach the trail to the lake, go west from Buena Vista on Crossman Avenue, which is Chaffee County Road 350. After approximately two miles, turn right on Chaffee County Road 361. You cannot miss this turn, since

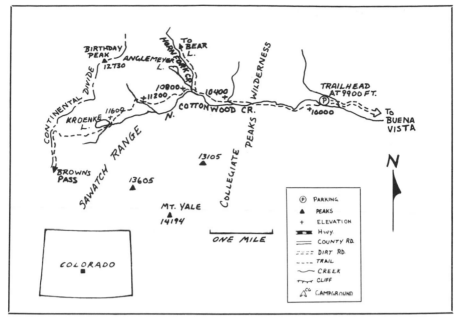

Kroenke Lake

Crossman Avenue (County Road 350) deadends here. After a short while, County Road 361 will veer to the left (northwest). After 1.2 miles from your original turn onto this road, take a sharp left. You will be heading south again. Shortly afterward the road will turn west again. From this point it is approximately nine miles along an extremely bumpy road to the dead-end at the trailhead.

The trail begins by crossing North Cottonwood Creek via a wide, sturdy bridge about 50 yards from the trailhead. It then continues on the south side of the North Fork of Cottonwood Creek through a lush forest of spruce and fir with scattered small stands of aspen and stays close to the stream.

After approximately 1.5 miles, the trail will cross the stream over a second bridge. Shortly therafter, it will cross a minor brook over some wobbly logs. As you continue on, you will occasionally have good views of the north face of Mt. Yale, which is composed of brecciated gneisses and granite. Approximately one mile after your last stream crossing via the second bridge, the trail crosses North Horn Creek.

From this point the hiker might decide to go right to Bear Lake, another four miles, or go straight ahead to Kroenke Lake. After another long mile, the trail crosses another small brook and then proceeds for less than one mile to Kroenke Lake.

All along your hike you will have seen small meadows with many wildflowers in summer. Kroenke Lake is surrounded by evergreens and is directly below the Continental Divide in a glaciated valley where there are vast alpine meadows, as well. It is a very beautiful area and the lake promises good fishing. You may want to stay awhile and just enjoy your surroundings or ascend to the summit of Mt. Yale (14,196), or go to Brown's Pass on the Continental Divide, or any of the other high peaks in the area. Then you will want to return as you came.—*Peter Dahmen*

33 *Missouri Trail*

General description: A day hike to a "hanging valley" and beyond to Elk
    Head Pass and the summit of Mt. Belford, a "fourteener."
General location: Approximately 20 miles northwest of Buena Vista.
Maps: Mt. Harvard 15 minute USGS quad; San Isabel National Forest Map.
Degree of difficulty: Difficult.
Length: 9 miles round trip.
Elevations: 9,600 to 14,196 feet.
Special attractions: Opportunity to climb a fourteener; beautiful views of the
    Missouri Basin.
Best season: Summer and early fall.
For more information: San Isabel National Forest, Leadville Ranger District,
    Post Office Building, 130 W. 5th St., P.O. Box 970, Leadville, CO 80461;
    (303) 486-0749.

The Missouri Trail will truly give you a Rocky Mountain experience, taking
you through stands of aspen, evergreen forest, alpine meadows and over the
delicate tundra to Elk Head Pass and the 14,196 foot summit of Mt. Belford in
the Collegiate Range.

To reach the trailhead, drive north from Buena Vista on State Highway 24
for 17 miles to the Clear Creek Road just north of Clear Creek Reservoir. Turn
left on this gravel road towards the ghost towns of Vicksburg and Winfield.
After 7.9 miles, you should encounter the parking lot for the trailhead marked
by a sign stating, "Missouri Trail Parking."

Allow at least eight hours hiking time for this nine mile round trip—you will
want extra time to enjoy the views from the summit of Mt. Belford and the
wildflowers you'll see as you cross the tundra.

Almost immediately after you've started your hike, you will cross Clear
Creek on a sturdy bridge and head into the Collegiate Peaks Wilderness Area.
After a short walk through a lush stand of aspen, you will start your ascent up
a very steep slope covered with evergreens, taking on more than 10
switchbacks to reach the top of the first steep portion of the Clear Creek
Valley.

At the top you will enter the Missouri Gulch Valley, a hanging glacial valley.
Here the trail levels off to a somewhat more gradual slope and continues thus
for about .5 miles through more aspen. You will then encounter another
stream as you cross Missouri Gulch on some wobbly logs and climb through a
meadow where there are young aspen and evergreens growing, probably a sign
that this meadow was beaten by avalanches.

At the end of this climb you will come across a miner's log cabin. A short
way farther you will reach timberline and have your first view of Missouri
Mountain. At this point you have hiked about two miles. Soon, the summit of
Mt. Belford comes into view.

It is possible to begin the climb of Mt. Belford a mile before timberline is
reached, via a very steep ridge just south of a prominent gulch. This climb
would save you 1.5 miles. However, if you have the time, and if you don't like
steep grades, proceed to Elk Head Pass. The beautiful tundra you'll see,
carpeted with wildflowers in summertime, will be worth the extra time. Please
be careful in walking across the tundra, however, as it is very fragile.

From time to time you will be crossing small boulder fields. At Elk Head
Pass the trail disappears. This should not create any problems, however, since

the pass and ridge to Mt. Belford are within view.

From Elk Head Pass you have a commanding view of the Missouri Basin, which is a glacial basin with numerous cirque lakes and patches of snow surrounded by sharp mountain peaks such as Mt. Harvard, Emerald Peak, Iowa Peak and Missouri Mountain. You will also have a fantastic view of the Sawatch Range south of you with its numerous fourteeners and the Continental Divide.

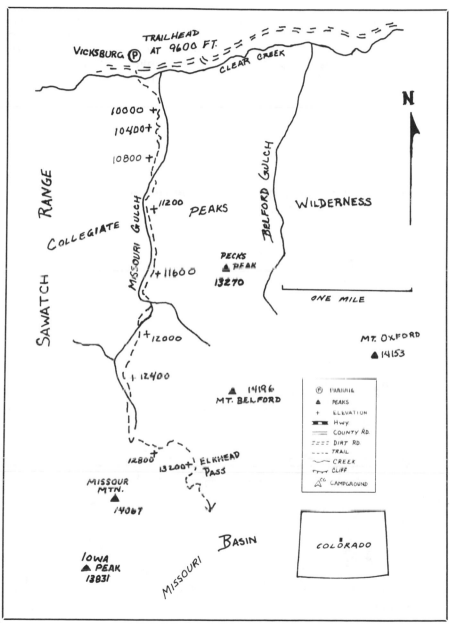

Missouri Trail

To reach the summit of Mt. Belford from Elk Head Pass, climb the ridge to your east, a gradual slope. After .3 miles on the ridge, you will have to turn north to reach the peak.

From the summit of Mt. Belford, at 14,197 feet, the view is even grander than at the pass. In addition to the mountains you have already seen, you will now be able to view the Sawatch Range north of you, a group of impressive peaks including Huron Peak to the west, and the Mosquito Range and South Park to the east.

In addition to enjoyable day hikes, there are many possibilities for long backpacks in this area. It is possible to reach the Texas Creek Basin from here by crossing the Continental Divide. You can also climb the rest of the fourteeners in the immediate area: Oxford, Harvard, Columbia, Huron peak and Missouri Mountain. You will also discover many hidden basins.—*Pieter Dahmen*

34 *Buffalo Meadows Loop*

General description: A long day hike or overnighter to a beautiful high mountain park in the Mosquito Range.
General location: 15 miles southwest of Fairplay.
Maps: South Peak and Jones Hill USGS quads; Pike National Forest Map.
Degree of difficulty: Moderate.
Length: 11 miles round trip.
Elevations: 9,950 to 11,500 feet.
Special attractions: A beautiful loop trail in the proposed Buffalo Peaks Wilderness Area; opportunities to see elk, bear and bighorn sheep.
Best season: Summer and fall.
For more information: Pike National Forest, South Park Ranger District, P.O. Box 218, Fairplay, CO 80440; (303) 836-2404.

Buffalo Meadows.

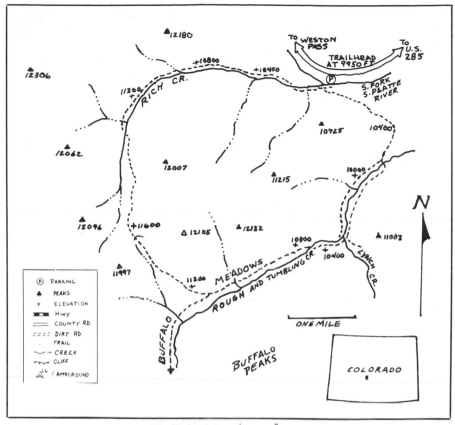

Buffalo Meadows Loop

Located at the base of Buffalo Peaks near the southern end of the Mosquito Range, Buffalo Meadows is an outstanding example of an undisturbed high mountain park, a flat, open area of grasses and willows, surrounded by forested mountains. The open character of this area provides an unlimited supply of good camping spots, easy access to the surrounding mountains, and the opportunity to spot elk, deer and even bighorn sheep on the slopes of Buffalo Peaks.

The trail to the meadows follows a loop by way of two beautiful streams, Rich Creek and Rough and Tumbling Creek, and traverses a variety of both open and forested terrain. This wild area is part of the proposed Buffalo Peaks Wilderness and is well worth preserving for its outstanding wildlife and its uniquely gentle terrain.

To reach the trailhead to Buffalo Meadows, take U.S. Highway 285 south of Fairplay about five miles to the Weston Pass Road (Park County Road 5). Follow this gravel road west, bearing right at a fork seven miles along and on to the Pike National Forest Boundary at about 10 miles. The national forest boundary is marked by a fence and cattle guard. Immediately past the cattle guard is a small parking area on the left with a sign indicating the South Fork of the South Platte River. This is the trailhead.

To begin your hike, take the footbridge across the South Fork and follow the trail upstream about 100 feet to an intersection, which marks the beginning

West Buffalo Peak in the proposed Buffalo Peaks Wilderness.

of the loop trail to Buffalo Meadows. The entire loop is about 11 miles and it is an equal distance to the meadow in either direction. The trail to the left takes you up and over a ridge to Rough and Tumbling Creek, which you follow for the remainder of the way to Buffalo Meadows. Traveling the loop in this direction takes you downhill for the last portion of your hike, while a hike around the loop in the opposite direction will require a final climb of this same ridge. The trail straight ahead, as opposed to the trail to the left, follows Rich Creek to a divide overlooking Buffalo Meadows and is probably the more scenic of the two directions. If you are planning just a short day hike, this is the trail you'll probably want to take. However, for fishing, the short 1.5 miles hike over the ridge to Rough and Tumbling Creek is well worth the effort (fishing is good for small brook trout).

If you take the fork to the left, the trail climbs steeply to the top of a broad ridge with stands of aspen intermingled with spruce, limber pine, bristlecone pine and open meadows. The descent from the ridge to Rough and Tumbling Creek offers some good views of West Buffalo Peak and the surrounding country. When you reach the valley bottom, there is a sign indicating that the trail crosses through the willows to the other side of the valley and this is how the trail is indicated on both the U.S. Forest Service and USGS maps. However, the work of beavers and the thickness of the willows have made this crossing nearly impassable. A better route follows a well-worn trail upstream along the near side of the valley about one mile to the intersection with Lynch Creek where the willows are crossable.

After crossing Rough and Tumbling Creek, you enter an area where hunters have camped. The trail to Buffalo Meadows takes off to the right of this spot and goes uphill. If you are traveling in the opposite direction, look for the trail to the left crossing through the willows at this same well-used camping spot; if you end up crossing Lynch Creek, you've passed it.

As it enters the timber, the trail climbs steeply and crosses Rough and Tumbling Creek once again. The many waterfalls visible along this section of the trail no doubt are responsible for the name of this beautiful stream. After about one mile of good steady climbing, you will reach the east end of Buffalo Meadows. It is another 1.5 miles to the junction with the trail from Rich Creek.

At Buffalo Meadows, there are many possibilities for camping and exploring. It is best to camp well away from the trail and at the edge of the forest in one of the many small side drainages, both for seclusion and for observing wildlife. Water is readily available, but should be treated, as both cattle and sheep graze here.

The forest surrounding the meadows is fairly open, providing easy cross country hiking. A good destination would be the top of West Buffalo Peak, which can be climbed along a ridge from the south side of Buffalo Meadows.

The Buffalo Peaks are volcanic mountains, marking the south end of the Mosquito Range. The view from their summits includes South Park, Pikes Peak, the Sangre de Cristo Range, the Sawatch Range, and the Collegiate Peaks. If you should spot some of the small herd of bighorn sheep on your climb, please respect the privacy of these intrusion-sensitive animals and watch them from a distance.

To return to your car by way of Rich Creek, look for the trail leaving through a saddle at the north end of the meadows. It is indistinct in many places as it passes in and out of willows, but generally follows the right (east) edge of both sides of the saddle. When you reach the top of the saddle, pause to look back at the view of Buffalo Meadows and West Buffalo Peak. On the Rich Creek side of the saddle, the trail passes in and out of the willows for about one mile, slowly becoming easier to follow as you descend. As the valley bends around towards the east, the trail crosses the creek and begins to steepen as it drops into the forest of the lower valley. It is along this lower portion of the trail that you may notice occasional anthills that have been dug up: an indication that black bears pass this way, too.—*Peter Boddie*

35 Trail Gulch

General description: A day hike or overnighter taking you into the Bureau of Land Management (BLM) Beaver Creek Wilderness Study Area.
General location: Approximately 20 miles southwest of Colorado Springs.
Maps: Phantom Canyon USGS quad; BLM SE-1 quad.
Degree of difficulty: Moderate.
Length: 10 to 11 miles round trip.
Elevations: 6,100 to 8,700 feet.
Special attractions: A wild area with beautiful views, virtually unchanged by the influences of man; interesting geology and varied vegetation; good fishing.
Best season: Late spring to early fall.
For more information: Bureau of Land Management, Royal Gorge Resource Area, 831 Royal Gorge Boulevard, P.O. Box 1470, Canon City, CO 81212; (303) 275-7578.

Trail Gulch takes you along Beaver Creek on the south end of the Front Range and into the BML's Beaver Creek Wilderness Study Area.

To reach the trailhead, take Interstate 25 to State Highway 115 in Colorado

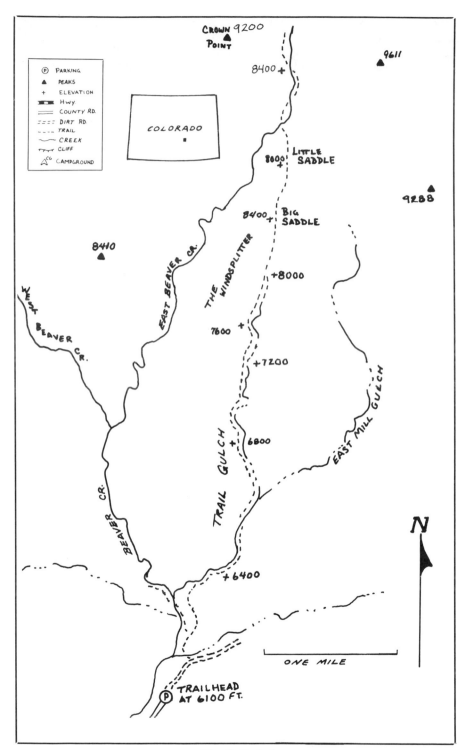

CROWN 9200
POINT ▲

9611 ▲

8400 +

P PARKING
▲ PEAKS
+ ELEVATION
▬▬ HWY
═══ COUNTY RD.
┅┅┅ DIRT RD.
┄┄┄ TRAIL
~~~ CREEK
✓✓ CLIFF
▲cg CAMPGROUND

COLORADO

8000 + LITTLE
        SADDLE

9288 ▲

8400 + BIG
        SADDLE

EAST BEAVER CR.

8410 ▲

THE WINDSPLITTER

+8000

WEST BEAVER CR.

7600 +

+7200

EAST MILL GULCH

TRAIL GULCH

+ 6800

BEAVER CR.

+ 6400

N

ONE MILE

TRAILHEAD
AT 6100 FT.
P

Trail Gulch

Springs. Drive south on 115, 33.6 miles through Penrose to State Highway 50 and turn right (west). After 4.2 miles turn right on Fremont County Road 67 (Phantom Canyon Road). After 1.7 miles, turn right on County Road 123, then turn left on Beaver Creek Road in .3 miles. Follow this road 10.8 miles to its end and the trailhead. Park next to the fence.

Begin your hike by going through the gate and following the old road several hundred yards. Then turn left near an east-west running pipeline. The trail then crosses a small, nearly dry gulch, around a steep cliff and along a fence. In another several hundred yards you will come to a fork in the trail. The left fork will lead you along the bed of Beaver Creek and eventually dead-end at a bend in the canyon. Take the right fork of the trail along a ridge paralleling Beaver Creek.

The Beaver Creek Wilderness Study Area consists of some 26,000 acres, in an area cut by very steep drainages. Beaver Creek itself is a stream of excellent water quality and sustains a good cold water fishery. Wildlife in the area includes species that thrive in this extremely rough and unroaded terrain: mule deer, bighorn sheep, mountain lion, and black bear. A pair of endangered peregrine falcons have also been sighted here, so keep your eyes peeled.

The area also contains a diversity of vegetation and interesting geology. Pinon pine, juniper, ponderosa pine, Douglas fir, white fir and spruce are some of the evergreen species present. You will also come upon stands of aspen. The major rocks in the area are granites and migmatitic gneisses and schists. The trail follows the ridge for a short way, then passes through an old ranch gate and eventually drops into Trail Gulch which it follows closely, crossing the creek many times. The valley is forested with evergreens and lush grass grows near the creek, with cactus away from the water.

About 1.5 miles along the trail you will enter a broad meadow, carpeted with clover. At its northern end, the stream surfaces from beneath an embankment offering water of good quality.

Continue the gradual ascent along the gulch for a total of 3.25 miles until the trail becomes much steeper. There are several sharp bends and then it straightens again for a very steep .5 miles to the Big Saddle. From this pretty spot you have excellent views of the cliffs of the Windsplitter to the west and of the Canon City-Florence basin to the southwest. The headwaters of Trail Gulch are near this saddle. There is no water available from this point to your destination at East Beaver Creek.

From the Big Saddle, head down the switchbacks (there is a total elevation loss of about 500 feet), through the lush vegetation at the bottom of the hill (notice the wild iris!) and begin a short ascent of 200 feet to the Little Saddle. Another short drop will take you into a small meadow bordered on the west by East Beaver Creek. This is a good place to camp. Stay at least 200 feet away from the creek and be careful in choosing your tent site. Grasses are lush and relatively undisturbed and there are several open areas of soil.

East Beaver Creek supplies water for cooking and other needs, but the water is of poor quality and tastes bad even after purification. The soils surrounding the creek are also porous and the cleaning of any dishes and dumping of liquids should be done at a considerable distance from the creek.

If you want, you can follow the trail on from the meadow along East Beaver Creek and into a more developed trail designated as a seasonal use road. The road eventually follows Gould Creek and joins Gold Camp Road between Rosemont and Clyde. You would have to arrange for a car shuttle in this case. Otherwise, return as you came.—*Mary Lucas*

General description: A long day hike or overnighter in the foothills country
of the Rampart Range.

General location: 20 miles north of Colorado Springs.

Maps: Palmer Lake and Mount Deception USGS quads; Pike National Forest
Map.

Degree of difficulty: Moderate.

Length: 15 miles round trip with several possibilities for short trips.

Elevations: 7,520 to 9,400 feet.

Special attractions: Easily accessible; steep canyons and interesting rock
formations; good views of Pikes Peak.

Best season: Spring, summer and fall.

For more information: Pike National Forest, Pikes Peak Ranger District,
320 West Fillmore, Colorado Springs, CO 80907; (303) 636-1602.

The North Monument Creek Trail Loop winds through the rocky and
forested area of the Rampart Range. The loop trail circles the North Monument Creek Canyon, rocky and steep with numerous interesting formations
that resemble shapes from eagles to Ayatollahs. In addition, the trail occasionally provides spectacular views of Pike's Peak. Portions of the trail that
climb from the trailhead to above the canyon are steep, but the rest is
moderate to easy hiking. It should be noted that, because of its proximity to
the Front Range Metropolitan area, parts of this trail receive heavy use from
four-wheelers and trailbikers.

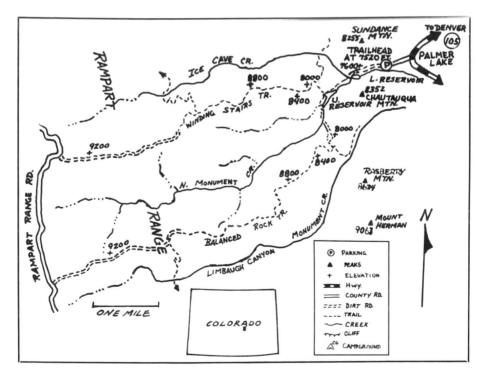

North Monument Creek Loop

To reach the trailhead take Interstate 25 to the Larkspur exit; the first exit south of Castle Rock. From here travel south on State Highway 18 to the town of Palmer Lake. In Palmer Lake, take the main westward road to the old waterworks. At this location there is a parking area where you can leave your vehicle and begin your hike.

A jeep road climbs westward from the trailhead into the North Monument Creek Canyon and through mountain brush and ponderosa pines for about .25 miles to the Lower Reservoir and then an additional .75 miles to the Upper Reservoir. The two reservoirs are water sources for the Town of Palmer Lake. At the Upper Reservoir the trail enters a relatively flat area—a good spot for camping.

Several trails merge at the Upper Reservoir and care should be taken to assure proper trail selection. Travel southward along the western shore and ignore any trails leading to the north or west until you are completely south of the reservoir. Travel southward about .75 miles to another trail fork, and follow the trail to the west. You are now on Balanced Rock Trail. This trail climbs steeply to the west up a ridge above North Monument Creek Canyon for about 2.5 miles. It takes you through ponderosa pine and aspen and occasionally provides beautiful views down into the rocky canyon.

After about 2.5 miles Balanced Rock Trail reaches the ridgetop of the canyon and becomes less steep. At this point it continues westward and provides excellent views into both North Monument Creek Canyon to the north and Monument Creek Canyon to the south. Also, at strategic locations, Pike's Peak is conspicuous on the southern horizon. This portion of the trail wanders through aspen, spruce and fir. After about two miles, the trail turns into a four-wheel drive road on which you may meet other recreational users. This road continues westward through terrain and vegetation similar to those on Rampart Range Road.

Several options are available at Rampart Range Road. The hike can be terminated at this point if arrangements have been made for transportation. As a second option, hikers can go northward along Rampart Range Road for two miles to Winding Stairs Road. This four-wheel-drive road goes eastward and narrows to a trail after about two miles. It then parallels the northern rim of North Monument Creek Canyon and goes back to the Upper Reservoir. Otherwise, hikers can return by Balanced Rock Trail to the trailhead.

One note of caution: hikers should be careful in traveling the canyon bottom and should not count on camping in the bottom or hiking it for any distance. There are extensive rock formations in the canyon that make a trip down worthwhile. However, access to the bottom is limited and paths should be selected with care. The canyon bottom is filled with large boulders that make footing difficult, and there are numerous beaver ponds.—*Bill and Kay Humphries*

37 Colorado Trail

General description: A day hike or the starting point for an extended backpack through the mountains along the north end of South Park.

General location: About 45 miles southwest of Denver.

Maps: Jefferson and Mount Logan USGS quads; Pike National Forest Map.

Degree of difficulty: Easy.

Length: 2 or more miles one way.

Elevations: 10,000 to 11,000 feet.

Special attractions: Easily accessible; offers many options for long and short hikes; beautiful aspen groves and views of South Park.

Best season: Spring, summer and early fall.

For more information: Pike National Forest, South Park Ranger District, P.O. Box 218, Fairplay, CO 80440; (303) 836-2404.

The Colorado Trail is a beautiful, long distance route which will one day extend from Denver to Durango. One particularly pretty section of the trail, now completed, skirts the northern edge of South Park in the Pike National Forest.

The easiest access point is at the summit of Kenosha Pass on U.S. Highway 285 about an hour's drive southwest of Denver. From this point the trail heads southeast along the Kenosha Mountains and into the Lost Creek Wilderness Area or to the west past the Jefferson Creek campgrounds and to the summit of Georgia Pass at the Continental Divide. Many options exist for day hikes and extended backpacks in either direction.

An enjoyable day hike goes southeast from the summit of the pass. To reach the trailhead, turn onto the road across from the sign for the Kenosha Pass summit and Kenosha Campground. Follow this road across a meadow to the edge of the aspen grove where you will see the sign for the Colorado Trail. Park here.

Follow the old jeep trail south through the meadow and then east into the aspens. A short distance along, you will come to a fork where a trail marker tells you to go to the right. As you continue on through alternating clearings and aspen groves, you will have some good views of South Park. The occasional pine trees you encounter along the way are bristlecone pines, which in some areas of South Park have been found to be more than 2,000 years old.

Starting down the trail.

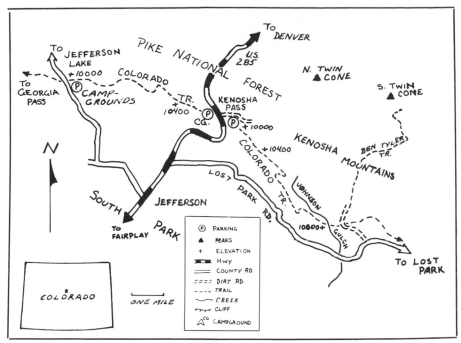

Colorado Trail

These trees are easily identified by their dense clusters of pine needles with globules of sap or pitch, their "bristly" cones (pick one up and feel), and their often gnarled and contorted shapes.

About .5 miles along, after several small openings, you will hike a long, level stretch through an aspen grove, especially beautiful in early fall. Beyond the trunks, as you look back, there are mountains.

Again the trail enters into open areas and smaller stands of aspen. Many of the aspens grew in after ancient forest fires burned through the spruce forests of the area. In places, the aspen stands are old and many spruce are growing in: a natural succession from aspen back to spruce once again.

The trail climbs to a saddle where you will encounter a jeep road. Follow the markers indicating the trail leading to the right and up to a ridgetop. You will hike atop this ridge for another mile and then descend to Johnson Gulch. From the ridge you have many splendid views of South Park, the Continental Divide, and the Tarryall and Kenosha mountains.

The ridgetop is a good destination for a short, easy hike of about two miles one way. Or you can continue on towards Lost Park and the Lost Creek Wilderness. In another eight miles you will reach the Lost Park Road.

An alternate route can be taken from the Kenosha Pass Campground west about seven miles to the Jefferson Creek Road and Aspen Campground where you could shuttle a car. This hike follows similar aspen, meadow and ridgetop terrain with many beautiful views.

Because the Colorado Trail is still under construction in many areas, you might want to check with the Forest Service for up-to-date trail routes and conditions for travel beyond the routes described here. Also, if you like this trail, you may want to get involved in funding and supporting its completion.—*Peter, Caryn and Crystal Boddie*

38 *Mount Silverheels*

General description: A day hike to the top of Mount Silverheels overlooking
  South Park.
General location: 5 miles north of Fairplay.
Maps: Alma and Como USGS quads; Pike National Forest Map.
Degree of difficulty: Moderate.
Length: 5 miles one way
Elevations: 10,250 to 13,822 feet.
Special attractions: Spectacular views of South Park and many high peaks.
Best season: Summer.
For more information: Pike National Forest, South Park Ranger District,
  P.O. Box 218, Fairplay, CO 80440; (303) 836-2404.

A few miles northwest of Fairplay, just up Buckskin Gulch from the town of
Alma, are the remains of the old mining camp called Buckskin Joe. It was here
during the boom of the 1860s that Mount Silverheels, the destination of this
hike, got its name.

Local legend has it that one day a beautiful dance hall girl came to town and
quickly earned the nickname of "Silverheels" for the silver slippers she always
wore. One winter, an epidemic of smallpox spread through the camp, killing
many of the miners and leaving many others terribly scarred. Throughout the
epidemic, Silverheels became nurse to the diseased miners, traveling from
cabin to cabin through the long winter. Then one day she herself contracted
the disease, but after many weeks was nursed back to health and survived.
When spring came, the disease had run its course and the town began to
recover its once thriving nature. In appreciation of her tireless efforts, the local
miners decided to take up a collection for Silverheels. They raised over five

Mount Silverheels.

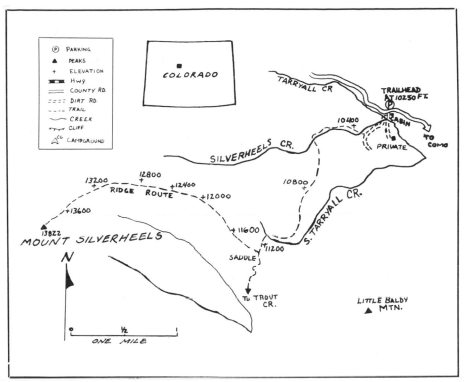

Mount Silverhells

thousand dollars, but when they went to her cabin to present their gift, the dance hall girl was gone, having fled town because of her scarred face. To commemorate her beauty and her untiring charity, the miners named the beautiful peak overlooking South Park in her honor.

So, as you begin your climb of Mount Silverheels, recall the story of the beautiful dancehall girl. Picture, as well, the many mining camps which once surrounded the base of this mountain and trace the footsteps of the many miners, trappers and Indians who may have preceeded you.

To reach the mountain, take U.S. 285 to the town of Como, about ten miles north of Fairplay. From the highway follow the county road northwest through town and to the turnoff to Boreas Pass Road. After about .5 miles bear left at the next fork. In about another .5 miles look for a log cabin on the left side of the road. This cabin will have the number 1187 on it. Pull off the county road and park near the cabin.

Begin your hike at the small dirt road marked "Private," next to the cabin. This road leads to a house on private property across Tarryall Creek. Please respect it and don't block the road. Follow it down towards the creek and take the right fork which fords the creek. There is a small footbridge here and once you cross the creek you will be on National Forest land.

Follow the jeep road across a second creek (Silverheels Creek) and up along the meadow into the trees to the right. After about .25 miles you will come to a small clearing where the jeep road forks. Take the trail down to the right into the trees and in a short distance you will again cross Silverheels Creek, then begin to climb steeply.

After the steep part of the climb, you will pass some old cabins, evidence of the mining heritage of this country. In another .25 miles the trail levels out and parallels a large opening full of willows. Follow the old road and near the upper end of this opening, look for it as it crosses through the willows. In this area the trail may become obscure. On the other side of the willows it bends to the right and climbs steeply through a thick forest of lodgepole pine and spruce. As you gain elevation, you are afforded occasional glimpses of Little Baldy Mountain and out into South Park. When the trail bends to the west, look for limber pine along the drier southfacing slopes. You will also hear the tumbling waters of South Tarryall Creek below you.

Eventually you come to a large open bowl with many wildflowers. This is an opening left by an old forest fire. Shortly after crossing South Tarryall Creek, you will reach a small saddle separating Little Baldy Mountain and Mount Silverheels. From here the trail continues on to Trout Creek, a stream which does not live up to its name. For those not wishing to make the summit climb up Silverheels, the saddle or the meadows on the banks of Trout Creek are good destinations (about 2.5 miles one way to the saddle). Keep an eye open for deer and elk in this area.

To climb Mount Silverheels follow the ridge from the saddle northwest and then west about 2.5 miles to the summit. The ridge is moderately steep and provides a good steady climbing grade. About .25 miles from the top you will encounter a false summit. Continue on southwest to the true summit. Sign the register and enjoy the view. From this vantage point you can see all of South Park, the Mosquito Range, (Mts. Bross, Lincoln and Democrat are directly to the west), the Tenmile Range and the Continental Divide as it skirts Summit County, as well as countless other peaks and ranges.—*Peter Boddie*

39 Homestake Mine Trail

General description: A day hike into a beautiful and historic area, ending at a high mountain lake and the Homestake Mine.
General location: 10 miles north of Leadville.
Maps: Homestake Reservoir and Leadville North USGS quads; San Isabel National Forest Map.
Degree of difficulty: Moderate.
Length: 3 to 4 miles one way.
Elevations: 10,400 to 11,700 feet.
Special attractions: Beautiful scenery; high mountain lakes; interesting history.
Best season: Summer.
For more information: San Isabel National Forest, Leadville Ranger District, Post Office Building, 130 W. 5th St., P.O. Box 970, Leadville, CO 80461; (303) 486-0749.

Taking you up into the beautiful Holy Cross Wilderness with its gorgeous scenery and high mountain lakes, the Homestake Mine Trail also gives you a look at some of the mining works the Leadville area is famous for.

To reach the trailhead, take U.S. Highway 24 north from Leadville for about 10 miles, turning left on Forest Route 100, the road to Lily Lake. Drive two miles on this road and park at the turn-about approximately .25 miles before the lake. (The road is rough for passenger cars to the turn-about and can be traveled only by four-wheel-drive vehicles beyond this point).

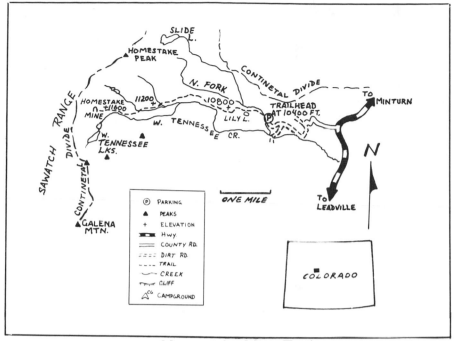

Homestake Mine Trail

Be sure you're wearing good waterproof boots before you set out. There are some marshy areas at the end of the trail near the Homestake Mine that you'll have to negotiate.

Begin your hike at Lily Lake by starting up the main jeep road. (There is a lesser-used one to your right.) The road will take you the entire three miles to a small, unnamed lake at the base of the Homestake Mine Area.

After hiking .5 to .75 miles, you will begin to skirt the edge of some high mountain meadows with streams running through them. Then, about two miles into your hike, you'll come into the Holy Cross Wilderness Area. Shortly beyond the wilderness sign you will see a boulder field on the right and, farther along in the trees, you will begin to see the occasional remains of the lodgings of miners who once lived here.

This area was once a thriving mining community, but it is also notorious as a slide area where loose rock from the surrounding mountain ridges buried many cabins and mines. Several people, even rescue parties, lost their lives in these rock and snow slides.

At the end of the jeep road you will come to the unnamed, high mountain lake. Above you is the Continental Divide, beautiful glacial cirques, and many snowfields.

An almost forgotten trail to the Homestake Mines (located in a large cirque) takes off to the right from here. The hiking trail to the left of the lake leads up into the cirque containing West Tennessee Lakes. Along the way, it passes many small waterfalls and affords the best view of the Homestake mining area.

Beautiful scenery, historical interest, and the fact that this trail is one of the lesser know ones combines to make this hike a truly enjoyable experience.—*Ruth and Sandy Mooneyham*

40 Midland Railroad Trail

General description: A unique day hike along the Midland Railroad Route, which passes through Hagerman Tunnel underneath the Continental Divide.

General location: About 13 miles west of Leadville.

Maps: Homestake Reservoir and Mt. Massive USGS quads; San Isabel National Forest Map.

Degree of difficulty: Easy.

Length: 5 miles round trip.

Elevations: 10,950 to 11,550 feet.

Special attractions: You will be hiking along the old railroad grade of the Midland Railroad; beautiful scenery.

Best season: Summer.

For more information: San Isabel National Forest, Leadville Ranger District, Post Office Building, 130 W. 5th St., P.O. Box 970, Leadville, CO 80461; (303) 486-0749.

The Midland Railroad Trail offers a unique hike, taking you up through the San Isabel National Forest along the old railroad bed to the Continental Divide and the old Hagerman Tunnel.

To reach the trailhead, take the Turquoise Lake road from Leadville west to Turquoise Lake. Then follow Forest Route 105 across the dam and continue on until you reach the Hagerman Pass Road turn-off four to five miles from

Cutthroat trout. Colorado Division of Wildlife photo.

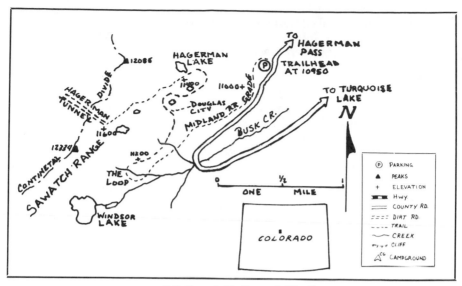

Midland Railroad Trail

the dam. Turn left onto this road and drive another two to three miles until you come to a Forest Service sign for the old railroad route of the Midland Railroad on the left. (Watch carefully for the sign, as it is small and set back 10 to 20 feet form the road.)

Park and begin your hike at the Forest Service sign, starting up the historic bed of the Colorado Midland Railroad, known in its day as perhaps the most scenic railroad route in America.

At the end of the first mile, you will drop into a meadow. This was the site of the famous Colorado Midland "Loop" bridge. A construction camp existed here once for the sole purpose of building a giant wooden bridge, now non-existent. Photographs of the famous bridge are abundant throughout the town of Leadville.

From the "Loop," continue on to the sign that marks a trail to Douglas City, an old railroad town now overgrown with trees. Continue on the old grade and you will come to beautiful, secluded Hagerman Lake, a great spot for camping (stay 200 feet away from the lake and off-trail) and fishing, which is fair for small cutthroat trout.

Continue on past Hagerman Lake another .75 miles and you will come to the large, cavernous opening in the rocks that is the long-abandoned Hagerman Tunnel. It once provided one of the last narrow gauge routes through the Rockies. Trains would travel through the tunnel to Lake Ivanhoe on the other side and then on to Basalt and Glenwood Springs. After having a good look, return as you came.

We're sure you'll agree this is a beautiful and interesting hike, well worth your effort.—*Ruth and Sandy Mooneyham*

41 Lostman Pass

General description: A day hike or overnighter into the high glacial basins which feed the Roaring Fork River and one of its tributaries, Lostman Creek.

General location: About 18.5 miles east of Aspen.
Maps: Mt. Champion, Independence Pass and New York Peak USGS quads; White River National Forest Map.
Degree of difficulty: Moderate.
Length: 8 miles one way.
Elevations: 11,600 to 12,00 feet.
Special attractions: A variety of ecotones from montane to krumholz to alpine; a number of glacial cirques and lakes.
Best season: Summer.
For more information: White River National Forest, Aspen Ranger District, 806 W. Hallam, Aspen, CO 81611; (303) 925-3445.

The trails in the glacially-formed basins which spawn the Roaring Fork River and its tributary, Lostman Creek, make high country more than ordinarily accessible. Because the area is easily reached from Independence Pass, it receives moderate to heavy usage. However, the trails—of varying lengths—provide quick access to nearby country which is less traveled.

The hiking alternatives in the Roaring Fork and Lostman drainages range from the short climb of less than a mile to Linkins Lake, to the full eight mile traverse between the Roaring Fork Basin and Lostman Reservoir. Backcountry of the Hunter-Fryingpan Wilderness is accessible here, as well. (See the following hike.)

The trail into the basin from the Roaring Fork Drainage starts 18.5 miles east of Aspen where State Highway 82 crosses the Roaring Fork River. Those following the full eight mile horseshoe from here to Lostman Reservoir should leave an auto at their destination, Lostman Campground, west of the trailhead.

From the parking area on the north side of the highway, there are trails ascending on either side of the river. To reach Linkins Lake where there is fair fishing for brook trout, follow the short trail on the west (left) side of the river, which soon goes off to the left away from the river, and follows a short, intermediate ridge into tundra. The lake is .25 miles beyond. This is a good picnic hike, or a nice introduction to high country traveling.

To reach Independence Lake or Lostman Pass, take the trail which parallels the river on the eastern (right) bank. It follows the course of the Roaring Fork through willows and Pre-Cambrian metamorphics and granites for 1.5 miles, then bears east and is marked by cairns up the rocky slope to the lush and marshy ground surrounding Independence Lake. Fishing in Independence Lake and in the Upper Roaring Fork is fair for brook trout.

The environs of Independence Lake demonstrate the adaptability of tundra flora to the cold, high altitude and short growing season. The area is also an excellent study in a process of succession—alpine lakes to tundra meadows: a glacial lake slowly filled by sediment, then taken over by tundra mosses and plants to become a marsh, which will in turn be drained by the erosion of creeks formed by summer runoff. Substantial evidence of mineralization, as well as textbook examples of glacial erosion forming cirques, moraines, and glacial lakes, is also present in the area.

The impressive walls surrounding Independence Lake to the northwest are broken by the low saddle of Lostman Pass, another 300 vertical feet above. Hikers can minimize impact through the tundra enroute to the talus-covered pass by staying on the main trail. Once you encounter the talus slopes below the pass, follow the cairns to the trail's summit at 12,800 feet.

Looking back to the south, Grizzly Peak is visible in the distance, as are several bench-like moraines containing alpine lakes, including Linkins and Independence Lakes. Over the pass and to the north, the trail drops in a steep descent to Lostman Lake. Farther north, along the jagged ridge to the right, lies South Fork Pass, and beyond it the eastern slopes of the Williams Mountains, which form the drainage of the Fryingpan River.

The descent to Lostman traverses down the righthand (northerly) slope of the basin, passes the lake and becomes somewhat obscure until it reaches the meadows surrounding Lostman Creek. The easiest traveling and the main trail lies on the west side of the creek. The trail becomes obvious once it crosses the creek at the head of the willow-covered upper valley. The remainder of the route is a leisurely grade past serpentine falls, with wide panoramas of the Continental Divide to the south, and ends at Lostman Reservoir. Fishing in the reservoir is good for rainbow and brook trout. Fishing in Lostman Creek and Lostman Lake is fair to good for brook trout.

Backpackers should be aware of the stove-only regulations in this area and should be sure to camp at least 200 feet away from the lakes, streams and trails.—*Chris Frye*

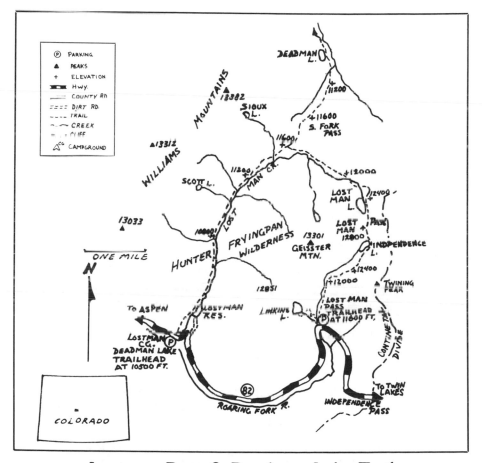

Lostman Pass & Deadman Lake Trails

42 Deadman Lake

General description: An overnighter taking you into the Hunter-Fryingpan Wilderness.

General location: 14 miles east of Aspen.

Maps: Independence Pass, New York Peak and Mt. Champion quads; White River National Forest Map.

Length: 5.5 miles one way.

Elevations: 10,500 to 11,900 feet.

Special attractions: Hunter-Fryingpan Wilderness; great scenery; two interesting and different glacially-formed alpine valleys.

Best season: Summer.

For more information: Contact White River National Forest, Aspen Ranger District, 806 W. Hallam, Aspen, CO 81611; (303) 925-3445.

This hike is recommended as an overnight trip. Not only do steep grades on South Fork Pass make a one-day roundtrip difficult, but the beauty of the Hunter-Fryingpan Wilderness is best savored at leisure.

To reach the trailhead, drive east from Aspen on State Highway 82 for 14 miles to the Lostman Campground parking area.

Follow the trail beginning on the north side of the highway. It parallels the Lostman Reservoir outlet channel about .25 miles to the reservoir, follows the west (lefthand) shore of Lostman Reservoir through a beautiful, mature stand of spruce and fir, and then wanders through the willows and gentle meadows to the west of Lostman Creek, a fast, pretty stream bounding over pink and grey granites.

Within three to four miles—a comfortable walk of no more than two hours—the trail crosses one of the upper forks of Lostman Creek. This is an ideal rest stop before the climb to the pass on the switchback trail immediately to the left.

The view from the beautiful tundra of South Fork Pass is well worth the required effort. To the south lies the Continental Divide; to the north, the green slopes of the Fryingpan drainages.

The trail continues northwest and descends 1.5 miles below timberline on the other side of the pass, then into a wide enchanting meadow. Across the meadow, along a faint trail marked by lonesome poles, lies Deadman Lake.

The broad expanse of the meadow and wooded hills around and below Deadman Lake are rich habitat for deer and elk, and the upper reaches of the Fryingpan offers fishing for brook trout. The area is a diverse mixture of alpine meadow, spruce-fir forest, and high country marsh. Water is readily available in the area, except on the pass, but it should be purified.

Deadman Lake itself really is dead in that it is a nonproductive fishery. This may be due to the fact that it is isolated from streams in the area, is spring fed, and is probably subject to hard freezes in winter. The lake does provide good habitat for waterfowl and a variety of mammals, and the rolling, sparsely wooded hills which surround it provide numerous attractive campsites. (Be sure to camp at least 200 feet from the lakeshore and use a backpacking stove, if possible, rather than building a fire.) What's more, the surprising mixture of meadow, woods and steep glacially-scoured ridges entices one to exploratory wandering.

One obvious topographic feature in the area below Deadman is a very large glacial moraine which forms an intricate network of ponds behind its dam of massive hardrock blocks.

The river and South Fork trail continues over steep hills and through heavy timber below and beyond the moraine and upper meadows. Eventually, the trail meets a road at Nast, which descends along the main Fryingpan River past Ruedi Reservoir to Basalt. Most hikers, however, return the way they came, over South Fork Pass, back to Lostman Reservoir.—*Chris Frye*

43 Hunter Creek Trail

General description: A beautiful day hike beginning within the city limits of Aspen and following roaring Hunter Creek.
General location: Eastern city limits of Aspen.
Maps: Aspen USGS quad; White River National Forest Map.
Degree of difficulty: Easy.
Length: 3.5 miles one way.
Elevations: 8,000 to 9,000 feet.
Special attractions: Easily accessible from Aspen; follows beautiful Hunter Creek; good views.
Best season: Late spring, summer and fall.
For more information: White River National Forest, Aspen Ranger District, 806 W. Hallam, Aspen, CO 81611; (303) 925-3445.

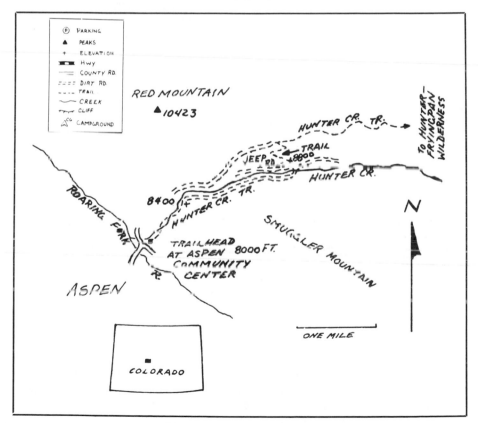

Hunter Creek Trail

Despite the proximity to civilization, this is truly a hike worth taking for the luxuriant foliage and aspen groves, turbulent Hunter Creek and the views of Aspen and surrounding country. You might take this hike when you're in Aspen for a weekend. It can easily be fit into a visit to this historic mountain community.

The trail begins at the Aspen Community Center. Take State Highway 82 into the town of Aspen and turn north just east of the Jerome Hotel. Follow this road down the hill and across the bridge and turn right a short way up the next hill. You can't miss the community center and anyone can direct you to it if you do.

Soon the trail touches Hunter Creek in a dense grove of aspen and begins its winding course toward the ridges of the Elk Mountains to the east.

After crossing a wooden bridge and stretches of log "corduroy," you climb rather abruptly for about 1.5 miles beside the rushing stream (definitely more than a "creek," particularly in early summer). There are frequent, broad pools that invite you to cast a line. Fishing is good for small brook and rainbow trout.

The trail eventually follows a jeep road for a mile, climbing about .25 miles to Hunter Valley, a broad valley of dense grasses and wildflowers and then goes around the valley to an abandoned homestead.

You may extend your hike by following the signs for the Hunter Creek Trail, which eventually enters the Hunter-Fryingpan Wilderness. Camping is allowed at several points, but only at designated sites. You should contact the Aspen Ranger Station for details should you plan to backpack.—*Gib and Buzzy Frye*

44 West Snowmass Trail

General description: A day hike or backpack taking you to a saddle overlooking the Maroon Bells-Snowmass Wilderness.
General location: Approximately 15 miles west of Aspen.
Maps: Capitol Peak and Highland Peak USGS quads; White River National Forest Map.
Degree of difficulty: Difficult.
Length: About 5.5 miles one way.
Elevations: About 8,500 to 12,000 feet.
Special attractions: Magnificent views of the high peaks, including several 14,000 foot summits; dense aspen groves; pretty meadows with many wildflowers; abundant wildlife.
Best season: Summer.
For more information: White River National Forest, Aspen Ranger District, 806 W. Hallam, Aspen CO 81611; (303) 925-3445.

If there were a typical "Aspen-Snowmass country" trail, this would be it. It would be hard to find another one that outdoes it in sheer beauty or range of vistas and attractions, including the fact that this is a lightly-used stretch of trail in a heavily-used area.

To reach the trailhead, take State Highway 82 about 14 miles northwest of Aspen. Turn south at the Forest Access sign at Old Snowmass. After about two miles, turn left at the sign for Snowmass Campground. Follow this road about 10 miles to the campground. Bear right past the campground and follow the road to a parking area about .5 miles beyond. This is the trailhead for the

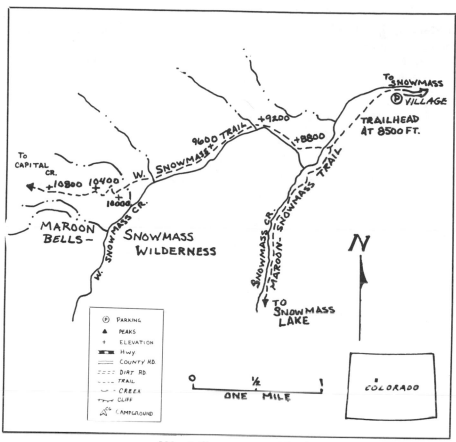

West Snowmass Trail

Maroon-Snowmass Trail. From the trailhead, hike about one mile along the main trail (which leads to Snowmass Lake) until a sign directs you to the West Snowmass Trail.

The trail is as challenging as it is scenic. Almost immediately it leads across Snowmass Creek (cold and swift) and climbs sharply, switching back many times for about 1.5 miles through stands of spruce, fir and huge aspen.

Across the first ridge, the country opens into several meadows from which the higher ridges and peaks can be seen. It climbs again steeply then for another three miles to the top of the ridge between the Snowmass and Capitol Peak valleys.

As the trail climbs ever higher, it passes beneath Mt. Daly and Haystack Mountain and leads upward to timberline, eventually reaching nearly 12,000 feet in elevation at the saddle between the two mountains. From here you have clear views of such beautiful peaks as Capitol Peak (14,130 feet), the Maroon Bells (14,014 and 14,156 feet), Snowmass Mountain (14,092 feet) named for the great snowfield between its two summits, and Mt. Sopris (12,953 feet), as well as the surrounding country. This is the Elk Mountain Range with fourteeners formed of both igneous rock eroded into thin sharp ridges like those you see on Snowmass Mountain and Capitol Peak and the obvious layered, stratified rock of Castle, Pyramid and Maroon Peaks. Spectacular mountains!

Hiking the West Snowmass Trail. Elizabeth Frye photo.

You can return as you came or continue on the trail as it drops abruptly for another 2.5 miles to Capitol Creek, again through stands of aspen and meadows luxuriant with wildflowers, grasses and ferns.

Especially in the upper reaches, you'll meet few, if any, hikers. It is excellent backpacking country, with numerous campsites, though steep grades and high elevations call for good conditioning, footwear and clothing. Fishing is rated fair to good in Snowmass Creek for six- to 12-inch brook trout.

You may want to explore any of the number of trails that thread through this country, particularly the Maroon-Snowmass Trail following Snowmass Creek to Snowmass Lake where fishing is good for a few natives and rainbows usually around 11 inches. The scenery is fantastic here, too. The Capitol Creek Trail takes you through the northwest end of the Maroon Bells-Snowmass Wilderness to the Crystal River north of Redstone.—*Gib and Buzzy Frye*

45 *Lonesome Lake*

General description: A day hike or overnighter to a beautiful cirque lake in the Holy Cross Wilderness.

General location: About 15 miles northwest of Leadville.

Maps: Homestake Reservoir USGS quad; White River National Forest Map.

Degree of difficulty: Moderate.

Length: Nine miles round trip.

Elevations: 10,200 to 11,600 feet.

Special attractions: Beautiful high mountain lake with good fishing; roaring Homestake Creek; wildflowers; wildlife.

Best season: Summer.

For more information: White River National Forest, Holy Cross Ranger Dis-

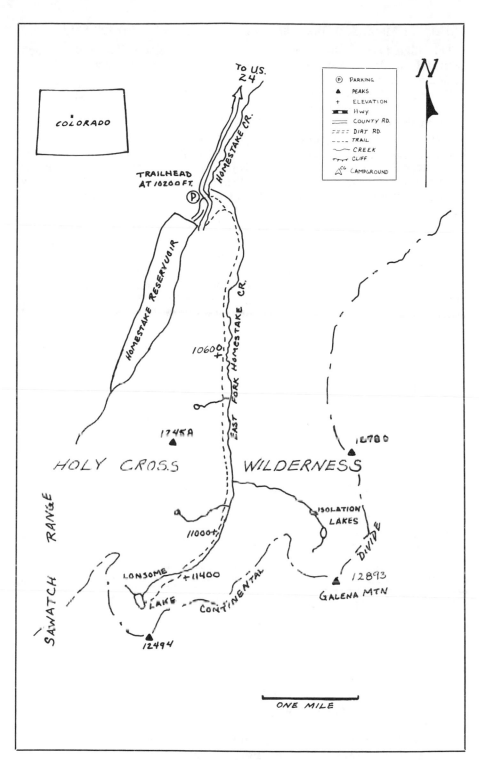

Lonesome Lake

trict, 401 Main, P.O. Box 190, Minturn, CO 81645; (303) 827-5715.

This hike takes you through a long, deep glacial valley and through beautiful meadows to one of the many alpine lakes in the Sawatch Range: Lonesome Lake.

To reach the trail to the lake, drive south from Minturn on U.S. Highway 24 for about 10 miles or drive north from the summit of Tennessee Pass about 12 miles to the signed junction with Forest Route 703, leading to Homestake Reservoir. Turn southwest on this road and follow it for about 10 miles, past the Gold Park Campground and to a signed junction at the base of the Homestake Reservoir dam. Park at this junction or, if you want to tackle the steep climb in your car, continue on to the crest of the dam. From here follow the aqueduct eastward into the valley of East Fork Homestake Creek. The aqueduct ends at a small diversion pond.

This diversion, a part of the Homestake Project, is one of many which capture water from tributaries to Homestake Creek and diverts it to Homestake Reservoir. From here the water flows beneath the Continental Divide through a tunnel to Turquoise Lake near Leadville. Recently, the Homestake Project has been the center of much controversy concerning a planned extension of the diversion project to Cross Creek within the Holy Cross Wilderness Area. The water ultimately is used by the cities of Colorado Springs and Aurora.

The trail begins along the west (right) side of the pond. Follow the cairns as it crosses an open area and then follows along the creek for about .5 miles through stands of evergreens. Then you will reach the first of two large meadows, this one being more than a mile in length. This beautiful spot where wildflowers bloom profusely in the summer might make a good destination if you are most interested in fishing.

Follow the trail around the west side of this mile-long meadow and then re-enter the woods. You will have to climb at a little steeper grade. Soon you will pass a small stream (a good spot to rest) and then come to the second of the meadows. Follow the creek to the other end of the meadow where you will find evidence of the avalanches that may have roared down from the obvious avalanche chute during the previous winter. The trail then re-enters the woods and begins a steady climb toward the lake. When you reach an open basin, keep to the left side for the last .5-mile climb to the grass-covered bench and Lonesome Lake. The trail is faint in several places. Watch for wildflowers and small mammals along your way, including marsh marigolds and marmots.

Lonesome Lake is one of many beautiful lakes to be found in this faulted anticline known as the Sawatch Range. Fishing is said to be good for cutthroat trout in the 12- to 14-inch range. Please be sure to camp at least 200 feet away from the lake and trails to preserve the beauty of the area and be sure to watch for deer and elk on your return hike.—*Jim Haynes, Don Wagner, Tyler Garbonza*

46 Wheeler and Gore Range Trails

General description: A long day hike or moderate overnighter, or a long backpack into the Gore Range.

General location: West of Dillon.

Maps: Mt. Powell, Squaw Creek, Dillon, Willow Lakes, Frisco and Vail Pass USGS quads; Arapaho National Forest Map.

Degree of difficulty: Moderate to difficult.

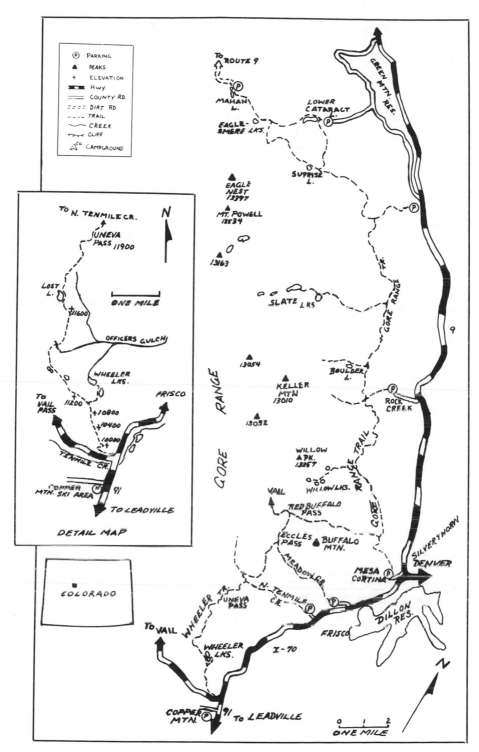

Wheeler & Gore Range Trails

Length: 6 mile round trip to Wheeler Lakes; 54.5 miles for the length of the Gore Range Trail.

Elevations: 8,800 to 11,600 feet.

Special attractions: Long trail with a lot of variety; beautiful views and wildflowers; big game; good fishing.

Best season: Summer through early fall.

For more information: Arapaho National Forest, Dillon Ranger District, 101 W. Main, Drawer Q, Frisco, CO 80433; (303) 668-5404, 668-3314.

Named for Sir St. George Gore, a nobleman from Ireland who led a hunting expedition here in the 1800s with the famous Jim Bridger as his guide, this is a superb hiking and backpacking trail that runs nearly the length of the Gore Range from Mahan Lake junction in the north to Copper Mountain in the south. There are numerous possibilities for long and short backpacks and day hikes.

Beginning at the southernmost end of the trail is an easily accessible portion of the trail that takes you to Wheeler Lakes (a six-mile round trip). From

Elk. Colorado Division of Wildlife photo.

Wheeler Lakes you can continue on for any number of miles on the Gore Range Trail, exiting at any of the many access points.

To reach the Wheeler-Gore Range trailhead, drive to Copper Mountain at the junction of Interstate 70 and State Highway 91. Park at the ski area near the intersection, then walk back over the overpass to the "No Parking" sign where the trail begins.

At first, the trail cuts across the south-facing slope along the highway. It may seem like a strange place to begin a hike. Keep going, though, and you'll soon be climbing away from the highway and into forests of aspen, Englemann spruce and lodgepole pine. You will cross meadows where mountain asters, lupine, chiming bells, cinquefoil and paintbrush grow abundantly.

After you've hiked a mile or so, you'll cross a small stream and, a short distance beyond, come upon the Eagles Nest Wilderness Area sign in a small stand of Englemann spruce. You are entering the wilderness at its southern edge.

The Eagles Nest Wilderness extends for over twenty miles to the north and includes some of the most rugged backcountry in Colorado. The Gore Range Trail follows the eastern edge of the Wilderness for its length. The section of the trail that will lead you to Wheeler Lakes is fairly steep.

A short way into the wilderness, you will come across a trail register. Be sure to sign it.

From the register, the trail continues to gain elevation steadily. For a distance of .75 miles it leads you through spruce and pine forest and then crosses a large meadow. At this point, the majority of the climb is behind you. Pause to look back at the Ten Mile Range and northwest across the meadow to the ridge above Shrine Pass.

The trail now continues for another .5 miles through intermittent meadow and forest and climbs steeply through a meadow to the top of a ridge. Here the view of the Ten Mile Range, including Crystal and Pacific Peaks, is even more spectacular.

At the ridgetop the trail forks. Take the right fork to Wheeler Lakes. A hike .25 miles downhill brings you to the first of the lakes. Keep going over the hill and you will come to the second and larger lake. Fishing is good here for 10- to 12-inch cutthroat trout. However, fishermen should limit their catch, because this lake is popular and easily accessible.

There are numerous camping spots in the meadows and forest surrounding the lakes. Camp away from the water to preserve the beauty of the spot. Check with the Forest Service about campfire policies and fire danger. We recommend you use a backpack stove.

Water is available in a small stream at the northwest end of the second lake. Boil or chemically purify it before using.

From the ridge at the north end of the second lake, you can look down into Officer's Gulch and Ten Mile Canyon and see Dillon Reservoir beyond. To the northwest is Uneva Pass and the Gore Range Trail winding up and over.

You may either return as you came from here or go on following the Gore Range Trail for as many of its 54.5 miles as you like. Along its length, it traverses an amazing variety of terrain and provides access to numerous lakes, valleys, and trails in the rugged and spectacular Gore Range.

There are numerous access points to the trail, but you will have to arrange a car shuttle if you plan a longer hike. These access points and mileages between them as given by the U.S. Forest Service are listed as follows (from south to north) with the appropriate USGS quads:

Copper Mountain to North Tenmile	10.0 miles
(Vail Pass quad)	
North Tenmile to Meadow Creek	3.0 miles
(Frisco, Vail Pass quads)	
Meadow Creek to Mesa Cortina	6.25 miles
(Dillon, Willow Lakes, Frisco quads)	
Mesa Cortina to Brush Creek	10.5 miles
(Dillon, Willow Lakes quads)	
Rock Creek to Brush Creek	10.5 miles
(Squaw Creek quad)	
Brush Creek to Surprise	6.5 miles
(Mt. Powell, Squaw Creek quads)	
Surprise to Eaglesmere	3.0 miles
(Mt. Powell quad)	
Eaglesmere to Mahan Lake Junction	4.5 miles
(Mt. Powell quad)	

This mileage does not include the mileages of the access trails taking you to the Gore Range Trail. One good, short hike to it in the center of the range is at Rock Creek (see description of Rock Creek).—*Peter and Caryn Boddie*

47 Pitkin Lake

General description: A day hike to Pitkin Lake in the Gore Range near Vail.
General location: 4 miles east of Vail.
Maps: Vail East USGS quad; White River National Forest Map.
Degree of difficulty: Moderate.
Length: About 5 miles one way.
Elevations: 8,400 to 11,400 feet.
Special attractions: Spectacular glacial valley with beautiful waterfalls; alpine
    lake; wildflowers; good fishing.
Best season: Summer.
For more information: White River National Forest, Holy Cross Ranger District, 401 Main, P.O. Box 190, Minturn, CO 81645; (303) 827-5715.

This easily accessible hike just east of Vail takes you to the beautiful setting of Pitkin Lake, a glacial bowl just below the crest of the Gore Range. Along the way the trail climbs through a steep glacial valley with stands of aspen and evergreens, alpine meadows, and picture postcard waterfalls. Because of its proximity to Vail this hike is recommended for day use, although an overnight trip would be possible.

To reach the trail to Pitkin Lake drive east on Interstate 70 from Vail Ski Area about four miles to an unmarked exit. This exit takes you to the north side of 1-70 and up a road that leads to several groups of condos where it dead-ends. Park just before the last group of condos at the trailhead and register at the Forest Service register.

Hike along the stream for a short distance and cross the bridge at the gaging station. You will pass several condos as you begin your hike. Initially, you will climb over switchbacks that take you in a northeasterly direction. At the top of this first steep pitch you head north on a good foot trail and up the Pitkin Creek Valley. As in most hanging valleys, the first part of the hike poses the

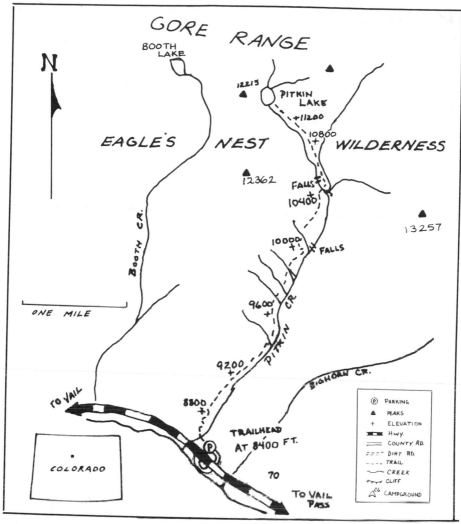

Pitkin Lake

more difficult pitches. After this initial exhilarating climb, the stream and trail converge to afford easier hiking and good fishing in Pitkin Creek, which has been known to yield 10 to 12-inch brook and native trout. As the trail carves its way through the valley, aspen stands give way to evergreens and the grasses and shrubs in the meadows become shorter in resistance to the harsher conditions at higher altitudes. Please leave as little an impact on this delicate environment as you can.

About 1.5 miles up the valley the first of five small stream crossings is made. Just past the last stream crossing, some 200 feet to the east, is the first of two spectacular waterfalls on Pitkin Creek. This would make a good destination for a shorter day hike. Another mile farther, just below the second falls, the trail crosses Pitkin Creek. From here it climbs steeply again up several switchbacks and then climbs less steeply for the final 1.5 miles to Pitkin Lake.—*Doug Crocker*

48 Rock Creek

General description: A day hike to timberline in the Gore Range-Eagle's Nest Wilderness.

General location: 8 miles northwest of Silverthorne.

Maps: WIllow Lakes USGS quad; Arapaho National Forest Map.

Degree of difficulty: Easy.

Length: Approximately 3.5 miles round trip.

Elevations: 9,500 to 10,200 feet.

Special attractions: Beautiful views of the Gore Range.

Best season: Summer.

For more information: Arapaho National Forest, Dillon Ranger District, 101 W. Main, Drawer Q, Frisco, CO 80443; (303) 668-5404, 668-3314.

Taking you from North Rock Creek to timberline and the old Boss Mine, the Rock Creek Trail offers an easy and enjoyable day hike into the Eagles Nest Wilderness.

To reach the trailhead, exit Interstate 70 at Silverthorne and drive north on Colorado Route 9 for eight miles to Rock Creek Road just across from the Blue River Campground. Drive southwest on Rock Creek Road, turning left when you come to the fork in the road 1.3 miles along, and head toward Rock Creek. Go right .5 miles after entering the Arapaho National Forest and continue 1.2 miles to park at the trailhead.

Begin your hike at the Forest Service sign after taking note of the special regulations governing this wilderness area.

As you follow the old jeep road away from the sign, (climbing away from North Rock Creek) you will pass a beaver pond in a small meadow. Look up to your left for a good view of one of the many unnamed peaks in the Gore

The Gore Range at North Rock Creek.

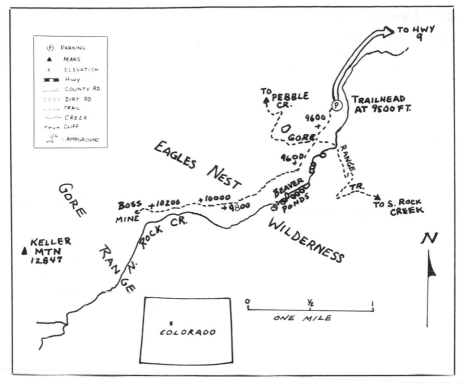

Rock Creek

Range.

Enjoy the wildflowers you see at the beginning of your hike. As you enter the forest of lodgepole pine and begin to climb toward the top of the ridge, which leads eventually to the summit of Keller Mountain, you will see few of them.

Soon you will come to a crossroads. You are crossing the Gore Range Trail (see Wheeler-Gore Range Trail), which runs the length of the Gore Range. The Rock Creek Trail is often used as an access point for this trail, which, to your right, leads to Pebble Creek and to your left, continues on to South Rock Creek. (It can be followed for many miles beyond these points in either direction.) To follow the Rock Creek Trail, continue ahead up the steep old jeep road until it tapers into a trail and then past a lot of deadfall to the top of the ridge.

This is what you came for! From the edge of timberline, you have beautiful views of the North Rock Creek Valley, sculpted by glaciers. The quality of water in North Rock Creek is excellent, coming as it does from the snowfields which have remained in the cirques high atop the peaks at the head of the valley. Notice that of all the peaks you see above North Rock Creek, only one is named and that is Keller Mountain, which you can climb by comtinuing along this ridge.

After you spend some time taking in the rugged peaks surrounding you (and, perhaps, naming one or two just for fun) continue along the ridge to the Boss Mine, and, if you like, to the summit of Keller Mountain (13,085 feet). Then return as you came.—*Caryn Boddie*

49 Lenawee Trail

General description: A day hike to the ridge on Lenawee Mountain with beautiful views and historic interest.

General location: 10 miles east of Dillon.

Maps: Montezuma and Grays Peak USG quads; Arapaho National Forest Map.

Degree of difficulty: Moderate.

Length: 3.5 miles one way.

Elevations: 10,400 to 13,200 feet.

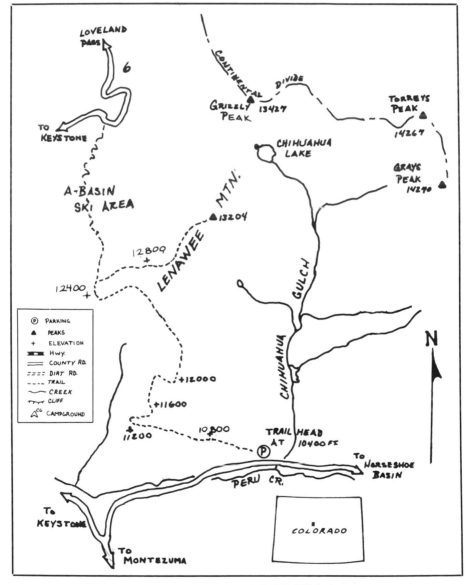

Lenawee Trail

Special attractions: Beautiful views; interesting boulder outcroppings; old
mines and ruins.
Best season: Summer.
For more information: Arapaho National Forest, Dillon Ranger District, 101
W. Main, Drawer Q, Frisco, CO 80443; (303) 668-5404, 668-3314.

The Lenawee Trail climbs from the Peru Creek Road to the summit ridge of
Lenawee Mountain. This point offers a panoramic view of Summit County,
including many historic mining areas and other points of interest.

To reach the trail head, drive east on U.S. Highway 6, 6.5 miles past Dillon
to the Montezuma Road. Turn right, bear left, and travel 4.6 miles to the Peru
Creek Road. Turn left and look for the Lenawee Trail sign, .6 miles past the
creek crossing. Park along the side of the road. There is no water source along
the trail, so be sure to take plenty of water with you.

From the trailhead, you climb at a moderate grade and traverse westward
along the north side of the Peru Creek Valley for about one mile and then the
trail begins one of several switchbacks, taking you to the top of the ridge. As
you reach timberline, take the time to look around and enjoy the alpine environment. The trail becomes less evident here and you will have to follow the
rock cairns marking it.

The trail continues to the ridge near the top of Lenawee Mountain and eventually takes you to the summit at 13,200 feet. From here the views are spectacular. You can see Grays (14,270 feet) and Torreys (14,267 feet) peaks to the
northeast of you, two fourteeners named for the famous botany professors
form Harvard and Princeton. Below you is Chihuahua Gulch and Peru Creek.
To the south is Montezuma and the headwaters of the Snake River. This entire
area is dotted with hundreds of mines. Way down the valley to the west is
Dillon Reservoir and beyond it, the Tenmile and Gore Ranges. To the north
and directly below you is the A Basin Ski Area and beyond it, the highway
ascending Loveland Pass. To the northeast and south you can see the ridgeline
of the Continental Divide extending for many miles.

After enjoying the views, return as you came.—*Caryn Boddie*

50 Too Long Trail

General description: A day hike to Bergen Peak in Means Meadow Park.
General location: About 20 miles west of Denver.
Maps: Squaw Pass and Evergreen USGS quads; Means Meadow Park Map.
Degree of difficulty: Moderate.
Length: 4.3 miles one way.
Elevations: 7,800 to 9,700 feet.
Special attractions: A wide diversity of ecosystems; opportunities to see
wildflowers and wildlife; good views east and west.
For more information: Jefferson County Open Space Department, 1801 19th
St., Golden, CO 80401; (303) 277-8332.

The Too Long Trail to the summit of Bergen Peak in the Front Range near
Bergen Park and Evergreen, offers a pleasant day hike through a variety of
ecosystems and culminates with scenic vistas of the Front Range peaks and the
eastern plains.

To reach the trailhead, drive west on Interstate 70 from Denver to Exit 252,
the El Rancho exit. Turn left (south), then right to Bergen Park on State

Means Meadow.

Highway 74. About one mile south of Bergen Park, look for a small parking area on your right. Park there and begin your hike at the trailhead.

Begin your hike through Means Meadow on the Means Meadow Trail. This .9 miles takes you through an environment of grasses, wildflowers and open, rolling park land. Stately, widely-spaced ponderosa pines grow in scattered stands and small mammals, such as badgers, pocket gophers, and the Richardson ground squirrel, make the meadow their home. Several colonies of prairie dogs are also found in the area.

As you skirt the northern edge of the meadow and begin to climb into stands of Douglas fir interspersed with aspens, you will come to a fork in the trail. A turn to the left will take you down and around the meadow. Go to the right and you will begin climbing steeply on the Too Long Trail leading to the summit of Bergen Peak. Keep an eye out for deer as you climb.

Soon you will find yourself along steep slopes forested with lodgepole pine. Keep on the lookout for blue grouse and porcupines. After 2.4 miles you will come to another fork in the trail. Take the steep right fork, which switchbacks another mile to the top of Bergen Peak.

Once at the summit of the peak you will be well rewarded for your efforts. The views are magnificent. From here you can see Mt. Evans, Mt. Bierstadt and Long's Peak in the distance and Squaw and Chief mountains before them. To the east you can see the plains and Denver.

You have a number of options for your return trip once you descend Bergen Peak to the last fork in the trail. You can go to your right (south) on the Bergen Peak Trail, which connects with the Meadow Trail in 2.7 miles; from this junction you can go south to a parking lot at Stagecoach Road (in which case you will have had to shuttle cars). Or you can follow the Bergen Peak Trail to the Meadow Trail and then hike around the edge of the meadow back to your car, a 5.1 mile hike. Or you can return as you came.

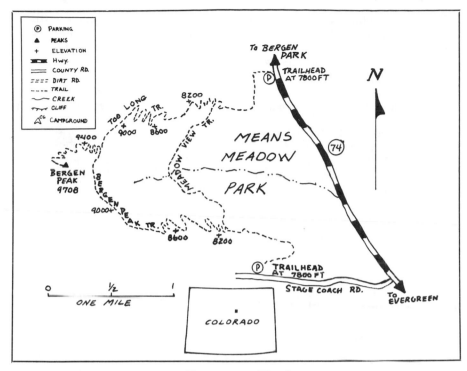

Too Long Trail

In any case, I'm sure you'll appreciate the good work of the Jefferson County Open Space people who provided all these easily accessible and enjoyable trails with the help of Denver Mountain Parks and the Colorado Division of Wildife. Contact the department for brochures on this and other open spaces and trails.—*Caryn, Peter and Crystal Boddie*

51 *Frazer Meadows*

General description: A day hike into Golden Gate Canyon State Park in the Front Range.

General location: About 15 miles northwest of Golden.

Maps: Black Hawk USGS quad; Golden Gate Canyon State Park.

Degree of difficulty: Easy to difficult.

Length: 1.5 to 5.9 miles one way.

Elevations: 8,150 to 9,100.

Special attractions: Easily accessible from Denver; beautiful foothills scenery.

Best season: Spring and fall.

For more information: Golden Gate Canyon State Park, R. Rt. #6, Box 280, Golden, CO 80403; (303) 642-3171.

This hike takes you into Golden Gate Canyon State Park on historic trails that were once traveled by gold miners, lumberjacks, and homesteaders. A Visitor's Center offers information on the history and natural history of the area.

To reach the state park from Golden, take Highway 93 two miles north to Golden Gate Canyon Road. Turn left and continue for 14 miles. In the park, a number of trails interconnect and offer possibilities for hikes ranging from two to about six miles one way.

One good short day hike takes you from Ralston Creek to Frazer Meadow. The trail winds through dense forests and open meadows, with beautiful views, is rated easy and offers a good getaway for those who don't have a lot of time.

To begin, park your car at the trailhead roughly .5 miles northeast of the Visitor's Center. From here the trail ascends an intermittent tributary of Ralston Creek. Gradually gaining elevation, it passes through thick stands of aspen and cottonwoods interspersed with blue spruce. Hiking in the fall is especially enjoyable because of the golden show these trees put on, set against the backdrop of deep green ponderosa pines.

The trail continues up the canyon, traverses the creekbed several times, then swings to the left into Greenfield Meadow. Located about .75 miles from the trailhead, the meadow is the first significant clearing you will encounter.

Immediately beyond the meadow the trail forks to the right and continues uphill at a more gradual rate. The canyon becomes less steep as you proceed and the timber less dense. Outcrops formed of granitic and gneiss bedrock are interesting features along the way. At approximately 1.5 miles past Greenfield Meadow, the trail intersects Mule Deer Trail. A right turn takes you across the creek to Frazer Meadow.

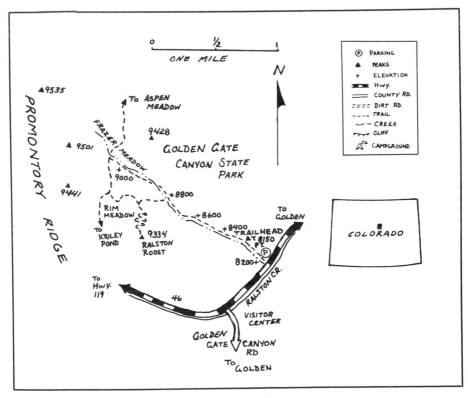

Frazer Meadows

Old homestead in Frazer Meadow. Tim Shangraw photo.

Frazer Meadow, large and open, was probably once used for livestock grazing and contains a partially collapsed homestead. The homestead is a large single-room house with an attached barn or storage room. Evidence of reconstruction over the years is indicated by the types of building materials used—square instead of round head nails, rough hewn instead of mill cut lumber, wooden instead of tin roofing. The homestead setting is very picturesque, with snow-capped mountains to the west, rock promontories to the north, and the serene meadow to the south.

From Frazer Meadow several other trails lead to other areas in the park. The 3.5-mile-long Mule Deer Trail will take you to Panorama Point, which offers a beautiful view of the Continental Divide. The 2.2-mile-long Coyote Trail, rated difficult, will take you back to a park road at Promontory Ridge, where you'll see interesting rock outcroppings. Several other choices are also possible (consult your maps). One strong word of caution is in order, however: In selecting alternate return routes, be careful about interpreting trail markers; they can easily be misinterpreted.

Watch for mule deer, elk, and the elusive blue grouse, as well as beaver and muskrat in stream courses. Occasionally, you will see soaring raptors and maybe coyotes, badgers, marmots, and raccoons.—*Janet and Tim Shangraw*

52 *Mt. Nystrom Trail*

General description: An easily accessible day hike along broad ridgetops above timberline near Berthoud Pass.
General location: About 45 miles west of Denver.
Maps: Berthoud Pass, Fraser and Byers Peak USGS quads; Arapaho National Forest Map.
Degree of difficulty: Easy to moderate.
Length: From 2 to 8 miles one way.
Elevations: 11,300 to 12,650 feet.

Special attractions: Easy access to timberline and the Continental Divide; great views; wildflowers.

Best season: Summer and fall.

For more information: Arapaho National Forest, Sulphur Ranger District, Intersection Highways 40 and 34, Star Route, Grandby, CO 80446; (303) 887-3331.

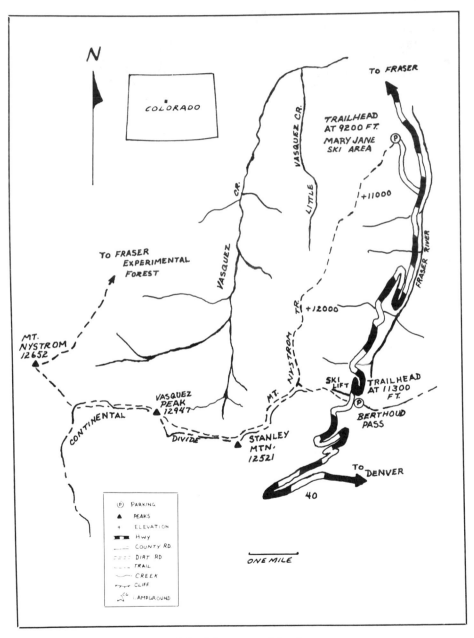

Mt. Nystrom Trail

The Mt. Nystrom Trail follows a long and broad ridge of the Continental Divide and a side ridge from Mt. Nystrom to the Mary Jane Ski Area. This route provides beautiful views of the surrounding mountains and a chance to see the spectacular wildflowers of this alpine environment. An easy access to this trail, which also provides the least elevation gain, is from Berthoud Pass. From this point you have options for short or extended day hikes and an extended backpack, as well.

To reach Berthoud Pass, take Interstate 70 west to U.S. Highway 40 and follow it to the summit of the pass. Park at the ski lodge on the east side.

To begin your hike, cross the highway and climb the ski slopes to the top of the chairlift. For an easier start of your hike, you can take the chairlift, which is operating most weekends and holidays during the summer.

From the top of the chairlift, follow the ridge west to its intersection with another broad ridge from the north. Here you should be able to locate the Mt. Nystrom Trail, marked with rock cairns. From here out your hike will be an easy walk in either direction. To the right the trail follows the ridge for about seven miles to the Mary Jane Ski Area. You can shuttle a car to the parking lot there. To the left the trail follows the Continental Divide about two miles to Stanley Mountain and another six miles to Mt. Nystrom.

This area is part of the Vasquez Mountains and is characterized by broad, rolling ridgetops with steep-sided, glacial cirques carved into them. In general the larger cirques are found on the eastern sides of the ridges where the prevailing winds have deposited snow to form the glaciers. This pattern is repeated over and over again here.

From Berthoud Pass, Stanley Mountain is a short day hike of about 3.5 miles one way, with an elevation gain of about 1,200 feet. From the top of the mountain you can look directly south and down the path of the famous Stanley Slide, a huge avalanche chute. This is one of the most dangerous chutes in the Front Range because it crosses U.S. Highway 40 in two separate places and can bury the highway under as much as 20 feet of snow.

From Stanley Mountain you can continue on towards Mt. Nystrom and beyond to intersect with trails to St. Louis Peak and the Fraser Experimental Forest, or you can return as you came. Whatever you choose to do, be sure to keep an eye out for signs of impending thunderstorms, as this is no place to be caught unaware.—*Brian Dempsey*

53 *Devil's Thumb Lake*

General description: A long day hike or overnighter to an alpine lake in the Indian Peaks Wilderness Area.
General location: About 20 miles west of Boulder.
Maps: East Portal and Nederland USGS quads; Roosevelt National Forest Map.
Degree of difficulty: Moderate.
Length: 10 miles one way.
Elevations: 9,000 to 11,200 feet.
Special attractions: Beautiful scenery; the Devil's Thumb; good fishing.
For more information: Roosevelt National Forest, Boulder Ranger District, 2995 Baseline Rd., Room 16, Boulder, CO 80303; (303) 444-6001.

One of the most scenic areas n the Indian Peaks Wilderness surrounds Devil's Thumb Lake. Its greatest attraction is the Devil's Thumb, a 600 foot

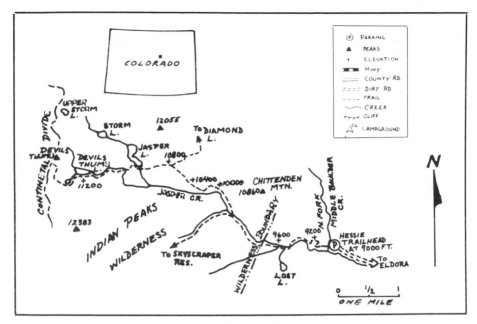

Devil's Thumb Lake

tower of granite which stands above the lake on the north. There is also good fishing to be had in the lower lakes and creeks of the area.

To reach Devil's Thumb Lake, drive west from Boulder on State Highway 119 to the town of Nederland. Go southwest through town, and turn right toward Lake Eldora Ski Area and the town of Eldora. Follow this road past the turnoff to the ski area and continue through town, and then another 1.5 miles to the settlement of Hessie, located where the valley forks.

Begin your hike along the trail which leads west from town and climbs steeply to the hanging glacial valleys of the South Fork of Middle Boulder Creek and Jasper Creek. Two miles from town you will pass the turnoff to Lost Lake, from which there is a beautiful view of the Devil's Thumb. Continue on about .25 miles to cross a sturdy Forest Service bridge, then up Jasper Creek to your right. The trail takes you through open meadows and tall stands of evergreen and aspen. Fishing is good here in Jasper Creek and farther along in Jasper Lake, with natives and brook trout as the predominant catch.

About 1.5 miles along Jasper Creek you will come to a fork in the trail. The left fork leads to Woodland Lake and Skyscraper Reservoir. Continue right for three miles to another fork in the trail. Here the right fork leads into the North Fork of Middle Boulder Ceek drainage and to Diamond Lake. Take the left fork and continue on 1.3 miles to Jasper Lake. Here there is a well-preserved cabin (just southeast of the dam on the southeast side of the lake) which has offered refuge to more than one hiker caught in a storm. From Jasper Lake follow the trail west to Devil's Thumb Lake.

Devil's Thumb Lake holds no fishing prospects due to its shallowness and high altitude. It does, however, offer beautiful scenery and options for further hiking excursions.

One option for hiking farther is to continue up the Devil's Thumb trail west to the top of Devil's Thumb Pass where you will have a splendid view as the

Indian Peaks Wilderness Area. U.S. Forest Service photo.

world seems to drop away in all directions. Winter Park Ski Area is plainly visible below, as is Middle Park. You can extend your hike from the pass by traveling north to the base of Devil's Thumb and farther to Mt. Neva along the Continental Divide. South from the pass, a well trodden path takes you six miles to Rollins Pass and the Corona site where an old snow house, used to shelter trains in the winter, still remains.

After you enjoy this beautiful area, return as you came, perhaps leaving yourself enough time to take a sidetrip, bushwacking northwest along the creek from Jasper Lake past Storm Lake to Upper Storm Lake just below the Continental Divide. This is a tough hike which gains 1,500 feet in elevation, but it is rewarding.

There are numerous good camping spots throughout this area. However, because of the heavy use that the Indian Peaks Wilderness Area receives, much care should be taken in selecting a site. Always use a camping stove as opposed to a campfire and stay well away from all water and trails. Abide by any other rules set by the Forest Service for this wilderness area.—*Doug Crocker*

54 Hell Canyon

General description: A rigorous day hike or overnighter into Hell Canyon, a steep glacial valley in the Indian Peaks Wilderness.

General location: 12 miles east of Granby near the southern edge of Rocky Mountain National Park.

Maps: Monarch Lake and Isolation Peak USGS quads; Arapaho National Forest Map.

Degree of difficulty: Difficult.

Length: 9 miles one way.

Elevations: 8,400 to 11,400 feet.

Special attractions: Rugged backcountry with alpine lakes in a steep, glacial valley; good fishing.

Best season: Summer.

For more information: Arapaho National Forest, Sulphur District, Star Route, Granby, CO 80446; (303) 887-3331.

Hell Canyon is very aptly named, a fact that becomes clear to anyone hiking up the unmarked trail that climbs to a saddle leading into Rocky Mountain National Park. Still, this is a hike well worth taking. Hell Canyon, as it rises above Buchanan Creek, cuts deeply into the landscape of this semi-primitive area where wildlife abounds.

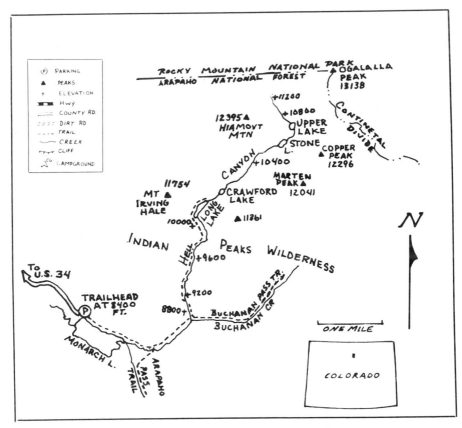

Hell Canyon

To reach Hell Canyon, take U.S. Highway 34 northeast from Granby towards Rocky Mountain National Park and Shadow Mountain National Recreation Area. About six miles north of Granby, take a right on the road which follows the southern shore of Lake Granby. Go on past Granby to road's end at Monarch Lake. Here a large parking lot serves as the trailhead for both the Arapaho Canyon and Buchanan Creek trail systems. Follow the Buchanan Creek Trail along the northeastern shore of Monarch Lake past the Forest Service cabin, then southeast to the trail register at the east end of Monarch Lake. From the register continue two miles along Buchanan Creek to the intersection with the first major drainage from the north. This is Hell Canyon. A good bridge here marks the spot where you want to leave the Buchanan Creek Trail and head north up the unmarked Hell Canyon Trail.

Rumor has it that a USGS party was caught in the canyon during a mid-November snow storm while surveying. They were forced to bushwack for several days in order to make good their retreat through fresh snow and over ice that made travel precarious at best. The party demanded that the canyon be named Hell Canyon when they finally reached their headquarters.

Monarch Lake. U.S. Forest Service photo.

No doubt, you will understand how the canyon earned its reputation as you make the long, steep climb to Long Lake some 2.5 miles from Buchanan Creek. Fishing in the lake is good and Mt. Irving Hale, which rises 1,500 feet, provides a magnificent setting. You may be tempted to make this your destination, but you will find it worthwhile to continue on beyond Long Lake. The terrain bcomes less steep (but remains challenging) and the trail becomes a rough foot path, as Forest Service maintenance is provided only to Long Lake. Crawford Lake, .5 miles farther up the canyon, is worth pushing on for, set as it is in a large and unexpected meadow. The terrain beyond becomes very interesting as you approach Stone Lake and timberline. Boulders as large as houses dot the landscape, and trees give way to grasses and shrubs.

From Stone Lake you climb a final 600 feet to the saddle that is your destination. A sign marking the southern boundary of Rocky Mountain National Park indicates the top of Hell Canyon. Travel north takes you into the park and Paradise Park. After enjoying this beautiful area, return as you came.—*Doug Crocker*

55 *St. Vrain Mountain*

General description: A day hike to the summit of St. Vrain Mountain in the Indian Peaks Wilderness Area.

General location: About 1.5 miles south of Allens Park; about 20 miles northwest of Boulder.

Maps: Allens Park USGS quad; Roosevelt National Forest Map.

Degree of difficulty: Moderate.

Length: 9.8 miles round trip.

Elevations: 8,800 to 12,126 feet.

Special attractions: Panoramic views of Rocky Mountain National Park, the Indian Peaks Wilderness, the foothills and the eastern plains.

Best season: Summer and fall.

For more information: Roosevelt National Forest, Boulder Ranger District, 2995 Baseline Rd., Room 16, Boulder, CO 80303; (303) 444-6001.

This hike takes you into the edge of the beautiful Indian Peaks Wilderness Area and to the summit of St. Vrain Mountain, with its panoramic view in all directions.

To reach the trailhead, take State Highway 7 south from Estes Park or west and north from Lyons to Allenspark. At Allenspark take the dirt road leading south to the Rock Creek Ski Area. About 1.5 miles along, turn right at the Forest Service sign pointing to Meadow Mountain and the St. Vrain Glaciers. From the sign it is .5 miles to the trailhead and parking area.

The trail begins through stands of lodgepole pine and aspen and climbs gradually along a lateral glacial moraine until it breaks into a large opening—an old forest fire area. It then climbs more steeply across the top of a bowl that once held a minor valley glacier.

About two hours of hiking brings you to a saddle south of Meadow Mountain. For those wishing a shorter hike with a good view, it is only about .25 miles due north to the top of the mountain. Here you'll have a magnificent view of Mt. Meeker, Longs Peak, Pagoda Mountain, and the peaks ringing Wild Basin in southern Rocky Mountain National Park. From the saddle continue about .7 miles south along the trail through a small stand of trees and back into the open. Then head due west up St. Vrain Mountain by any route

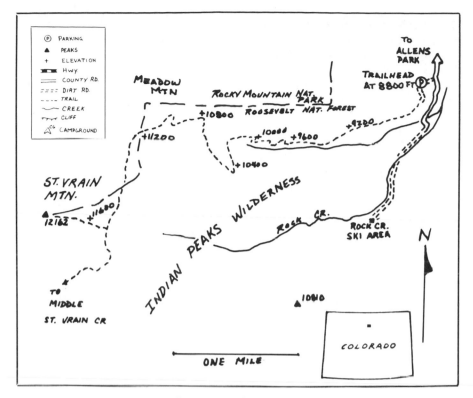

St. Vrain Mountain

you wish. The view from the peak is a 360 degree panorama of the Great Plains, Longs Peak, Wild Basin, the St. Vrain Glaciers, and the northern Indian Peaks.

This part of the Front Range is heavily glaciated and includes some of the last moving bodies of ice in Colorado. Some of the most spectacular remnants of the Great Ice Age are the St. Vrain Glaciers directly west of you at the head of Middle St. Vrain Canyon. All of the landmarks with the name St. Vrain, including the glaciers, the rivers, and the mountain are named for Ceran St. Vrain, an early trader in the area.

On your return from St. Vrain Mountain, two additional trail routes are possible when you reach the trail. To the right (south) the trail continues on and descends into the middle St. Vrain drainage where you can connect with other trails going into the Indian Peaks Wilderness. In addition, an old trail leads down Rock Creek directly to the east of St. Vrain Mountain. It has largely disappeared from lack of use, but eventually intersects with old roads constructed to build the defunct Rock Creek Ski Area. These connect back to the road to Allenspark. You won't get lost on this route as long as you stay in the Rock Creek drainage.

Portions of the St. Vrain Mountain hike traverse the southern edge of Rocky Mountain National Park, the boundary of which has been extended to the drainage divide connecting Meadow Mountain and St. Vrain Mountain. Therefore, you should be prepared to follow park regulations and register for any overnight trips in this area. Be sure to take plenty of water with you on your hike and enjoy the view.—*Norm Nielsen*

56 *Lion Gulch Trail*

General description: An easily accessible day hike to Homestead Meadows, a beautiful area of historical interest.

General location: 13 miles northwest of Lyons.

Maps: Panorama Peak USGS quad; Roosevelt National Forest and Homestead Meadows Trail System maps.

Degree of difficulty: Easy.

Length: 5 miles round trip.

Elevations: 7,360 to 8,400 feet.

Special attractions: Easily accessible; pretty wildflowers and meadows; historic Homestead Meadows is your destination.

Best Season: Late spring through late fall.

For more information: Roosevelt National Forest, Estes-Poudre Ranger District, 148 Remington St., Fort Collins, CO 80521; (303) 482-3822.

The Lion Gulch Trail takes you through stands of lodgepole pine, ponderosa pine and Douglas fir to aptly named Homestead Meadows. There you will find the remains of many old homesteads as well as a multitude of wildflowers and scenic views.

To reach the trailhead, take State Highway 36, 13 miles northwest of Lyons or seven miles southeast of Estes Park. Look for the Lion Gulch Trail on the west side of the road—it is clearly marked and a parking area is provided.

Begin your hike through a forest of lodgepole pines. Chiming bells grow in abundance on the forest floor and the whir of hummingbird wings is in the air. Stop at the trail register to sign in.

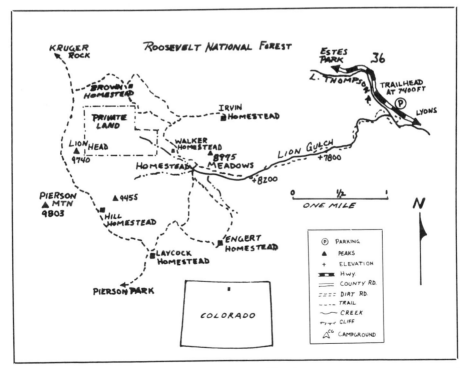

Lion Gulch Trail

Lion Gulch.

At first the trail winds gently down to a footbridge crossing the Little Thompson River, then bears right after the bridge and heads back into the pines. Soon the trail drops again and crosses another footbridge over Lion Gulch at its mouth. From this point, the trail will ascend Lion Gulch while crossing the stream several more times as it follows both the north and south sides of the canyon. This provides an excellent opportunity to observe the distinct differences in moisture conditions and vegetation between the two canyon slopes. As you climb steeply up the north (south-facing) slope of the canyon during the first part of the trail, the intense Colorado sun may provide you with the first clue to this difference. This slope receives the greatest amount of solar radiation during the year and is consequently much drier and more open. It is characterized by grasses and mountain brush species interspersed with ponderosa pines, Douglas firs and junipers. The stand of dead trees you encounter along the way are ponderosa pines killed by pine bark beetles.

After dropping down and crossing another footbridge, you follow along the canyon bottom for about one mile. During this section, the trail crosses the stream several times, but without the benefit of footbridges. Due to the small size of the stream, however, these crossings should not present any problems, except perhaps during spring runoff.

Along the canyon bottom you will encounter several beautiful stands of aspen, riparian vegetation such as willows and alder, and a mixture of plants representative of both north- and south-facing slopes. This combination of vegetation types provides an outstanding variety of wildflowers which, combined with the occasional small waterfalls along the way, make for some excellent picture taking opportunities. You may also want to keep your eyes open for wild strawberries along this stretch of the trail.

As you make progress along Lion Gulch, the trail slowly steepens and eventually begins to climb steeply along the south (north-facing) slope of the canyon. This is the best place along the hike to observe the moist conditions and dense vegetation found on steep, shaded north-facing slopes. There are lodgepole pines, Englemann spruce and a profusion of mosses covering the ground. The cool air along this section of the trail compensates for its steepness and the many small waterfalls below you provide good excuses to stop and rest.

After crossing the stream once again, the trail leads out and enters into a long, open meadow. Another .5 miles brings you to an upland park surrounded by forested mountains. This is Homestead Meadows. At this point, a sign indicates several trails leading to the many homesteads in the area. The closest of these, the Walker Homestead, is about .25 miles straight ahead. The weathered remains of cabins, corrals, and ranch buildings provide for many photographic possibilities, and one could easily spend several days exploring this historic area. In doing so, please do not remove artifacts or disturb any of these historic sites.

After taking time to explore the old homesteads (and keeping an eye out for deer and elk) return as you came.—*Caryn, Peter and Crystal Boddie*

57 Greyrock Trail

General description: A day hike taking you to Greyrock Mountain and back through Greyrock Meadow.
General location: 17 miles west of Fort Collins.
Maps: Poudre Park USGS quad; Roosevelt National Forest Map.
Degree of difficulty: Moderate.
Length: Approximately 7 miles round trip.
Elevations: 5,560 to 7,600 feet.
Special attractions: Panoramic views of northern Colorado plains and mountains; beautiful meadows.
Best season: Year 'round.
For more information: Roosevelt National Forest, Redfeather Ranger District, 1600 N. College Ave., Fort Collins, CO 80524; (303) 482-3834.

The Greyrock National Recreation Trail takes you from the canyon of the

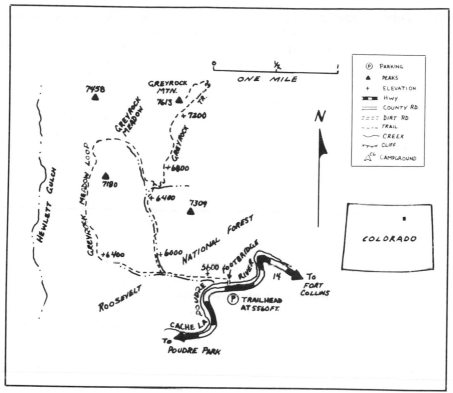

Greyrock Trail

Cache la Poudre River through beautiful foothills to the summit of Greyrock Mountain, a unique landmark of the northern Front Range. This popular trail was built in the 1930s by the Civilian Conservation Corps, and a loop trail, taking you through a pristine meadow, was added in 1978.

This hike can be done in any season (provided there is no snow) but is best in spring and fall when temperatures are milder and the rattlesnakes are hiding. Be sure to take plenty of water.

To reach the trailhead, drive 17 miles west of Fort Collins on State Highway 14 through Poudre Canyon and look for the trailhead parking on the left (south) side of the road.

To begin your hike, find the trail (on the opposite side of the highway) and the footbridge across the Cache la Poudre River. Once across the river, you begin to climb along a small foothills gulch going west. During the storm that caused the deadly Big Thompson Canyon flood of 1976, the water in this small, usually dry gully was more than 100 feet wide where it entered the Poudre River. The river itself crested the footbridge and took out the railing. As you walk along the edge of the Poudre River and then along this foothills stream, look for evidence of this flash flood in the form of boulders, gravel bars, logs and other debris. Although much of this evidence is now hidden by new vegetation, you can still get an idea of the power of summer flash floods.

About .5 miles into the hike you will encounter a fork in the trail. A left here will take you along a 2.3-mile loop through Greyrock Meadow and back to the main trail. This route offers great views of Hewlett Gulch and Poudre Canyon as it climbs to a spectacular saddle at the edge of the meadow. The right fork is the main trail to the summit of Greyrock Mountain. As it climbs the gulch, you pass through stands of ponderosa pine and Douglas fir. (Please do not cut across switchbacks. This causes erosion.) After a good steady climb the trail intersects again with the meadow loop and then levels off somewhat.

Through the trees you can see the domelike summit of Greyrock Mountain, an intrusive dome of granitic, igneous rock which was forced upward and then cooled while still beneath the earth's surface. After the region uplifted, exposing this dome, the release of pressure from the overlying rocks caused it to slowly exfoliate (expand and crack) dividing into great slabs that split and then slid from its sides.

Continue on climbing steeply to the base of the mountain and then follow its southeastern slope until the trail turns and ascends the east side. Once on the dome hike southwest (the trail climbs gently through intermingled rock, grass and forest) to the barren high point at the southwest end which is the summit. Along the way you will pass an unexpected, small, rain-fed lake trapped in the granite.

From the top of Greyrock Mountain you have a spectacular view of the plains, the foothills and the peaks of the northern Front Range. To the southeast is Fort Collins. To the west are the Medicine Bow Mountains and the Rawah Wilderness. To the southwest you can make out the prone shape of The Mummy (giving its name to the Mummy Range at the northern end of Rocky Mountain National Park) and the newly designated Comanche Peak Wilderness. Below you lies Greyrock Meadow. On your return, you might want to follow the loop trail through this beautiful meadow. —*Caryn, Peter and Crystal Boddie*

58 McIntyre Creek Trail

General description: A day hike or overnighter into the Shipman Park Area and the Rawah Wilderness.
General location: Approximately 50 miles west of Fort Collins.
Maps: Glendevey and Shipman Mountain USGS quads; Roosevelt National Forest Map.
Degree of difficulty: Moderate.
Length: 7 miles one way.
Elevations: 8,400 to 9,600 feet.
Special attractions: A hike along two beautiful mountain streams to an upland park; prime elk habitat; numerous beaver ponds with trout.
Best season: Summer and fall.
For more information: Roosevelt National Forest, Redfeather Ranger District, 1600 N. College Ave., Fort Collins, CO 80524; (303) 482-3834.

This hike to Shipman Park takes you up the McIntyre Creek Trail from the junction of McIntyre Creek and Jinks Creek into a series of upland parks and follows McIntyre and then Housmer Creek, two beautiful mountain streams.

The 14-mile round trip from the trailhead to Shipman Park along steep terrain makes a strenuous two-day hike, the trail gaining 1,200 feet in elevation along the way. Figure on five to seven hours in and three to five out.

As an alternative, you can camp the first night in Shipman Park and then hike another two miles the next day to Ute Pass. At this point, the trail joins

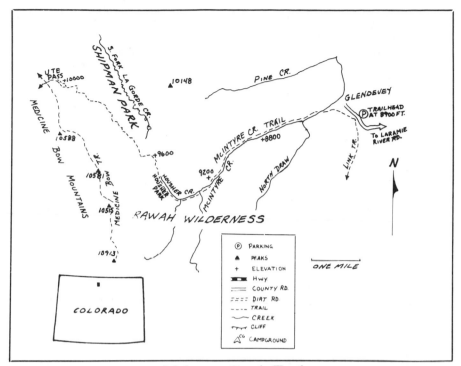

McIntyre Creek Trail

the Medicine Bow Trail and ties into the major trail network in the Rawah Wilderness Area. Therefore, several alternative hikes of varying lengths and difficulty can be added.

To reach the McIntyre Creek trailhead, drive west from Fort Collins on State Highway 14 for 59 miles. Turn right (north) on the Laramie River Road and follow it 17 miles to the Glendevey turnoff, which is well-marked. Turn left (west) on Glendevey Road and travel approximately three miles to the parking lot provided for the trailhead.

The trailhead has been relocated from the Hooligan Roost Camp Group as it is shown on the USGS Glendevey quad to a joint trailhead with the Link Trail, approximately .75 miles east of the old location. At the trailhead, follow the trail sign for McIntyre Creek Trail along the powerline cut for approximately .5 miles to the junction with the old trail. At this point, there is a registry box for the wilderness area. After you register, follow the trail winding downward among the ponderosa pines to cross McIntyre Creek.

For the next four miles, the trail will follow the north side of McIntyre Creek in a steep canyon where occasional side canyons enter. In this section you will climb gradually (sometimes steeply) through ponderosa pines, aspen, Englemann spruce and subalpine fir. Willows are also present along the creek, which is a good water source at this point.

After about four miles you will enter Housmer Park, a narrow upland park about one mile in length where there is a pretty meadow and good campsites for those not interested in continuing on to Shipman Park. The creek through Housmer Park is dammed by beavers in several locations, creating small ponds that look potentially good for fishing.

After exiting the north end of Housmer Park, the trail climbs up about .25 miles to a divide. An unmapped trail joins the main trail at this point. Be sure to continue to your left. The trail then drops another .25 miles to the edge of Shipman Park. This end of the park is boggy and it may be necessary to wade through some standing water. However, as you move northward and westward, the ground rises and becomes drier.

Shipman Park is an upland meadow approximately 4.5 miles long and as much as a mile wide at its widest point. A fun day hike from a base camp takes you to fishing at several small ponds. In addition, the area is frequented by deer and elk, most often seen at dusk and dawn.

Several possibilities exist for a continued hike. As noted, the trail goes on to Ute Pass. At the pass there is a spectacular view into North Park, as well as a junction with the Medicine Bow Trail, from which much of the Rawah Wilderness Area, with its numerous alpine lakes, can be explored.—*New Hope Community Church High School Youth Group*

59 Baker Gulch

General description: A day hike or backpack beginning in Rocky Mountain National Park and following Baker Gulch to Baker Pass in the Never Summer Range.

General location: Approximately 6 miles from the west entrance in Rocky Mountain National Park.

Maps: Bowen Mountain and Mount Richthofen USGS quads; Arapaho National Forest Map.

Degree of difficulty: Moderate.

Length: 6 miles one way.

Elevations: 8,940 to 11,250 feet.

Special attractions: Lightly used, undeveloped area; beautiful views from Baker Pass; good fishing in Baker Gulch Creek; lots of wildlife, including bighorn sheep and blue grouse.

Best season: Summer and fall.

For more information: Arapaho National Forest, Sulphur Ranger District; Star Route, Granby, CO 80446; (303) 887-3331.

The Baker Gulch Trail takes you from Rocky Mountain National Park into the Arapaho National Forest and up to Baker Pass, where you'll have beautiful views in all directions.

To reach the trailhead, enter Rocky Mountain National Park at the west entrance and follow Trail Ridge Road for 6.4 miles to the Camp Kawuneeche exit. Park in the picnic area parking lot and hike up the dirt road .5 miles to the "Baker Trailhead" sign.

Rising from the Kawuneeche Valley through lodgepole pine, the trail follows Baker Gulch at a moderate grade. Up the trail 1.3 miles, a worn spot to the right indicates the way to a large beaver pond fishermen will find inviting. The trail then continues through an area of deadfall and follows several switchbacks before leveling off to cross a boulder field. As you cross the boulders, look for the small mammals that make this boulder field their home. The marmots shouldn't be too difficult to spot, but not so for those little, squeaky picas. You will also pass the Grand Ditch road carved into the steep south-facing slope above the trail. The ditch, built in the 1890s, provides the eastern plains with runoff water for irrigation.

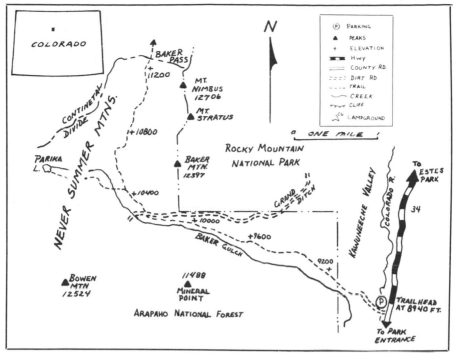

Baker Gulch

After switching back through stands of aspen, the trail passes through a lush meadow alive with wildflowers, particularly columbine and the unusual American bistort. Look for Longs Peak to the east here and for the cliffs of Bowen Mountain above Baker Gulch to the southwest. You can also see the green of the Kawuneeche Valley below.

Shortly after leaving the meadow, the trail crosses the Grand Ditch service road. There is then a wooden bridge across the ditch itself, and you enter a forest of Engelmann spruce and subalpine fir. Four miles from the trailhead you will meet a stream which becomes difficult to cross during spring runoff. On the opposite bank is a sign marking the Parika Lake turn off. Follow the Baker Gulch Trail which continues north and to the right, crossing several small streams and meadows where deer and elk can frequently be seen grazing. The large barren mountain to the right is Baker Mountain (elevation 12,397 feet). Rock cairns mark the last .5 miles of the hike, which follows a gentle slope through marshy alpine meadows (a fragile environment) to the saddle of Baker Pass.

To the east are the "cloud mountains" of the Never Summer Range, which form the boundary between the Routt National Forest and Rocky Mountain National Park. The southernmost of these is Mount Stratus, named after low altitude horizontal clouds. Looking north of Mount Stratus is Mount Nimbus. Farther to the north is Mount Cumulus. Mount Cirrus, named after high altitude clouds, is the highest of the cloud mountains with a summit of 12,797 feet. Between Cirrus and Cumulus is Howard Mountain, said to have been named after Luke Howard, the man who first classified cloud forms. North of the cloud mountains is Mount Richthofen, at 12,940 feet, the highest mountain in the Never Summer Range.

Another trail from Baker Pass leads southwest, traversing the slope just below the Continental Divide to Parika Lake. You can also continue on into the Routt National Forest along the Michigan River Trail and the Jack Creek Trail, known as Baker Pass Trail. Otherwise, return as you came once you have enjoyed this beautiful view. Be sure to watch for wildlife including bighorn sheep and blue grouse as you return.—*U.S. Forest Service.*

Looking northeast from the summit of Parkview Mountain to the Never Summer Range.

60   Parkview Mountain

General description: A day hike to the summit of Parkview Mountain, the high point of the Rabbit Ears Range.

General location: About 35 miles southwest of Walden and 20 miles northwest of Granby.

Maps: Parkview Mountain and Radial Mountain USGS quads; Arapaho National Forest Map.

Degree of difficulty: Moderate.

Length: 5 miles one way.

Elevations: 9,500 to 12,296 feet.

Special attractions: Beautiful views of North and Middle Parks and the mountains of northern Colorado; wildflowers; big game.

Best season: Summer.

For more information: Arapaho National Forest, Sulphur Ranger District, Star Route, Granby, CO 80446; (303) 887-3331.

An imposing and aptly named landmark in northern Colorado, Parkview Mountain is the high point of the Rabbit Ears Range, which separates North and Middle Parks. A hike to its summit offers beautiful alpine wildflowers, herds of elk and spectacular views of the surrounding mountains and mountain parks.

Drive south from Walden (or north from Granby) on State Highway 125 to the summit of Willow Creek Pass. Proceed south over the pass for about .6 miles to the second timber road on your right. You can park or drive on, but the road becomes increasingly rough and steep as you proceed, and it may not be suitable for passenger cars. Your hike will be longer if you park here, but the walking is easy up this old road.

Begin your hike by crossing a small stream and make a right and then a left turn at two forks encountered as the road climbs in the first .25 miles. From here keep to what is obviously the main road, as it switches back many times for about two miles through old timber sales on the lower slopes of Parkview Mountain.

This area was once clearcut and has since been reseeded. As you climb, you can use this opportunity to observe the reestablishment of a new forest. At the upper end of the timber sale the road steepens and switches back several times more until it crosses a steep bowl and avalanche chute below timberline. Just past this point, the road reenters forest as it rounds the end of a ridge. At this point, you have a choice of two routes leading to the summit.

One possibility (and the easier of the two) is to climb to your right directly up the ridge from the road. This route climbs steadily through scattered timber to timberline. From here it is a short, but steep, climb to the long ridge leading west and then south to the summit. This route provides beautiful views of North Park along its length. Look for elk on the broad grassy slopes on the north sides of the mountain.

An alternate route begins another .5 miles along where the road ends in a beautiful glacial cirque below the peak. From this point you can see the small lookout shelter on the summit. Set out around the cirque and intersect the ridge on the south side. Take time to notice the wildflowers here: American bistort, columbine, Indian paintbrush, and many more. The climb is very steep here to the summit ridge, but the last quarter-mile is nearly level. Keep an eye out for the tiny alpine flowers which thrive in this harsh environment, including tiny blue forget-me-nots.

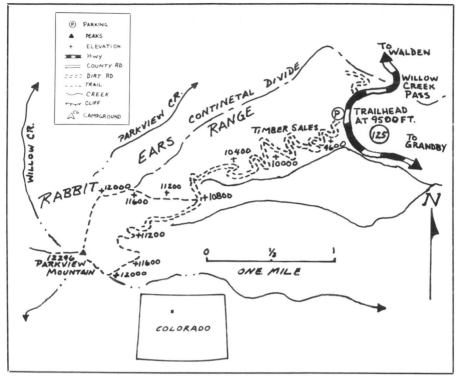

Parkview Mountain

Once at the summit, sign the register and enjoy the view. To the north is the beautiful green expanse of North Park, bordered on the west by the Park Range and the Mount Zirkel Wilderness Area and on the east by the Medicine Bow Mountains and the Rawah Wilderness Area. On a clear day you should be able to discern the outline of the sand hills of North Park, which lie at the base of the Medicine Bow Mountains, a much smaller version of those found at Great Sand Dunes National Monument. To the east is the Never Summer Range, and beyond it, to the southeast, are Longs Peak, the Indian Peaks, and Berthoud Pass. To the south lies Middle Park and to the southwest are the Gore Range and the Flat Tops. To the west you may be able to discern the distinct shape of Rabbit Ears Peak, marking the end of the Rabbit Ears Range at Rabbit Ears Pass. From this one point you can see most of the course of the Continental Divide throughout northern Colorado.—*Caryn, Peter and Crystal Boddie.*

61 Service Creek

General description: A backpack along Service Creek in the northern part of the Gore Range.

General location: Approximately 15 miles east of Yampa.

Maps: Blacktail Mtn., Walton Peak, and Lake Agnes USGS quads; Routt National Forest Map.

Degree of difficulty: Moderate.

Length: About 12 miles one way.

Elevations: 7,000 to 9,240 feet.

Special attractions: Very primitive area; historic log flumes and homesteads present; opportunity to view elk and deer.

Best season: Summer.

For more information: Routt National Forest, Yampa Ranger District, 300 Roselawn, P.O. Box 7, Yampa, CO 80483; (303) 638-4516.

This hike following Service Creek (originally named Sarvis Creek after the Sarvis Timber company's logging operations in the area), takes you through a very primitive area in the Gore Range, one which has been recommended for wilderness designation.

To reach the trailhead drive north on State Highway 131 from Yampa for eight miles to County Road 14. Follow County Road 14 east four miles to County Road 18A. Follow County Road 18A east .6 miles to County Road 18. Follow County Road 18 for 3.2 miles and then cross the Yampa River to the trailhead.

To shuttle a vehicle to your ending point at the east end of the trail (at Buffalo Park) or to begin there, follow State Highway 131 9.5 miles south from Yampa to State Highway 134. Follow Highway 134 east 11 miles to Forest Route 250. Follow Forest Route 250 north nine miles to Forest Route 100, then take Forest Route 100, 8.5 miles to the trailhead at the north end of Buffalo Park.

Beginning at the west end, the trail leaves the parking area and rises through stands of spruce into the Service Creek Canyon on the western side of the Gore Range, a faulted anticline with Precambrian rocks at its core. Further upstream, where the valley widens, there is evidence of glaciation (apparent as you look at your topographic map, an essential on this hike).

Although this portion of the Gore Range is below timberline, during glacial periods it received sufficient snowfall for small glaciers to form in the many tributary drainages to Service Creek. The small glaciers then combined to form a larger valley glacier. From the landforms evident on the topographic maps, this valley glacier terminated before reaching the main valley of the Yampa River. As you climb the Service Creek Canyon, you may want to look for glacial boulder and moraine deposits, indicating the terminus point.

Continuing southeast, the trail enters a small mountain park. Notice the Douglas fir at the far end of the park on the steep slopes of the canyon. From this point, you pass through stands of aspen and finally enter dense spruce-fir forest at an elevation of 7,800 feet. For the next .9 miles the trail remains fairly level until it crosses a bridge over the creek.

Now, on the north side of the creek, you will notice that the creek disappears for several hundred yards. In another .3 miles the trail crosses a small open park. Remains of the Sarvis Timber Company's logging operations still exist here in the form of logging flumes built around 1913. Not long after, the company folded.

At mile post 4.5 the remains of an old homesteading cabin are visible on the other side of the river. Then the trail enters a series of small parks along the creek's edge: a good spot to camp, provided you can stay at least 200 feet back from the creek and the trail. At mile 6.5 you will enter a small lot of private land—the cabin and lodge are used for guided hunting and fishing trips—then, after another .8 miles, the trail leaves the main drainage, crosses through stands of lodgepole pine and connects with an old road. A short way along this road you come into Buffalo Park—an alpine meadow that once served as

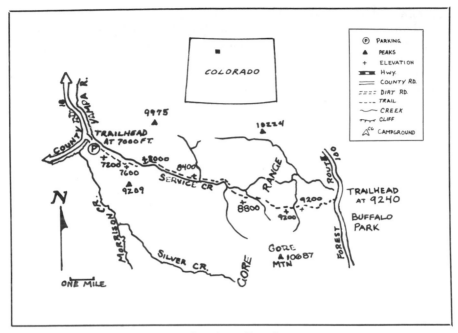

Service Creek

range for buffalo—and then connect with Forest Route 100, your destination if you are meeting a vehicle here.

You have several options from this point. You might want to camp in Buffalo Park and then return the way you came.

Another option would be to walk south on Forest Route 100 about five miles to the Silver Creek trail which will take you back to County Road 18A some seven miles southeast of the junction of County Roads 18A and 18, and about 10 miles southeast of the Service Creek trailhead. If this is what you plan to do, you will want to shuttle a vehicle to the Silver Creek Trailhead before you start out on your hike.

While you are hiking this area keep your eyes open for big game animals, and be sure to wear blaze orange in the fall. This is a popular hunting area. Other denizens that may be seen in the Routt National Forest are bear, bighorn sheep, mountain lion, coyote, beaver, marmot, ptarmigan, and various raptors. Fishing is considered excellent in the upper part of Service Creek in Buffalo Park for small brook trout. The lower part is heavily fished.—*U.S. Forest Service.*

62 Encampment River Loop

General description: A 2 to 3 day backback along two forks of the Encampment River in the northern end of the Mount Zirkel Wilderness Area.

General location: Approximately 30 miles northwest of Walden.

Maps: USGS West Fork Lake, Davis Peak and Mt. Zirkel quads; Routt National Forest Map.

Degree of difficulty: Moderate.

Length: 17 mile round trip.

Elevations: 8,500 to 9,800 feet.

Special attractions: Two beautiful glaciated valleys leading into the Mount Zirkel Wilderness; great fishing; opportunities to see big game; pretty alpine lake in a spectacular setting.

Best season: Summer and fall.

For more information: Routt National Forest, North Park Ranger District, 612 5th St., P.O. Box 158, Walden, CO 80480; (303) 723-4707.

The Encampment River is one of the most pristine rivers in northern Col-

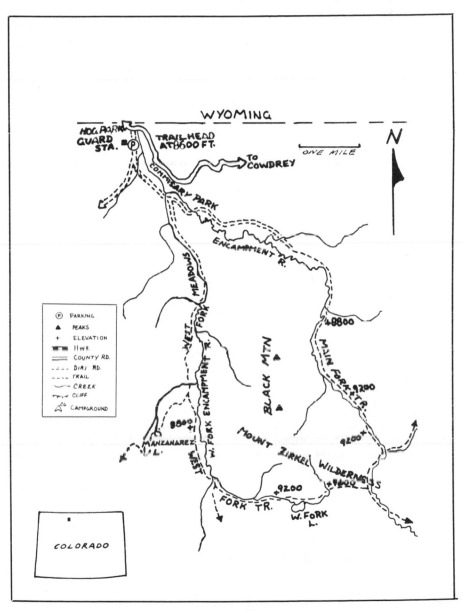

Encampment River Loop

orado and has been suggested for inclusion in the National Wild and Scenic Rivers System. With its headwaters in the Mount Zirkel Wilderness Area, this river provides excellent fishing and hiking opportunities. One enjoyable route combines trails along the Main and West Forks of the river, forming a loop of about 17 miles. This loop makes for an excellent two or three day backpack which can be extended by following connecting trails into the wilderness area.

To reach the trailhead for the Encampment River Loop, take State Highway 125 north from Walden about nine miles to Cowdrey. Turn left on County Road 6W and follow it for about 20 miles, past Pearl. Then turn left on County Road 6B toward Hog Park Reservoir. Continue west on this road, past the forest boundary, about 15 miles to Commissary Park. Turn left just past the bridge over the Encampment River and follow this small road south. Park just past the Hog Park Guard Station. From this point, the trailhead for the West Fork Trail is one mile straight ahead and the trailhead for the Main Fork Trail is two miles. However, parking at this spot is recommended: the jeep roads are rough and boggy and the wet meadows ahead especially fragile.

This meadow area, Commissary Park, was named for the town of Commissary located just north of the guard station in the early 1890s. The town was a supply depot for the tie hacks, those hardy souls who cut railroad ties and floated them down the Encampment River to the railroad in Wyoming.

As you begin your hike, the jeep road will fork. To the right is the Ellis Trail, which continues on towards the town of Columbine. To the left is the road which leads to the trailheads. Go left, and after fording the West Fork, you will come to another branch in the road. Another left turn leads to the Main Fork trailhead after fording the Main Fork of the Encampment River. A right turn takes you to the West Fork Trail.

If you take the West Fork Trail it is about six miles to West Fork Lake and another mile to the intersection with the Main Fork Trail. As you hike along what was once a popular jeep trail you head out of stands of lodgepole pine, cross the West Fork again (there is good fishing here for brook and brown trout) and come into West Fork Meadows. To the east looms Black Mountain, a recent addition to the Mount Zirkel Wilderness. Follow the trail marker posts across the meadow and into forest again. There is then practically no grade for several miles and the wide trail is easy to follow.

You will reach the boundary of the Mount Zirkel Wilderness Area just before you begin the steep climb to West Fork Lake, blessed with a spectacular setting and good fishing. Several beaten out campsites along the north shore attest to past years of heavy use. In order to protect this overused area, please camp well way from both the lake and trail (at least 200 feet.)

Next day, after making sure you've left no trace of your presence at your campsite, follow the West Fork Trail another mile through open stands of lodgepole pine and over the broad saddle to the Main Fork Trail. At this point you can go south (right) for a more extended backpack to Encampment Meadows, Gem Lake, or beyond into the Mount Zirkel Wilderness. Or you can go north (left) and down the Main Fork of the Encampment River to your vehicle in about eight miles.

As you follow the Main Fork downstream, you will notice that the meadows become smaller and the Encampment River ever larger, growing from a gently meandering brook to a boulder strewn rushing stream. Watch for mule deer and elk in the high meadows—good habitat in summer and fall.—*U.S. Forest Service.*

The Plateaus

West of Colorado's highest mountains lies the plateau country. To the uninitiated it is flat, dry and humdrum. But to hikers who have explored there it is an enchanted land. Nowhere else in Colorado have natural forces produced a greater variety of landscapes and life zones, from the tundra and glacial lakes of the highest plateaus to the meandering desert canyons cut by the west's great rivers.

The following hikes will take you through the various terrains of the plateau country. We hope you enjoy them.

Columbine.

63 Limestone Ridge

General description: An overnight hike to the high point at the eastern edge of the O-wi-yu-kuts Plateau.

General location: Approximately 100 miles east of Craig.

Maps: Irish Canyon and Big Joe Basin USGS quads.

Degree of difficulty: Moderate.

Length: 12 to 14 miles one way.

Elevations: 6,200 to 8,636 feet.

Special attractions: Views of Irish Canyon, the Vermillion Creek Basin, and Brown's Park—highly colorful examples of various geologic phenomena; a remarkable standing burnt pinyon forest; various archeological sites; a profusion of wildlife.

Best season: Spring, winter and fall, excluding hunting season.

For more information: Bureau of Land Management, Craig District office, 455 Emerson, P.O. Box 248, Craig, CO 81626; (303) 824-8261.

Limestone Ridge offers a unique opportunity to experience an area largely ignored by hikers. It is characterized by pinyon-juniper forests, sage and grass parks, and windswept ridges that command sweeping views of a fascinating area. The 12- to 14-mile round trip described here could be made in a day, but a night out helps to fully absorb the experience.

From U.S. 40 at Maybell, take State Highway 31B northwest for approximately 70 miles to Moffat County Road 10. Go north on County Road 10 about two miles. Turn left (west) onto a small dirt track passable, barring deep snow or mud, in any vehicle, 1.5 miles to a good camping spot (minus water). Park off the main gravel road; the land next to it is administered by the Bureau of Land Management.

A wide trail, built for cattle drives, leads from the parking area northwest through thick juniper stands that open up .6 miles on, where you pass through an old gate. Around 1970 a fire burnt this area, leaving the curious and haunting skeletons of pinyons and junipers and exposing the succeeding benches of red sandstone which build toward the ridges. The fire also made for easy off-trail walking, at a northeast bearing, from the gate toward the top of the high bench rising 500 feet. This climb is the most demanding part of the hike, but it is fun. Exertion can be minimized by careful inspection and route selection. The edge of this bench is a good place to camp and provides an excellent view of Brown's Park and the Green River as it cuts into the eastern-most finger of the Uinta Range, forming Lodore Canyon in Dinosaur National Monument.

If you left your car before 9:00 A.M., you'll probably want to leave most of your gear here and head on with day packs to the top of the ridge to your east. If you gain the ridge directly from your camp and head for the southern end first you can largely avoid the down and up of another drainage. In addition you'll have an excellent view of dramatic Irish Canyon, which displays twelve different geologic outcroppings and is noteworthy in that it was formed by two parallel faults rather than the cutting action of water.

The length of the ridge is an easy walk, climbing gradually to the north and offering excellent views in all directions. To the northeast the badlands of the Vermillion Creek drainage display their colors and to the north is rugged Wyoming rangeland above which, on a very clear day, the snowcapped peaks of the Wind River Range are visible. To the northwest and west the O-wi-yu-kuts Plateau stretches into the high Uintas. South of Cold Springs Mountain,

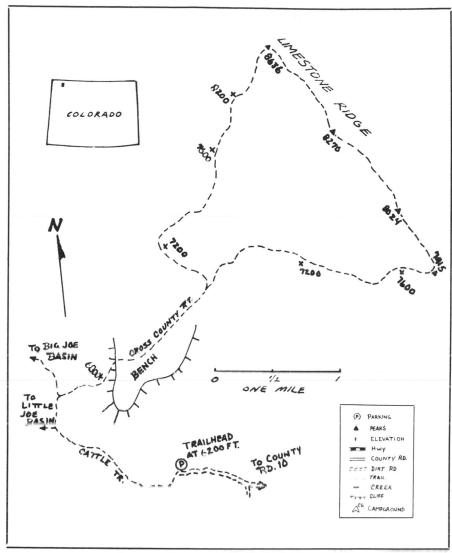

COLORADO

LIMESTONE RIDGE

8656

8200 +

7800 +

8270

8024

7815

7200 +

7200 x

7600 x

N

TO BIG JOE BASIN

CROSS COUNTRY RT.

BENCH

6800 x

TO LITTLE JOE BASIN

CATTLE TR.

TRAILHEAD AT 6200 FT.

TO COUNTY RD. 10

0   1/2   1
ONE MILE

(P) PARKING
▲ PEAKS
+ ELEVATION
▭ HWY
COUNTY RD.
DIRT RD
TRAIL
CREEK
CLIFF
▲cg CAMPGROUND

Limestone Ridge

at the end of the plateau, Brown's Park stretches west towards Red Canyon, flooded to form Flaming Gorge Reservoir. Southeast and east are the Flat Top Mountains and the Continental Divide.

The ridge top provides a good vantage point from which to observe golden and bald eagles, vultures, and an occasional peregrine falcon. Elk are numerous, with herds of over 200 grazing at times along the parks just below the ridge. You may be lucky enough to see mountain lion or moose, too, but are more likely to spot antelope, deer, coyote, or fox.

You can also select your route back to camp from the ridge or perhaps satisfy your curiosity with a detour into Big Joe Basin or Little Joe Basin. Be on the alert for pictographs or petroglyphs, as there is much evidence of earlier cultures throughout the region.

This area was dropped from the BLM wilderness inventory largely because of the extent of roads and stockpond improvements. Still under consideration is an area approximately seven miles to the west (extending into Utah) called Cold Springs Mountain. It deserves our support.

Hiking here in winter is recommended for several reasons. Summer means heat, rattlesnakes, and no snow to melt for safe drinking water.

Remember that this arid ecosystem is fragile and slow to regenerate when disturbed. The magic of the area would be diminished by clumsy camping, so please use a campstove, walk lightly, and let your spirit soar with the raptors of the area.

If you have a spare minute on your drive home, you will want to stop at the southern mouth of Irish Canyon and view the Petroglyphs.—*John Randolph*

64   Cross Mountain

General description: A day hike or backpack along Cross Mountain in northwestern Colorado.

General location: Approximately 45 miles west of Craig.

Maps: Lone Mountain and Elk Springs USGS quads; BLM Dinosaur and Maybell color quads.

Degree of difficulty: Moderate to difficult.

Length: 5 to 10 miles one way.

Elevations: 5,600 to 7,800 feet.

Special attractions: Cross Mountain Canyon; wildlife including bighorn sheep and raptors; panoramic views of surrounding semi-arid country and Dinosaur National Monument.

Best season: Late spring and fall.

Bighorn Lambs.

For more information: Bureau of Land Management, 455 Emerson Street, Craig, CO 81625; (303) 824-8261.

Cross Mountain is a beautiful and unique hiking experience in Colorado's northwestern plateau country. This Bureau of Land Management Wilderness Study Area features deep Cross Mountain Canyon on the Yampa River, several archeological sites, bighorn sheep and wild horses, and raptors such as bald eagles and peregrine falcons.

Cross Mountain is considered to be the eastern-most extension of the Uinta Mountains, an oblong, flat-topped mountain which trends 10 miles north to south and rises 2,200 feet above the floodplain of the Yampa River (on the east) and the Little Snake River (on the west). It is an easily distinguishable landmark, approximately four miles wide with the highest point (7,804 feet) in the north. There are no developed hiking trails but many good hiking routes traverse the side canyons and ridges.

One of the easiest routes into this spectacular area can be reached by taking U.S. Highway 40 to the Deerlodge Road about 16 miles west of Maybell. Follow Deerlodge Road along the west side of Cross Mountain to the turnout for the National Park Service parking area at the mouth of the Cross Mountain Canyon.

From the Park Service parking lot, by taking the first drainage to the south, you may begin a five- to six-mile round trip day hike along the south rim of the canyon up to the top of Cross Mountain and back to the rim. The terrain is at times steep and rocky but does not require any special climbing skills. Once on the rim, walking is easy through pinyon-juniper woodlands and you have a good view into the canyon while the roar of the river echoes below you.

The Yampa River has cut 1,200-foot-deep Cross Mountain Canyon through the south end of the mountain, an example of a superimposed westward flowing stream on the Cross Mountain anticline. It has entrenched the resistant Mesozoic and Paleozoic rock layers, all sedimentary, to form incised meanders within the canyon. Watch for turkey vultures, golden eagles (or bald eagles, when they migrate in winter), and prairie falcons soaring above the Yampa. Peregrine falcons nest in nearby Dinosaur National Monument and may be seen here, also. Continued protection of the cliffs where these raptors nest and maintenance of undisturbed roosting and hunting areas is critical to their survival, so do not harrass or disturb any nest or nesting area you come upon. The river itself has been the target of much controversy. The proposed Juniper-Cross Mountain hydroelectric project, tabled for now because of economic reasons, would flood the canyon to a depth of 100 feet.

Another hike is possible in the north end of the mountain, where there are many colorful wildflowers in late spring and early summer. This cross country route would follow the ridge that is the backbone of Cross Mountain to its highest point and beyond. Vehicle access to the north end of the mountain is generally good from Moffat County Road 10 when it is dry. Most of the mountain is covered with pinyon-juniper woodlands and vast sagebrush openings. The top is open, flat, and covered with grasses, allowing for panoramic views in all directions. On a clear day, you can see 80 to 90 miles eastward to the Continental Divide or westward over Dinosaur National Monument and into Utah.

Interesting geologic features along this route include colorful formations, up to a billion years old, exposed on the mountain. The Madison limestone, Pennsylvanian, Morgan and Chinle formations containing fossils and petrified

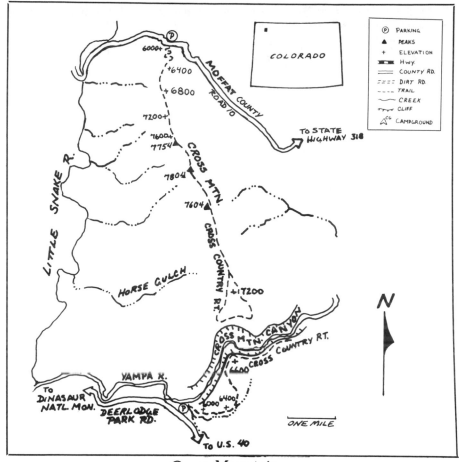

Cross Mountain

wood, outcrop on the mountain and in the canyon. Minor outcrops of the Morrison formation also occur (the same formatin containing the dinosaur bones found in Dinosaur National Monument to the west).

Be sure to watch for wildlife while hiking Cross Mountain. Five to eight wild horses roam here, and there are also elk, deer, antelope, mountain lion, coyote, small mammals, bats and bighorn sheep.

The bighorns, reintroduced here in 1977 by the Colorado Division of Wildlife and the BLM, inhabit upper slopes and grassy areas. They use the Yampa River as a water source and the north canyon rim as a lambing area. Maintenance of solitude, water sources, and grassland/mountain shrub vegetation is vital to their survival—another case for the establishment of a wilderness area here.

While I was hiking here in mid-canyon in October of '83, I stumbled upon a young ram snoozing behind the boulder on which I was standing. We were not more than three feet apart. I quickly sat down out of sight to get my camera ready when he suddenly and quietly jumped upon the rock right beside me. We looked each other straight in the eye, then he turned and ran down the canyon before I could snap a picture.

Keep your eyes open for archeological sites as you hike. It is believed that the diversity of topography and life zones on Cross Mountain attracted prehistoric peoples throughout the last 12,000 years. You may come upon rock art (petroglyphs and pictographs), granaries, campsites with lithic scatter from stone tool manufacture, and rock shelters and caves. Please remember that all archeologic sites and artifacts are protected by federal law and may not be disturbed or collected.

Remember these few things to have a safe and enjoyable hike on Cross Mountain:

☐ Carry all your drinking water.

☐ Watch for rattlesnakes.

☐ Use a stove if you're backpacking.

☐ If you're hiking during October and November, wear the requisite blaze orange and be very careful. There are many deer and elk hunters in the area during that time.

☐ Follow the minimum impact rules discussed at the beginning of this book.—*Dave Cooper*

65 K-Creek

General description: A day hike into the edge of the BLM Bull Canyon Wilderness Study Area with camping possibilities and great views.
General location: Just west of Dinosaur National Monument.
Maps: Plug Hat Rock and Snake John Reef USGS quads.
Degree of difficulty: Easy.
Length: 5.5 miles round trip.
Elevations: 6,850 to 7,529 feet.
Special attractions: Good views; lots of wildlife.
Best season: Spring and fall.
For more information: Bureau of Land Management, Little Snake Resource Area, P.O. Box 1136, Craig, CO 81625; (303) 824-4441.

A half-day hike that offers spectacular desert vistas, K-Creek is located at the edge of the Bureau of Land Management (BLM) Bull Canyon Wilderness Study Area, very near Dinosaur National Monument. You'll be hiking along a southern slope where it can be very hot, so the best times to visit are during the spring and fall.

To reach the area, drive east from the town of Dinosaur on State Highway 40 for one mile to the Dinosaur National Monument turnoff. Travel up the park road—Harper's Corner Road—11.6 miles. To the left is a graded dirt road named Miner's Draw Road. Although there is no sign, the road is obvious and there is a cattle guard across it. Drive down this road about .25 miles and park where you see a steep jeep road drop off to the left.

There are several sandstone canyons to explore in this little-visited Wilderness Study Area, including Middle Creek, Richardson Draw, Buckwater Draw and Bull Canyon. Together they form a very scenic canyon land. Cottonwoods line the rivers, while pinyon and juniper make up the remainder of the dominant vegetation. An extended backpack here would be a dfficult trip over rough terrain—but well worth it.

Eventually all drainages converge at the lush K Ranch (private property which should be respected), built on a campsite of the Escalante Expedition of 1776. Remember that you are on BLM land and that cattle are grazed on the

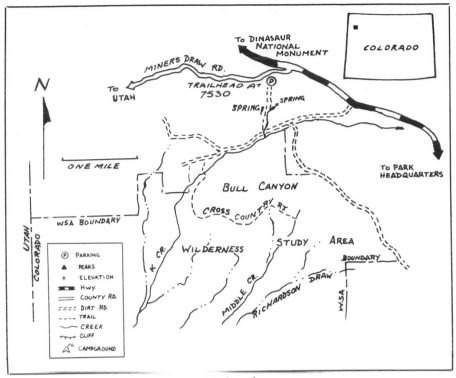

K-Creek

upper elevations during the summer, so if you open a gate, be sure to close it again.

Your hike begins as you walk down the jeep trail past some springs to the trail's end, climb a fence, and continue downhill along the creek, where you will encounter another road. Follow it west and downhill along the creek. Many small roads wander about in this area; just stay on the one that follows closest to the creek. After about a mile, cross the creek and follow it on the trail to your right. You will come to yet another road and an open area. Head in a southwesterly direction across this plateau. You will go through an ancient juniper stand to the plateau's edge. There are many rock outcrops from which to enjoy the spectacular views of the desert beyond and the canyons below. To the west are the impressive geologic folds of Blue Mountain. At the mouth of the canyon is the K Ranch. To the south are the other canyons making up this canyon land.

You'll encounter a variety of wildlife in K-Creek, including deer and predatory birds. We also encountered an unusual phenomenon while hiking in late July: migration of Mormon crickets, the large, wingless grasshoppers common in the arid West. When migrating, they move across the countryside by the millions, completely covering the ground in some areas. They are harmless—at least to hikers—and the migration is an astonishing thing to see.

K-Creek becomes brushy below the plateau, but for those who don't mind bushwacking, there are Indian petroglyphs to be found in the lower canyons. Otherwise, return from the plateau by the same route.—*Mary Menconi & Rich Boddie*

166

66   East Fork Trail

General description: A backpack along a beautiful valley in the northern end of the Flat Tops Wilderness.

General location: 15 miles southwest of Yampa.

Maps: Devils Causeway and Dunckley Pass USGS quads.

Degree of difficulty: Moderate.

Length: Up to 14 miles one way.

Elevations: 8,400 to 11,600 feet.

Special attractions: Varied terrain; beautiful views; fair to good fishing.

Best season: Summer and fall.

For more information: Routt National Forest, Yampa Ranger District, 300 Roselawn, P.O. Box 7, Yampa, CO 80483 (303) 638-4516.

This hike takes you across a narrow saddle in the Flat Tops at the base of the Devils Causeway and into the East Fork of the Williams Fork River valley, all within the Flat Tops Wilderness. Along the way the trail traverses a variety of

Pronghorn antelope. Colorado Division of Wildlife photo.

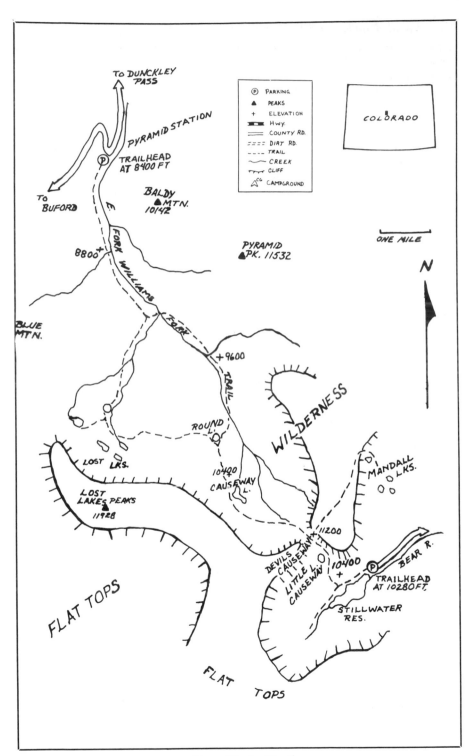

East Fork Trail

terrain (from tundra to thick forest) and passes alpine lakes. This hike can be a short day hike to the Devils Causeway or a 14-mile trip for the length of the trail, which requires a car shuttle. Side trips to numerous lakes in the area are also possible.

To reach the trailhead, turn west on the road along the Bear River at the south end of Yampa. Follow it as it becomes Forest Route 900 and leads to Stillwater Reservoir and a common trailhead for several trails. Begin your hike at the west end of the parking lot at the trail registration station where there is a map of the area.

If you plan on following the East Fork Trail to its end at the Pyramid Ranger Station you will want to shuttle a vehicle to that point. To do so, turn west at the north end of Yampa on the Dunckley Pass Road, which becomes Forest Highway 16. Follow this road northwest over Dunckley Pass and continue south, where the road forks, and on to Pyramid Station. Park in the area provided north of the Forest Highway.

For the first .8 miles the trail takes you along the north shore of Stillwater Reservoir and then it turns north at the junction with the Bear River Trail. The East Fork Trail then climbs slowly through scattered stands of spruce and fir, crosses the wilderness boundary at 1.2 miles from the trailhead and follows the talus slopes of the adjacent plateau. To the west, a short distance off the trail, is Little Causeway Lake with fair fishing for brook trout.

For the next .4 miles, the trail climbs steeply to a saddle at 11,600 feet on the ridge dividing the Bear River and Williams Fork drainages. There are beautiful views of the alpine environment of the Flat Tops from here.

If you would like to view the Devils Causeway, ascend the ridge to the southwest, a short climb of 200 feet that is well worth the effort. Here the plateau is only four feet wide and drops some 1,500 feet to the valley below.

Crossing into the Williams Fork Valley, you will pass the junction with the Mandall Lakes Trail and head down into thick stands of spruce, fir and aspen, dotted with alpine lakes. Legend has it that this valley was named after Old Bill Williams, a scout and trapper who explored Colorado's mountains in the 1830s.

You will descend slowly, coming to Causeway Lake at mile 5.2 and then, in another 1.2 miles, to Round Lake and the Lost Lakes Trail, which heads off to your left. These lakes are deep, offer good fishing, and make a good side trip or alternative hiking destination.

This part of the valley was burned by a forest fire around the turn of the century and has still not recovered. A lightning strike is believed to have been the cause.

Continuing in a northerly direction, East Fork Trail crosses the East Fork of the Williams Fork River, which offers fair to good fishing for brook, cutthroat and rainbow trout, and then meets the Black Mountain Trail, which follows Black Mountain Creek. The East Fork Trail goes straight ahead towards the Blue Mountain Slide.

At mile 10.2 you cross the river once again, climb a small hill via a series of switchbacks and meet the looping Lost Lakes Trail again. This crossing can be dangerous during high water.

For the next 3.6 miles the trail continues towards its destination at the Pyramid Ranger Station, meeting the Transfer Trail as it does, which heads off to the left. After continuing straight on from this junction and leaving the wilderness, the trail ends at some Forest Service buildings. Please, do not enter the buildings.

A short walk takes you to the parking area just north of Forest Route 16, where you should have a vehicle waiting for you, unless you are planning to return as you came. You can, of course, expand your backpack by exploring any of the trails you came into contact with as you followed the East Fork Trail.—*U.S. Forest Service.*

67 Hooper Lake

General description: A day hike or overnighter to a beautiful alpine lake at the base of the Flat Tops.

General location: 15 miles southwest of Yampa.

Maps: Orno Peak and Dome Peak USGS quads; Routt and White River National Forest Maps.

Degree of difficulty: Easy.

Length: 6 miles round trip.

Elevations: 10,300 to 11,300 feet.

Special attractions: Scenic view of the impressive basalt cliffs that rim the Flat Tops; good fishing.

Best season: Summer through early fall.

For more information: Routt National Forest, Yampa Ranger District, 300 Roselawn, P.O. Box 7, Yampa, CO 80483; (303) 638-4516.

The trail to Hooper Lake takes you into the Flat Tops Wilderness Area where you will find interesting geology, beautiful scenery and good fishing.

To reach the trailhead, drive 30 miles south of Steamboat Springs or 42 miles north of Wolcott on State Highway 131 to the town of Yampa. Leave the highway and go into town. In the southwest corner of town near the Antlers Bar there is a paved road which follows the Bear River and leads to the trailhead. Follow this road to its end at Stillwater Reservoir. It is about 15 miles or so and you can't get lost.

There is a relatively large parking area at the end of the road and it's likely to be packed with cars. Don't worry, this is the take-off point for numerous fishermen who are out for the day, as well as for other hikers heading off in many different directions. There is a sign pointing the way to Hooper and Keener Lakes near the end of the parking lot. Take a left turn and walk along the dam which impounds Sweetwater Reservoir. After about .25 miles or so (near the end of the dam) look for the Hooper Lake trail to the left. It isn't marked but is easy to pick out. There are no other forks from here to the lake.

You will travel through open country for several hundred yards after you leave the dam, then enter forest and begin to climb at a moderate grade. About .5 miles after entering the forest, the trail levels off and then bends to the right, passing a few small ponds. It then turns left and climbs along a small stream. The climb steepens considerably when it leaves this stream, but the views get better and better as you approach the divide which separates Sweetwater Reservoir from Hooper Lake. You reach the divide after one last short, steep climb.

This is a good spot to pause, rest and enjoy the panoramic views of the Sweetwater Lake area, the Flat Tops to the northwest, and Derby Creek valley to the south. To the east is Flat Top Mountain whose broad grassy slopes make for an easy climb and an even more spectacular view. The basalt cliffs to the

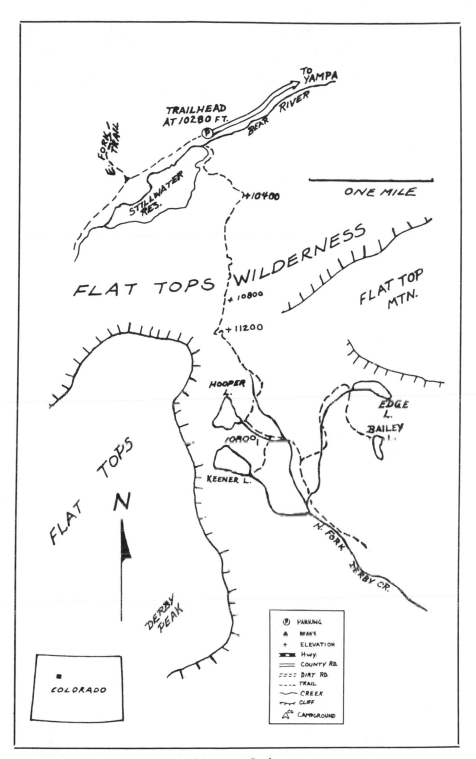

Hooper Lake

west of the divide are impressive, but cannot be ascended without technical climbing gear. This area is on the northeastern end of the Flat Tops Wilderness Area, one of the earlier wilderness areas to be established in Colorado. The Flat Tops area is the most uplifted part of the White River Plateau and includes extensive areas above timberline. Hooper Lake, like most of the lakes in the Flat Tops, was sculpted by glaciers which formed in the depressions or cirques along the rim of this high plateau. The spectacular cliffs which extend for many miles in all directions are formed by resistant basalt capping the top of the plateau.

The trail continues south from the divide, winding through gently sloping meadows. It becomes a bit obscure in places, but within a few hundred yards of the divide you can see Hooper Lake, sporadically good fishing for rainbow trout to 14 inches. There are good camping areas along the north and east sides of the lake; the south and west sides are rather rugged. Be sure to camp 200 feet from the lake itself, though. And one word of caution on selecting your campsite: many of the trees surrounding the lake are dead and may be blown over by strong winds. Our party didn't worry about it much when we camped here until about two o'clock in the morning when a storm blew through. Next day, we noticed some freshly-downed trees nearby.

The main trail continues past the lower end of Hooper Lake. Several hundred yards past Hooper Lake there is a right turn to Keener Lake. The main trail winds down along the North Fork of Derby Creek to a very scenic meadow about .5 miles below. A trail to the left in this meadow leads you to Edge and Bailey Lakes.—*Bill Bath*

68 Grizzly Creek

General description: An easily accessible day hike along Grizzly Creek, a fast-moving tributary of the Colorado River, which forms a deep canyon in the White River Plateau.

General location: 6 miles east of Glenwood Springs.

Maps: Glenwood Springs, Carbonate USGS quads; White River National Forest Map.

Degree of difficulty: Moderate.

Length: 6 miles one way.

Elevations: 6,000 to 8,000 feet.

Special attractions: Towering Grizzly Creek Canyon; good views of lower Grizzly Creek toward Glenwood Canyon and Glenwood Springs; excellent, though difficult, fishing.

Best season: Summer and fall.

For more information: White River National Forest, Sopris Ranger District, 620 Main, P.O. Box 248, Carbondale, CO 81623; (303) 963-2266.

This is a well-traveled trail due to its accessibility from Interstate 70. Yet, because of the dense foliage, there is little sense of overcrowding.

To reach the trailhead, drive east from Glenwood Springs about five miles on I-70 to Grizzly Creek. Turn left on the small dirt road just east of the bridge across Grizzly Creek. It is hard to spot so look carefully. This is the Grizzly Creek Road. Take it approximately .5 miles to Grizzly Creek Picnic Ground and the trailhead.

Grizzly Creek is a large creek which has sliced through the White River Plateau to drain south into the muddy Colorado. The White River Plateau is composed of sedimentary rocks that fold downward sharply along its south and west edges for 135 miles. The creek, starting high in the snows atop the plateau, runs clear and fast through the limestone canyon it has cut. It offers excellent but difficult fishing (big boulders and the narrow canyon hinder casting efforts) for 10-inch brook trout in the upper reaches and 12- to 14-inch whitefish along the lower stretches when they run from the Colorado River in mid-October.

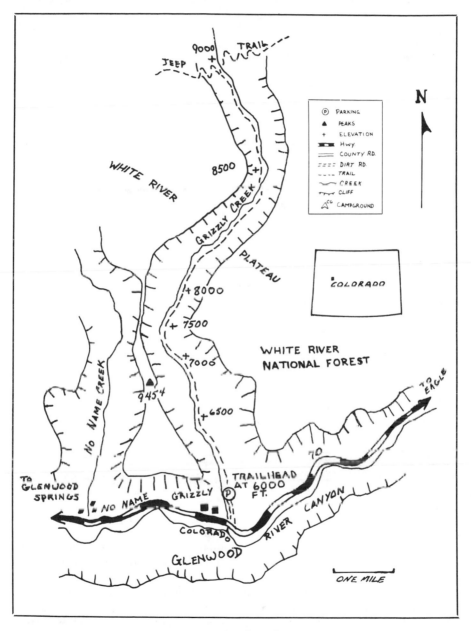

Grizzly Creek

Grizzly Creek. Gilbert Frye photo.

The Grizzly Creek Trail primarily follows Grizzly Creek through the narrow and very rocky (watch your footing) canyon. It begins in dense foliage, which obscures your views except of the river and the rims of the canyon overhead. As you hike, keep a lookout for some of the limestone solution caves along the cliffs. Water is available along the entire trail (you'll have to purify it, though).

After the first mile, the trail climbs at a steeper grade on the hillside, then descends again to the creek before rising sharply from 6,000 feet to the upper reaches of the canyon.

At points, the trail opens up briefly to offer views of mountain ridges ahead, and at about the three mile point, you'll have excellent views of lower Grizzly Creek and of Glenwood Canyon with its deep-cut gorges. At 8,000 feet, from higher ridges, you'll have a more extensive view down the canyon all of the way to Glenwood Springs.

At no point along the six-mile trail is the grade particularly severe, though the narrow tread and loose rocks do make footing treacherous. Good shoes are in order.

Your day hike can extend to a backpack to the top of the plateau. Simply continue on the Grizzly Creek Trail for about six miles and camp in the upper reaches of the canyon where it is more open. In another three miles you will connect with a jeep trail that will take you to the top of the plateau. Return as you came.

If you've marvelled at the colors and cut of Glenwood Canyon while driving I-70 to Glenwood Springs, then you'll find some special rewards in the canyon of Grizzly Creek, with its rushing water, towering walls, and evergreen forests.—*Gib and Buzzy Frye*

69 Spring Canyon

General description: A long day hike or overnighter into the canyons of the
Little Book Cliffs Wild Horse Area.

General location: 10 miles northeast of Grand Junction.

Maps: Cameo and Round Mountain USGS quads.

Degree of difficulty: Moderate to difficult.

Length: 9 miles one way.

Elevations: 5,000 to 7,000 feet.

Special attractions: Spectacular canyons; desert and semi-arid flora; intricate rock formations; opportunity to spot wild horses.

Best season: Spring.

For more information: Bureau of Land Management, Grand Junction
Resource Area, 764 Horizon Drive, Grand Junction, CO 81501; (303)
243-6552.

A hike into Spring Canyon in the Little Book Cliffs Wild Horse area provides an opportunity to spot some of Colorado's rare wild horses, as well as to
explore a seldom-visited canyon. The length of this hike can be varied accord-
ing to the time available and the hiker's ability, with the hike increasing in difficulty as you go along. If you choose to backpack, you could easily spend
several days exploring the many canyons and rolling upland areas of this BLM
Wilderness Study Area.

The Little Book Cliffs Wild Horse Area includes several deep (1,000 feet)
canyons which disect a gently sloping plateau. This plateau is bordered on the
west by the spectacular Book Cliffs, a 1,500-foot escarpment which extends
for many miles into Utah. The lower canyons are semi-desert with vegetation
consisting primarily of sagebrush, rabbitbrush and fourwinged saltbrush. The
upland areas include pinyon-juniper woodlands interspersed with sage and
grass meadows. A hike along the length of Spring Canyon will take you
through this entire range of topography and vegetation, culminating in a spectacular view from the top of the Book Cliffs. The chance to see wild horses
along the way adds to the intriguing nature of this hike.

To reach Spring Canyon, take Interstate-70 east from Grand Junction or
west from DeBeque to the Cameo exit. Follow the paved road alongside the
highway and across the bridge over the Colorado River to the electrical
generating plant. Continue straight past the plant, across an irrigation ditch
and on up the dirt road into the canyon ahead. There are several service roads
associated with the nearby coal mining and power plant operations, but it is
easy to determine which road continues on into the canyon. This road becomes
progressively smaller and more rugged as it makes several crossings of the Coal
Canyon streambed. However, when dry, it should be accessible to most
passenger cars. Should you find it necessary to park somewhere along the way,
it is only about 1.5 miles from the power plant to the take-off point for the
Spring Canyon hike.

The take-off point is reached where you see a road climbing to the right and
over a low saddle. Just ahead on the main road are a cattle guard and a BLM
boundary sign. Park at the base of the side road and begin hiking up to the
saddle. At the top there is a locked gate, which you will have to climb over or
around, and below you is Main Canyon which drains the wilderness study
area.

Descend from the saddle along the road to the canyon bottom. After cross-

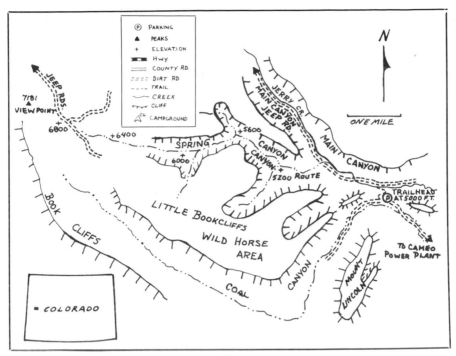

Spring Canyon

ing the often dry streambed of Jerry Creek, follow the jeep road up Main Canyon while crossing the creek several more times. This stretch of the trail along Main Canyon is notable for the inspiring views it provides many miles up the canyon to the headwaters of the creek on the plateau above. When these upland areas are cloaked in clouds and the canyons resound with thunder, be prepared for the dry streambed of Jerry Creek and its many side canyons to quickly change into a raging torrent of water, mud, rocks and logs. Because of its width, Main Canyon can be an excellent place to observe one of these flash floods, provided you stay well away from the streambed and are prepared to add several hours to your trip while you wait for the waters to recede. Should these same conditions occur while you are hiking in one of the smaller canyons, immediately seek the safety of higher ground and wait out the storm. Under no circumstances should you set up camp in a narrow canyon or near a creekbed.

Continue along Main Canyon for about 1.5 miles, past a small side canyon on the left, until you reach a much larger canyon. This is Spring Canyon. At this point, you will leave the jeep road and follow the streambed of Spring Canyon and occasional horse trails for the remainder of your hike. Spring Canyon provides an amazing variety of exploration possibilities—each bend reveals some new geologic features or plant type and there is always the chance of glimpsing one of the area's wild horses before it spots you.

Shortly after entering Spring Canyon, you will encounter an area of spectacular rock pedestals. These pedestals are formed when resistant blocks of sandstone, which have fallen from the cliffs above, form a cap, preventing erosion of the soft, underlying materials. As you continue, the canyon slowly steepens until you encounter sandstone ledges which block your way. These obstacles can all be overcome with a few minutes effort by backtracking to a point where you can climb up and around on one of the canyon slopes. In many cases, you may find a horse trail indicating the best route.

About two miles along in Spring Canyon, after passing a couple of side canyons on the left, you will come to a fork. The right fork takes you into a box canyon with some spectacular falls, a good destination for a day hike. The left fork follows Spring Canyon for another four miles to the top of the plateau. This route becomes progressively more rugged for some distance as you ascend the canyon and, in places, is quite overgrown with vegetation. However, these difficult spots are separated by enough easy stretches to make the hike enjoyable. You will be rewarded for your efforts by the continuing changes in vegetation and geologic formations and the appearance of water. You will also hear the cries of many types of raptors that nest in the upper canyons.

One particularly interesting spot is reached about .5 miles above the fork in the canyon. Here, where a side canyon enters, there is a stand of Douglas fir clinging to the shaded north-facing slope. A little farther along, if you are hiking during late spring, you may come across an equally surprising find—a few red columbines growing where water reappears in the streambed.

During the next couple of miles the canyon gradually opens into an upland area of pinyon and juniper-covered hills, benches and gullies. Go straight ahead and along the main channel until you reach a sage area and an old jeep road. You are now at the top of Spring Canyon. The ridge to the west of you can be followed in a northwesterly direction to a high point at the edge of the Book Cliffs. From here you have a spectacular view of the Grand Valley and Grand Junction below you. Southwest is Colorado National Monument and the Uncompahgre Plateau extending for many miles. To the south towers Grand Mesa and to the north are the extensive cliffs and plateaus which contain Colorado's vast deposits of oil shale. Directly below you to the south (paralleling Spring Canyon) is Coal Canyon, at whose bottom you left your car. From the high point you can return as you came or by way of Coal Canyon.

If, instead, you choose to take an alternate and longer route back or to spend an extended period exploring this fascinating area, you will need to remember a few important points. Always ascend and descend from the upland areas by way of the larger canyons near their headwaters; many of the smaller canyons end in steep drop-offs. Carry enough water for your planned trip and treat any water which you may find in the canyons. The best and safest camping spots are in Main Canyon and on the upland benches. The best season to hike here is spring, when the flowers are blooming and water is available. Fall and winter are also enjoyable, but summer is too hot with too many rattlesnakes. A good topo map is essential for making an extended hike in this area.—*Peter Boddie*

70 *No Thoroughfare Canyon*

General description: A long day hike or overnighter through a beautiful canyon in Colorado National Monument.

General location: Colorado National Monument, 5 miles west of Grand Junction.

Maps: Colorado National Monument and Glade Park USGS quads; National

Park Service map of Colorado National Monument.
Degree of difficulty: Moderate.
Length: 8.5 miles round trip.
Elevations: 5,000 to 6,800 feet.
Special attractions: Two ephemeral waterfalls; spectacular Wingate sandstone cliffs and canyons and many other interesting geologic features; semi-arid desert flora and fauna.
Best season: Spring.
For more information: Colorado National Monument, Fruita, CO 81521; (303) 858-3617.

Colorado National Monument was established in 1911 in recognition of its unique geological features. The red cliffs, canyons, and monoliths of this desert area are strikingly beautiful against the green pinyon-juniper forest, and the quiet solitude of these canyons gives one ample chance to "get away from it all."

There are a number of maintained trails throughout the Monument, as well as many canyon drainages and mesas which are very hikeable, particularly from October to April. (Summer temperatures, as well as swarms of "no-see-ums"—those irritating clouds of insects you never see cause many to avoid canyon hiking at that time.) One especially interesting unmarked trail follows the drainage of No Thoroughfare Canyon for 8.5 miles on the eastern edge of the Monument.

One access to No Thoroughfare Canyon is found at Devil's Kitchen Trail near the east entrance to the Monument, five miles west of Grand Junction. The other access is at the upper end of the canyon on Little Park Road where there is a sign and pullout. If you hike the entire canyon, you will need to shuttle a vehicle from one point to the other.

To begin your hike at the lower end of the canyon, park at the Devil's Kitchen Trailhead, follow the Devil's Kitchen Trail for about .5 miles until the trail intersects the No Thoroughfare Canyon streambed. Turn upstream and follow the drainage.

Along the streambed, dry except during spring runoff and after summer thunderstorms, there are two waterfalls that flow over the Precambrian rock of the area. The first you will come to is about 1.5 miles along and is 100 feet high. A primitive trail is seen on the right side of the canyon going up and around the waterfall. Follow this, keeping in mind that footing is hazardous in places. After reaching the top of the falls, follow the streambed again until you come to a side canyon in less than .25 miles. Take the time to explore. There is an old sheepherder's cabin immediately after the fork in the streambed and you'll discover many interesting rock formations within this extensive side canyon. There are numerous smaller waterfalls you'll need to climb around in order to get into the upper reaches of the canyons. In the upper reaches of one of these canyons is the Monument's only stand of Douglas fir.

Back in the main drainage, you proceed about .75 miles on until you reach the 200-foot cascade. This is one of the most impressive sites in the canyon, especially when the water is really flowing. If you are day hiking, you may want to turn around here. Otherwise, you will need to backtrack until an easy slope is found (try the right side of the canyon) to climb up and around the waterfall (again, be careful of footing) and continue upstream for about two miles.

At this point, it is best to climb to the bench on the right above the stream to

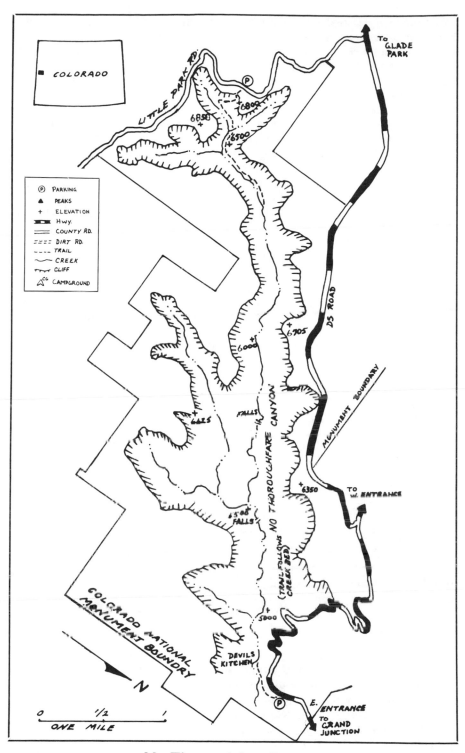

COLORADO

TO GLADE PARK

P

LITTLE PARK RD.

6850 +
6800
+ 6500

DS ROAD

MONUMENT BOUNDARY

+ 6705

+ 6000

FALLS

+ 6625

NO THOROUGHFARE CANYON

+ 6350

TO W. ENTRANCE

6505
FALLS

(TRAIL FOLLOWS CREEK BED)

+ 5800

COLORADO NATIONAL MONUMENT BOUNDRY

DEVILS KITCHEN

P

E. ENTRANCE
TO GRAND JUNCTION

N

0   1/2   1
ONE MILE

Legend

P PARKING
▲ PEAKS
+ ELEVATION
▬▬ HWY.
── COUNTY RD.
= = = DIRT RD.
─ ─ ─ TRAIL
∿∿ CREEK
⊤⊤⊤ CLIFF
⌂CG CAMPGROUND

No Thoroughfare Canyon

avoid the thick-tangled growth along the canyon bottom. The bench has waist-high (and later, in places, head-high) sagebrush and can be tick-infested during spring months. Keep an eye out for deer in this area. A small side canyon cuts through the bench at about mile eight. Here you will need to carefully descend the 80-foot dirt slope and climb up the other side. Further on, there is a very rough, but passable, trail that leads you out of the canyon to the trailhead on Little Park Road.

All along your hike, keep an eye on the intriguing geology surrounding you and watch for the wildlife typical of this semi-arid environment.

The hard, black crystalline metamorphic and igneous, erosion-resistant rock of the lower canyon bottom dates to the Precambrian age some 1.7 billion years ago. Towering 300 to 400 feet above this resistant layer are the Wingate sandstone cliffs, formed of windblown sand about 170 million years ago. They have weathered and continue to weather into fantastic shapes, including many alcoves and monoliths.

The reptile, animal and birdlife in the canyon is intriguing and varied: watch the stream drainage for lizards (the yellow-headed, collared lizard is most common); watch the skies for birds such as canyon wrens, rock wrens, broad-tailed and black-chinned hummingbirds, rufous-sided towhees, bushtits, titmice, blue-gray gnatcatchers, white-throated swifts, and violet-green swallows. There is a pair of golden eagles that nest in the vicinity, so you may have the opportunity to see one of them, as well. Watch also for rock squirrels, desert cottontails, ground squirrels, chipmunks, and mule deer, and keep an eye out for bobcat tracks.

During the spring, a profusion of wildflowers brings splashes of color to view. Three types of cactus grow here: fishhook, prickly pear, and claret cup. And sego lily, pepperweed, wild columbine, buttercup, Indian paintbrush, goldenweed, twin bladderpod. buckwheat, and many flowering shrubs bloom at nearly the same time. In the fall, the yellow flowers of rabbitbrush and broom snakeweed mixed with ocean spray, yucca and brickelia add their color to the scene.

Colorado National Monument is a little known hiking area and you will rarely meet other hikers. The beauty of the area, coupled with this solitude, will make your trip a special one. To preserve this special area and to have a safe trip, follow all Park Service regulations. Of special importance: you should register and pick up a backcountry permit (free) at the Visitor Center near the west entrance to the Monument if you'll be backpacking or if you're day hiking alone (try to avoid it); wood fires are not allowed in the Monument so you'll need a stove for backpacking; you'll also need to carry all your water.—*Beth Kaeding*

71 Indian Point

General description: A long day hike for the ambitious hiker or an excellent overnight to the top of Grand Mesa at Indian Point.
General location: 15 miles southeast of Grand Junction.
Maps: Indian Point USGS quad.
Degree of difficulty: Moderate to difficult.
Length: 15 miles round trip.
Elevations: 6,200 to 9,996 feet.
Special attractions: Many viewpoints of the west side of the Grand Mesa,

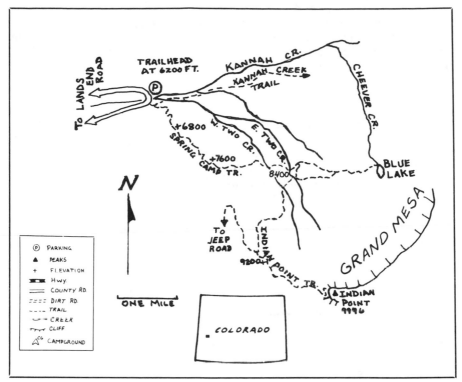

Indian Point

southwest Mesa County, Northwest Delta County; beautiful wildflowers and mountain meadows.

Best season: Late spring to early fall.

For more information: Grand Mesa National Forest, Collbran Ranger District, High St., P.O. Box 338, Collbran, CO 81624; (303) 487-3249.

This fifteen-mile round trip along the Indian Point Trail on Grand Mesa takes you from 6,200 feet at the trailhead to the lookout point at 9,996 feet—a gain in elevation of 3,796 feet. Figure on eight to nine hours minimum walking time for the round trip.

As an alternative to such a long day hike, you can camp in the aspen groves or meadows which occupy the bench just below the rim of Grand Mesa, then, next morning, walk the remaining two miles to the point, and finally in the afternoon, make the full return trip, downhill all the way.

To reach the trailhead, go 13 miles southeast of Grand Junction on State Highways 6 and 50 to County Road #F.S. (unmarked at present). Look for the Kannah Creek Wildlife Park marker at the entrance of the road. From here, following the Kannah Creek sign where the road splits, go approximately 11 miles northeast to Kannah Creek gaging station where the Spring Camp trailhead parking lot is just beyond the bridge. This trail takes you to the start of the Indian Point Trail, approximately five miles out.

The trail quickly climbs above Kannah Creek, heading into a pine forest (with nice cool morning shade) that gradually becomes scrub oak terrain. For three miles along open hillsides (on a very gradual slope) the trail overlooks scattered meadows, the Kannah Creek Valley below, and Lands End Point above. It then goes through two separate aspen groves and crosses East Two Creeks and West Two Creeks, about .5 miles apart. As the trail goes through the second aspen grove it winds around a series of beaver ponds. A short distance from here it splits—south to the Indian Point Trail, or straight ahead (two miles) to Blue Lake.

A short distance from the forks, the trail comes into open meadows with a beautiful variety of wildflowers from early summer to early fall. If you are quiet and alert early in the morning, you may see mule deer and elk here.

There is another fork in the trail here; stay to your right and look for trail markers as you cross the meadows and through the scattered aspen groves.

Another trail merges with the Indian Point Trail about two miles along. From this point things get confusing, with forks at various points. At the first fork stay to your left, then at the second to your right over a short hill. From the top you can see the Mesa's rim where it curves around to Indian Point. Just follow the trail up to the point. From here you can enjoy a spectacular view of the Colorado and Gunnison Valleys, the Uncompahgre Plateau and the San Juan Mountains to the south.—*Steve Adams*

72 Crag Crest National Recreation Trail

General description: A day hike along a narrow, rocky ridge overlooking Grand Mesa.

General location: Atop Grand Mesa 30 miles east of Grand Junction.

Maps: Grand Mesa USGS quad (trail information not current); Grand Mesa National Forest Map.

Degree of difficulty: Moderate.

Length: A 10-mile circular loop with possibilities for shorter outings.

Elevations: 10,150 to 11,189 feet.

Special attractions: A spectacular ridgetop trail overlooking Grand Mesa, one of the largest flat top mountains in the world, and beautiful views of other mountain ranges and nearby lakes.

Best season: Late summer through early fall.

For more information: Grand Mesa National Forest, Collbran Ranger District, High St., P.O. Box 338, Collbran, CO 81624; (303) 487-3249.

The Crag Crest National Recreation Trail takes you on a spectacular hike along a ridgetop from which you can view Grand Mesa, the San Juans and parts of many other mountain ranges.

There are two points of access to the trail: one at Island Lake, the other at Eggleston Lake. There are also three options with regard to the length of your hike: a 10-mile circular trip; a 6.5-mile trip from one of the trail to the other; and a short hike in from either end after which you retrace your steps to your starting point.

To reach the Island Lake trailhead, turn off Interstate 70 and go south on State Highway 65 (the junction is about 12 miles west of the exit to Debeque or seven miles east of Palisade) to Island Lake, about eight miles southeast of Mesa Lakes Resort. Watch for the sign indicating the Crag Crest parking lot just past Grand Mesa Lodge.

To reach the Eggleston Lake trailhead, continue past Island Lake and turn left on Forest Route 121 toward Ward and Alexander Lakes. Bear left at the junction you'll encounter some two miles along, continuing on toward Trickle Park and Collbran. After about one mile, look for the Crag Crest parking lot

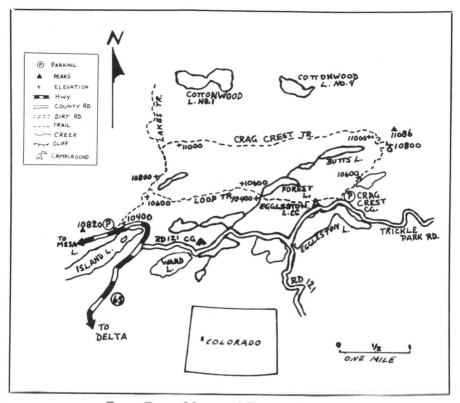

Crag Crest National Recreation Trail

on the right. It's on the shore of Eggleston Lake a short distance past Eggleston Campground.

Although the trail occasionally crosses small streams, it is recommended that you carry water with you. In the summer you can fill your bottles at the many nearby campgrounds before setting out.

Beginning at the east end of Eggleston Lake, you will start climbing gradually through the woods to Bullfinch Lake. You will come upon a junction with another trail on the left about a hundred yards from the trailhead. This is a 3.5-mile-long connection between Island and Eggleston Lakes, and makes possible a swifter return to your starting point than would retracing your steps.

After you reach Bullfinch Lake you will go up several long switchbacks on a fairly open hillside that overlooks the lake. As you climb, more and more lakes become visible in the distance (there are hundreds of them on the mesa). Just before you reach the actual crest you will cross an open boulder field of volcanic rock from the ancient lava flow that created the cap forming the top of the mesa. From here the trail traverses a narrow ridge for over a mile with spectacular drop-offs on each side. Be sure to notice the columbines here; they seem to thrive in rocky areas.

Looking off to the north, you will see the Cottonwood Lakes area and, in the distance, the Book and Roan Cliffs and Battlement Mesa. On the south side you will see long, narrow Butts Lake just below you and the San Juan and West Elk Mountains in the distance. To the west beyond the Uncompahgre Plateau, you may be able to see the La Sal Mountains in eastern Utah.

After dropping down off the crest the trail continues through the dense spruce-fir forest for about a mile before going through an open meadow, then joins the Cottonwood Lakes Trail. The next mile to the junction with the Crag Crest Loop Trail is mostly through the forest, except for an open area on the lower switchbacks that overlooks Wolverine Lake. Upon reaching the junction with the loop trail you can either continue straight for another .5 miles to the Crag Crest parking lot above Island Lake or turn left for the 3.5 mile return trip over rolling terrain to your starting point at Eggleston Lake. This lower trail goes through woods and open hillsides from which you can see some of the lakes to the south. It joins the main trail just above the Crag Crest Campground, about 100 yards from the trailhead.

Be prepared for cool temperatures at higher elevations and stay off the crest if thunderstorms are a possibility. If you backpack, be sure to camp at least 200 feet off the trail and away from water. The fishing is good in the many lakes, which, however, are easily accessible and receive a lot of use.—*Andy Berry*

73 Dillon Pinnacles

General description: An easily accessible day hike to some very interesting geologic formations in the Curecanti National Recreation Area.

General location: 21 miles west of Gunnison; 44 miles east of Montrose.

Maps: Sapinero USGS quads; Curecanti National Recreation Area Map.

Degree of difficulty: Easy.

Length: 4 miles round trip.

Elevations: 7,500 to 7,850 feet.

Special attractions: Intriguing geologic formations; beautiful views of Blue Mesa Reservoir; vegetation typical of West Slope Upper Sonoran Transition Zone.

Best season: Spring and fall.

For more information: Curecanti National Recreation Area, Box 1040, Gunnison, CO 81230; (303) 641-0407.

This easily accessible hike leads you through the sagebrush country of the Upper Sonoran Transition Zone (typical of western Colorado's plateaus) to the eroded, volcanic Dillon Pinnacles. To reach the trailhead, drive west from Gunnison 21.3 miles on State Highway 50 to the parking area and sign for the Dillon Pinnacles trailhead, located at the north end of the bridge crossing Blue Mesa Reservoir.

Begin your hike by following the well-marked trail along the northern shore of Blue Mesa Lake, the largest of three man-made lakes that make up the Curecanti National Recreation Area. Fishing in the lake is good for Kokanee salmon, rainbow, brown and Mackinaw trout. Browns and Mackinaw are especially large and catchable in May and June. You may also see shore and water birds along the lake in spring.

As you head away from the lake you will climb across open country covered with sagebrush, then drop across Dillon Gulch. Notice the vegetation change at the gulch. Cottonwoods, willows, juniper and scrub oak grow near this water source.

While climbing again on the trail, take time to stop and read the signs provided at viewpoints and notice the big old Douglas firs and ponderosa pines

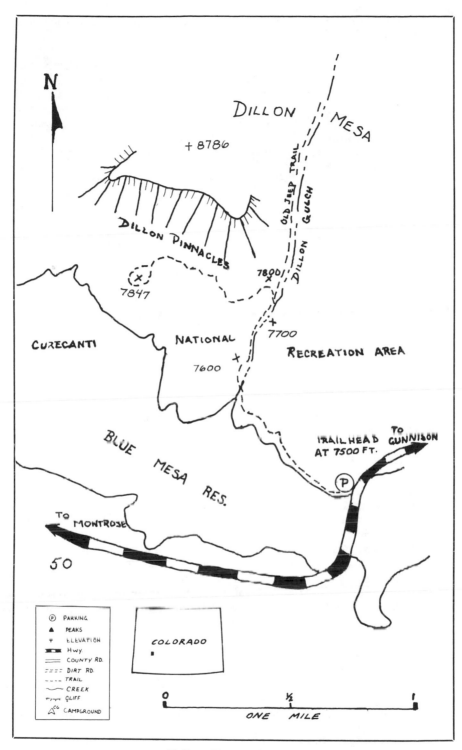

N

+ 8786

DILLON MESA

OLD JEEP TRAIL

DILLON GULCH

DILLON PINNACLES

X
7847

7800

7700

7600

CURECANTI

NATIONAL

RECREATION AREA

BLUE

MESA RES.

TO MONTROSE

50

TRAILHEAD
AT 7500 FT.

TO
GUNNISON

P

P PARKING
▲ PEAKS
┼ ELEVATION
▭ HWY.
═ COUNTY RD.
┅ DIRT RD.
┄ TRAIL
⌒ CREEK
┬┬ CLIFF
⌂CG CAMPGROUND

COLORADO

0   ½   1

ONE   MILE

Dillon Pinnacles

Dillon Pinnacles.

that dot the landscape. The rocks of the Dillon Pinnacles were formed 30-35 million years ago during a period of volcanic activity—which also formed the West Elk and San Juan Mountains. Lava, mud flows and rocks from exploding volcanoes formed the breccia, a conglomerate of sharp fragments of rock cemented together, then eroded to form pinnacles.

As you near these formations you will come to a fork with a jeep road heading up Dillon Gulch. Follow the trail to the left, paralleling the pinnacles to a lookout point with great views of these intriguing formations and the reservoir. Watch for golden and bald eagles, for red-tailed hawks, ravens and magpies as you rest here. Near the lake you may spot eared grebes, seagulls, or great blue herons.

Winter brings the elk down into this country, but you are more likely to see small mammals such as chipmunks, goldenmantled ground squirrels, cottontail rabbits, marmots and prairie dogs. And it is very unlikely that you will see the bear, shorttailed weasels, coyotes, and bobcats said to live here. Try to identify the many wildflowers you'll come upon spring through fall, including Indian paintbrush, bright yellow rabbitbrush (a favorite of butterflies) and others. Be sure to take plenty of water with you on this short but interesting hike.—*Caryn, Peter, and Crystal Boddie*

74 Crystal Creek Trail

General description: A day hike to a point overlooking Crystal Lake and the Black Canyon of the Gunnison in the Curecanti Recreation Area.
General location: Approximately 60 miles west-northwest of Gunnison.
Maps: Cimarron USGS quad; Curecanti National Recreation Area Map.
Degree of difficulty: Easy.
Length: 5 miles round trip.

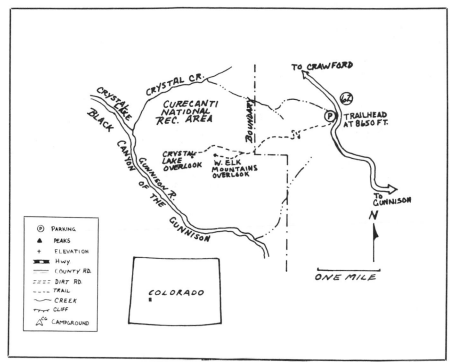

Crystal Creek Trail

Elevations: 8,510 to 8,894 feet.

Special attractions: Scenic views of Uncompahgre Peak, the West Elk Mountains, Poverty Mesa, Crystal Lake, and the Black Canyon of the Gunnison.

Best season: Summer and fall.

For more information: Curecanti National Recreation Area, Box 1040, Gunnison, CO 81230; (303) 641-0407.

The Crystal Creek Trail, located on the western end of the Curecanti National Recreation Area, is a fairly level path through wildflowers and stands of fir and aspen to a Crystal Lake overlook on the edge of the Black Canyon of the Gunnison. To reach the trailhead drive west from Gunnison on State Highway 50 for 28 miles to the junction with State Highway 92. Turn right (north) on Highway 92 and follow it for 24.1 miles to the parking area and sign for the Crystal Creek Trail.

The trail starts out through an open landscape of scrub oak and sagebrush. Stroll along at a comfortable pace and frequently scan the panorama as you criss-cross back and forth with each switchback. Benches at the base of some of these switchbacks are reminders to slow down and enjoy the distant views. As you move on down the trail you will soon enter a shady tunnel of juniper and Douglas fir ascending into scruboak, sagebrush, and the showy purple aster. You will find a stand of aspen a short distance ahead as you travel downgrade. You may see deer, coyotes, blue grouse and the golden eagle.

As you continue you'll have to overcome a fairly steep incline, but there is a breathtaking view at the end. Bear to the left where the trail splits and head towards the scenic view of the volcanic West Elk Mountains to the north. This is one of two overlooks.

Backtrack and take the right fork of the trail to the Crystal Lake overlook. On the way you will pass through an area ravaged in 1974 by a forest fire that destroyed over seventy acres. The trail ends with a bird's eye view of Crystal Lake—fifteen hundred feet below—and rock spires in the upper Black Canyon of the Gunnison.

This portion of the Black Canyon was surveyed as early as 1880 in the hopes of finding a railroad route from Cimarron through the canyon. Although the route was infeasible, interest in the canyon remained high when the possibility arose to divert water through a tunnel to the Uncompahgre Valley. Such efforts set the stage for the Gunnison River Diversion Project and tunnel of 1905, one of the most dramatic engineering feats of the time.

After enjoying the views, return to your starting point as you came. You may want to take advantage of the many other trails in the Curecanti National Recreation Area. They are easily accessible and relatively short, and well-suited to travelers with little time and a desire to get to know this beautiful area. (See Dillon Pinnacles.)—*Elizabeth Richards*

75   Transfer Trail

General description: A day hike along the Uncompahgre Plateau with access to Roubideau Canyon.
General location: Approximately 15 miles west of Montrose.
Maps: Davis Point USGS quad; Uncompahgre National Forest Map.
Degree of difficulty: Difficult.
Length: About 6 miles one way.
Elevations: 7,300 to 8,600 feet.
Special attractions: Beautiful forest and meadows along the plateau; good access to Roubideau Canyon.
Best season: Summer and fall.
For more information: Uncompahgre National Forest, 101 N. Uncompahgre Ave., P.O. Box 1047, Montrose, CO 81401; (303) 249-3711.

The Transfer and Coal Bank Trails form a loop which traverses alternating canyons and benches on the eastern slope of the Uncompahgre Plateau. Along the way you will travel through meadows, oakbrush, aspen, spruce, fir and pine, with occasional views to the east of the canyons which dissect this plateau. From this route, you can also descend into Roubideau Canyon for a more lengthy and primitive hiking experience.

To reach the trailhead, take the Jay Jay Road west from U.S. Highway 50 between Delta and Montrose. It becomes the Deadman's Drive. Turn right on Coal Creek Drive and, at the Coal Creek School, take a left onto Jasmine Road and then a right onto Hillside which winds around and becomes Holly. Finally turn left onto the Transfer Road and drive seven miles to the national forest boundary, then four miles farther to Oak Hill. A carved trailhead sign for the Transfer Trail stands on the right (west) side of the road in some bushes. Look carefully for it.

You will need a topographic map for this hike, which will test your orienteering abilities. This is cattle country and numerous stock trails criss-cross the Transfer Trail, which begins with switchbacks into Roubideau Canyon, down the bench that was your beginning. The path is wide and free of overgrowth.

Roubideau Canyon was named after Joseph Roubideau, who explored the

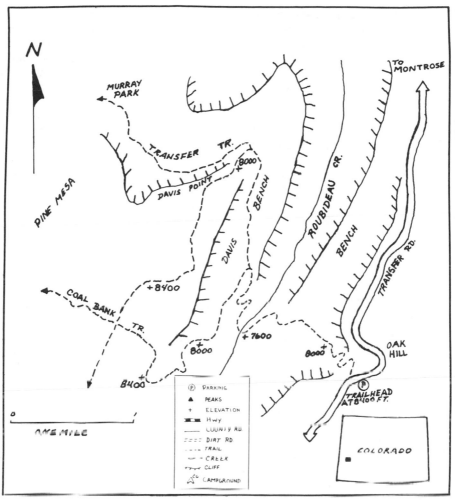

Transfer Trail

area in the early 1800s looking for beaver. Looking up and down the canyon from here, you have a full view of the surrounding area. The vegetation becomes lusher and greener upstream, close to the headwaters of Roubideau Creek. Atop the plateau flat areas of sage and grass mingle with stands of aspen, pine, fir and spruce. Downstream, the greenery gives way to exposed rocky cliffs and pinyon-juniper. Other mountain shrubbery in the area includes scrub oak, cliff rose, and many other species. In the spring many wildflowers are in bloom, starting with the delicate cactus flower and sego lilies and ending in the fall with the hardy gold rabbitbrush.

Roubideau Creek, with its headwaters near the Divide Road and Darling Lake, drains nearly straight northeast to the Gunnison River. It has sculpted this canyon, cutting through the hard caprock of sandstone atop the high plateau and down through brilliant red rock near Monitor Creek, north of the national forest boundary. Roubideau Canyon could provide a separate hike in itself, an exploration of its entire 25-mile length. The deepest part of the canyon occurs about five miles downstream from the Transfer Trail. In the lower levels significant archeological finds have been made.

After entering the canyon you'll reach another bench. Stagnant water pools dot the area. The trail then develops offshoots that test your attention, then meets a small creek with a beaver dam that you'll have to cross. The trail is vague in this area, not well tramped or marked, but keep to the right after the creek and the trail will lead you directly to Roubideau Creek. There is no bridge at the crossing but it should be no problem, except during spring runoff.

After crossing, proceed on switchbacks up the opposite side of the canyon. The trail curves to the left and becomes better defined. Here cow paths can be confusing. Maintain a northern course.

Looking ahead to your left (northwest) you will see Davis Point. Hike toward it. You will come across a refrigerator filled with salt blocks along the way—a confirmation that this is cattle country. Soon after, the trail becomes rocky and brings you through an open meadow, then through brush, and down to a small clearing with faint jeep tracks. Go left through this clearing and continue west toward the bottom of Davis Point. The jeep trail becomes more evident and rises to the top of the point as a steep and rocky road.

Here you will have a good view and find another refrigerator filled with salt blocks. The jeep trail continues through a forest of ponderosa pine, green meadows, and munching cattle. Look for the small cache of fallen logs on your left, just off the trail. There is a fresh water spring among the trunks: a good place to rest. The jeep trail continues another .25 miles to another meadow surrounded by aspen and intersects the Coal Bank Trail. The trail goes southeast through stands of aspen, then curves right to forests of juniper, pinyon and ponderosa pine.

Cattle trails once again make your way confusing, so watch for the old Coal Bank Trail signs. They are rusty and in disrepair, if even still standing, so be sure to read them correctly. Soon you will turn left off your present trail. If you go straight, you will come to a ledge with no marked trail down; to the right are only cattle trails. The main trail will skirt a swamp on the right and bring you back to the first refrigerator you discovered. You will then find your original jeep trail. Now refresh yourself and head home up the canyon; across the bench; and back up the clear, wide, rocky switchbacks to your car.

The best camping spots in this area are in Murray Park and on the flat area between the Transfer Road and Roubideau Creek. Wear blaze orange if hiking during hunting season: deer are numerous on this end of the Uncompahgre Plateau.—*Jeanne Vallez*

Aspen Grove

Afterword

Colorado's Wilderness Resources

By Clifton R. Merritt

This exceptional hiking guide by a knowledgable young Colorado couple introduces you to the best.

A remarkable feature of this book is that it deliberately selects areas off the beaten track where small numbers of hikers or backpackers can spend a day or a week without causing overuse. Yet this doesn't mean that the wildlands chosen are less desirable. Quite the opposite. Infrequently visited, they offer solitude, natural integrity and a quality outdoor experience that can't be matched in the more heavily used and impacted areas.

In fact, some of the areas mentioned in the guide book are among the most spectacular wild country on the continent. Here, untouched watersheds provide stable, clean flows of water for millions of downstream users. Trout, including native cutthroat, are found in the many beautiful subalpine lakes and streams. A wealth of wildlife inhabits the untamed tracts, including bighorn sheep, mountain goat, elk, deer, black bear, mountain lion, wolverine, lynx, marten, bald eagle and ptarmigan. Most of these species are known as wilderness-associated wildlife. Their fate is inextricably tied to the integrity of these wildlands.

The hiker may choose the more convenient tread of a man-made trail, follow the more erratic game-trail or occasionally bushwack over mountains with no trail at all. But, wherever he sojourns or camps overnight, he must learn to live lightly on the land—or those who come later will never know the joy of experiencing nature in all of its primeval splendor.

In 1981, in a study and report, "Wilderness Resource Economics," by the American Wilderness Alliance and Colorado State University, researchers found that there are potentially ten million acres of wilderness in the state. Most of the wild regions are on national forest land, but significant acreage also occurs on national park and Bureau of Land Management land.

Known as amenity resources, wilderness areas have long been overlooked in the traditional cost-benefit analysis. Wilderness benefits, we have often been told, are largely intangible and beyond price. As a result, when faced with making a decision as to what should be done with a wild area, public land managers have frequently favored the "tangible" benefits of commodity development. Yet we know that an unsullied watershed or a majestic elk herd that owes its health largely to wilderness also has economic values.

Working with Dr. Richard Walsh, John Loomis and Richard Gillman—natural resource economists at Colorado State University—the American Wilderness Alliance set out to measure some of these amenity values.

In a year-long scientific study, the researchers found that Colorado's citizens valued the 2.6 million acres of wilderness that has been set aside by law in the state at 1.9 billion dollars! For the first time in history, natural resource specialists had measured, in dollar terms, both recreation and preservation benefits of wilderness areas, preservation values based on the idea that citizens were willing to pay for the option of using these areas or simply to know that they exist and are bequeathed to future generations.

With the passage of the 1964 Wilderness Act, some 250,000 acres of administratively designated "wilderness areas" and "wild areas" in the national forests of Colorado gained legal protection. That landmark piece of legislation also provided for the study and addition of other suitable areas to the National Wilderness Preservation System—an opportunity that has not been overlooked by Colorado's wilderness supporters. Since 1964, they have successfully spearheaded major public campaigns against entrenched development interests to boost the state's total established wilderness to its present 2.6 million acres. And they are not finished yet. In the next few years they hope to augment Colorado's protected wilderness by another 1.5 million acres.

A wilderness designation by act of Congress is still the best assurance that these primeval places will remain always wild and beautiful. However, all four wilderness resource agencies—U.S. Forest Service, National Park Service, Bureau of Land Management, and U.S. Fish and Wildlife Service—have the authority to establish special management areas under the jurisdiction to be maintained essentially in their natural condition for outdoor recreation, scientific research and education. Mindful that such areas would make fine hiking areas, Colorado's conservationists are working even now with Forest Service and Bureau of Land Management officials to encourage them to establish several of these outstanding special management tracts.

But, as important as recreation values are, they are not the only benefits derived from wilderness. For example:

• Wilderness is crucial to many kinds of wildlife that are relatively intolerant of man and his works.

• Wilderness protects undisturbed watersheds and promotes stable, quality flows of water for the municipal, industrial, agricultural, and recreational use of millions of Americans downstream.

• Wilderness possesses tremendous scientific and educational values that will teach us how to manage our developed lands better.

• Wilderness preserves an important part of our rich American cultural heritage. In this regard, wilderness promotes freedom, self-reliance, hardihood and the spirit of adventure.

As one who has been intimately involved for 20 years in the effort to safeguard Colorado's special wild places, I am acquainted with the exceptional areas mentioned in this book, and I recommend them to you.

A few words of caution are in order, however. Although Colorado's wildlands may appear rugged, they are frequently fragile, easily disturbed and slow to heal. Conservationists and the public land managers have worked hard to gain lasting protection for these superb wild regions. As you visit the areas, you can help—by following the rules of minimum impact hiking and camping and leaving only footprints. And you can help after you leave these areas, by urging your congresspersons to preserve the wilderness you've enjoyed!—*Clifton R. Merritt is Executive Director of the American Wilderness Alliance, a national, non-profit conservation organization.*

Resources

Appendix I

Local Hiking Clubs and Conservation Organizations

American Wilderness Alliance
7600 E. Arapaho Road, Suite 114
Englewood, CO 80112
(303)771-0380

Colorado Open Space Council
2239 E. Colfax
Denver, CO 80206
(303) 393-0466

Environmental Defense Fund
1405 Arapahoe Avenue
Boulder, CO 80302
(303) 440-4901

Greenpeace Rocky Mountain
2029 E. 13th Ave.
Denver, CO 80206
(303) 355-7397

Sierra Club Rocky Mountain Chapter
2239 E. Colfax
Denver, CO 80206
(303) 321-8292

The Colorado Mountain Club
2530 West Alameda Ave.
Denver, CO 80219
(303) 922-8315

Colorado Wildlife Federation
P.O. Box 18887
Denver, CO 80218
(303) 321-5503

Friends of the Earth
1150 Filmore St.
Denver, CO 80206
(303) 399-2288

National Audubon Society
    Rocky Mtn. Regional Office
4150 Darley Ave.
Boulder, CO 80303
(303) 449-0219

Wilderness Society
1720 Race
Denver, CO 80206
(303) 388-5801

Appendix II
Federal Land Management Agencies

Bureau of Land Management (BLM)

Colorado State Office
1037 20th Street
Denver, CO 80202
(303) 837-4481

Canon City District Office
3080 E. Main Street
P.O. Box 311
Canon City, CO 81212
(303) 275-0631

Northeast Resource Area
10200 W. 44th Ave.
Wheat Ridge, CO 80033
(303) 334-4988

Royal Gorge Resource Area
831 Royal Gorge Blvd.,
P.O. Box 1470
Canon City, CO 81212
(303) 275-7578

San Luis Resource Area
1921 State Street
Alamosa, CO 81101
(303) 589-4976

Craig District Office
455 Emerson, P.O. Box 248
Craig, CO 81625
(303)824-8261

Kremmling Resource Area
P.O. Box 68
Kremmling, CO 80459
(303) 724-3438

Little Snake Resource Area
P.O. Box 1136
Craig, CO 81625
(303) 824-4441

White River Resource Area
P.O. Box 928
Meeker, CO 81641
(303) 878-3601

Grand Junction District Office
Grand Junction Resource Area
764 Horizon Drive
Grand Junction, CO 81501
(303) 243-6552

Glenwood Springs Resource Area
P.O. Box 1009 (50629 Highways
6 & 24)
Glenwood Springs, CO 81601
(303) 945-2341

Montrose District Office
2465 South Townsend
P.O. Box 1269
Montrose, CO 81402
(303) 249-7791

Gunnison Basin Resource Area
336 South 10th Street
P.O. Box 1269
Montrose, CO 81402
(303) 249-2244

San Juan Resource Area
Durango, CO 81301
(303) 247-4082

Uncompahgre Basin Resource
Area
336 South 10th Street
P.O. Box 1269
Montrose, CO 81402
(303) 249-2244

U.S. FOREST SERVICE (USFS)

Rocky Mountain Region
Regional Office
11177 W. 8th Ave., P.O. Box 25127
Lakewood, CO 80225
(303) 234-4185

Arapaho and Roosevelt
National Forests
Headquarters
Federal Building, 301 S. Howes,
P.O. Box 1366
Fort Collins, CO 80522
(303) 482-5155

Boulder Ranger District
(Roosevelt)
2995 Baseline Rd., Room 16
Boulder, CO 80303
(303) 444-6001

Estes-Poudre Ranger District
(Roosevelt)
148 Remington St.
Fort Collins, CO 80521
(303) 482-3822

Pawnee National Grassland
(Roosevelt)
2009 Ninth Street
Greeley, CO 80631
(303) 353-5004

Redfeather Ranger District
(Roosevelt)
1600 N. College Ave.
Fort Collins, CO 80524
(303) 482-3834

Clear Creek Ranger District
(Arapaho)
101 Chicago Creek
P.O. Box 730
Idaho Springs, CO 80452
(303) 567-2901, 893-1474
(Denver Metro Phone)

Dillion Ranger District
(administered by White River
National   Forest)
101 W. Main, Drawer Q
Frisco, CO 80443
(303) 668-5404, 668-3314

Middle Park Ranger District
(Administered by Routt National Forest)
210 South 6th, P.O. Box 278
Kremmling, CO 80459
(303) 724-3244

Sulphur Ranger District
(Arapaho)
Star Route
Granby, CO 80446
(303) 887-3331

Grand Mesa, Uncompahgre and
Gunnison National Forests
Headquarters
2250 Highway 50
Delta, CO 81416
(303) 874-7691

Collbran Ranger District
(Grand Mesa)
High St., P.O. Box 338
Collbran, CO 81624
(303) 487-3249

Grand Junction Ranger District
(Grand Mesa Uncompahgre)
Federal Building
4th and Rood Ave.
P.O. Box 1150
Grand Junction, CO 81501

Norwood Ranger District
(Uncompahgre)
East Grand Ave., P.O. Box 388
Norwood, CO 81423
(303) 327-4261

Ouray Ranger District
(Uncompahgre)
101 N. Uncompahgre Ave.,
P.O. Box 1047
Montrose, CO 81401
(303) 249-3711

Cebolla Ranger District
(Gunnison)
216 N. Colorado
Gunnison, CO 81230
(303) 641-0471

Paonia Ranger District
(Gunnison)
North Rio Grande St.
Paonia, CO 81428
(303) 527-4131

Taylor Ranger District
(Gunnison)
216 N. Colorado
Gunnison, CO 81230
(303) 641-0471

*Pike and San Isabel National
Forests Headquarters*
1920 Valley Dr.
Pueblo, CO 81008
(303) 545-8737,
    545-4328 (recording)

Carrizo Ranger District
(San Isabel)
(Comanche National Grassland)
212 E. 10th St., P.O. Box 127
Springfield, CO 81073
(303) 523-6591

Timpas Unit-Carrizo District
(San Isabel)
East Highway 50, P.O. Box 817
La Junta, CO 81050
(303) 384-2181

Leadville Ranger District
(San Isabel)
Post Office Bldg., 130 W. 5th St.
P.O. Box 970
Leadville, CO 80461
(303) 486-0749

Salida Ranger District
(San Isabel)
248 Dozier St.
Canon City, CO 81212
(303) 275-1626

Pikes Peak Ranger District
(Pike)
320 West Filmore
Colorado Springs, CO 80907
(303) 636-1602

South Park Ranger District
(Pike)
P.O. Box 218
Fairplay, CO 80440
(303) 836-2404

South Platte Ranger District
(Pike)
393 S. Harlan, Suite 107
Lakewood, CO 80226
(303) 234-5707,
    234-5706 (recording)

*Rio Grande National Forest
Headquarters*
1803 W. Highway 160
Monte Vista, CO 81144
(303) 852-5941

Alamosa Ranger District
Highway 285 North, Rt. 1,
P.O. Box 520 G
La Jara, CO 81140
(303) 274-5193

Creede Ranger District
Creede Ave., P.O. Box 270
Creede, CO 81130
(303) 658-2556

Conejos Ranger District
Highway 285 North, Rt. 1
P.O. Box 520 G
La Jara, CO 81140
(303) 274-5193

Del Norte Ranger District
810 Grand Ave., P.O. Box 40
Del Norte, CO 81132
(303) 657-3321

Sagauche Ranger District
444 Christy Ave., P.O. Box 67
Saguache, CO 81149
(303) 566-2553

Routt National Forest
Headquarters
Hunt Building, 137-10th St.,
P.O. Box 771198
Steamboat Springs, CO 80477
(303) 879-1722

Bears Ears Ranger District
356 Ranney St.
Craig, CO 81625
(303) 824-9438

Hahns Peak Ranger District
57-10th St., P.O. Box 771212
Steamboat Springs, CO 80477
(303) 879-1870

North Park Ranger District
612-5th St., P.O. Box 158
Walden, CO 80480
(303) 723-4707

Yampa Ranger District
300 Roselawn, P.O. Box 7
Yampa, CO 80483
(303) 638-4516

San Juan National Forest
Headquarters
Federal Bldg., 701 Camino del Rio
Durango, CO 81301
(303) 247-4874

Animas Ranger District
Federal Building
701 Camino del Rio, Room 100
Durango, CO 81301
(303) 259-0195

Dolores Ranger District
401 Railroad Ave., P.O. Box 210
Dolores, CO. 81323
(303) 882-7296

Mancos Ranger District
P.O. Box 369
Mancos, CO 81328
(303) 264-2268

Pagosa Ranger District
Building 180, 2nd and Pagosa St.
P.O. Box 310
Pagosa Springs, CO 81147
(303) 264-2268

Pine Ranger District
419 Pearl St., P.O. Box 406
Bayfield, CO 81122
(303) 884-2512

White River National Forest
Headquarters
Old Federal Bldg., 9th and Grand
P.O. Box 948
Glenwood Springs, CO 80602
(303) 945-2521

Aspen Ranger District
806 W. Hallam
Aspen, CO 81611
(303) 025-3445

Blanco Ranger District
361-7th St., P.O. Box 358
Meeker, CO 81641
(303) 878-4039

Eagle Ranger District
125 W. 5th St., P.O. Box 720
Eagle, CO 81631
(303)328-6388

Holy Cross Ranger District
401 Main, P.O. Box 190
Minturn, CO 81645
(303) 827-5715

Rifle Ranger District
1400 Access Road, P.O. Box 289
Rifle, CO 81650
(303) 625-2371

Sopris Ranger District
620 Main, P.O. Box 248
Carbondale, CO 81623
(303) 963-2266

NATIONAL PARK SERVICE

Rocky Mountain Regional
Office
655 Parfet, P.O. Box 25287
Denver, CO 80225
(303) 234-3857 or 234-3095

Bent's Fort
35101 Highway 194 East
La Junta, CO 81050

Black Canyon of the Gunnison
National Monument
P.O. Box 1648
Montrose, CO 81401

Colorado National Monument
Fruita, CO 81521

Curecanti National Recreation
Area
P.O. Box 1040
Gunnison, CO 81230

Dinosaur National Monument
P.O. Box 210
Dinosaur, CO 81610

Florissant National Monument
P.O. Box 185
Florissant, CO 80816

Mesa Verde National Park
Mesa Verde National Park, CO
81330

Great Sand Dunes National
Monument
Mosca, CO 81146

Rocky Mountain National Park
Estes Park, CO 80517

Appendix III

State Office and Land Management Agencies

Colorado Geological Survey
1313 Sherman, Room 423
Denver, CO 80203
(303) 866-3567

Department of Natural Resources
1313 Sherman St., Room 718
Denver, CO 80203
(303) 866-3311

Division of Parks and Recreation
1313 Sherman Street, Room 618
Denver, CO 80203
(303) 866-3437

State Historical Society
1300 Broadway
Denver, CO 80203
(303) 866-3682

Governor's Office
136 State Capitol Building
Denver, CO 80203
(303) 866-2471

Division of Wildlife
6060 Broadway
Denver, CO 80216
(303) 825-1192

State Climatologist,
    National Weather Service
2520 Galena Street
Denver, CO 80010
(303) 837-3788

State Office of Tourism
986 State Capitol Building
Denver, CO 80203
(303) 866-2205

Appendix IV
Information Sources

Books

We've listed the following books because they offer added information on hiking safety and backcountry ethics, as well as giving you that in-depth look at the various regions of the state we spoke of in the Introduction. Not listed below because of their sheer numbers are many interesting books available on Colorado history and natural history. Better bookstores carry them, as well as many Denver area libraries.

Backwoods Ethics: Environmental Concerns for Hikers & Campers by Laura and Guy Waterman. Stone Wall Press.

Colorado Hot Springs Guide by Rick Cahill, Pruett.

80 Northern Colorado Hiking Trails by Don and Roberta Lowe. The Touchestone Press.

50 West Central Colorado Hiking Trails by Don and Roberta Lowe. The Touchstone Press.

First Aid for Backpackers & Campers by Lowell J. Thomas and Joy L. Sanderson. HR&W.

Foothills to Mount Evans: A Trail Guide by Linda Rathbun & Linda Ringrose. Wordsmiths.

Hiking Trails of Central Colorado by Bob Martin, Pruett.

Hiking Trails of Northern Colorado by Mary Hagen. Pruett.

Hiking Trails of Southwestern Colorado by Paul Pixler, Pruett.

Hiking Trails of the Boulder Mountain Area by Vici DeHaan. Pruett.

Rocky Mountain Park Trails by Erik Nilsson. Anderson World Books, Inc.

Rocky Mountain Trails. Pruett.

The Fourteeners: Colorado's Great Mountains by Perry Eberhart and Philip Schmuck. The Swallow Press Inc.

The Summit Hiker by Mark Ellen Gilliland. Alpenrose Press.

The Wilderness Handbook by Paul Petzoldt. Norton.

Trails of the Front Range by Louis Kenofer. Pruett.

Walks with Nature in Rocky Mountain National Park by Kent and Dona Dannen. East Woods.

Front Range Resources

The following resources offer a variety of information to add to your enjoyment of Colorado's hiking trails. Though located in Front Range cities, they are valuable resources for people in all regions of Colorado—and to visiting hikers.

Boulder County Parks and
  Open Space Department
1045 13th St., P.O. Box 471
Boulder, CO 80306
(303) 441-3950

Colorado Heritage Center
Colorado Historical Society
1300 Broadway
Denver, CO 80203
(303) 866-3682

Colorado School of Mines
  Geological Museum
16th & Maple Sts.
Golden, CO 80401
(303) 273-3000

Denver Mountain Parks
City and County of Denver
Department of Parks and Recreation
1805 Bryant Street
Denver, CO 80204
(303) 575-3170

Denver Public Library
(Energy and Environmental
Information Center, Western History
Division, and Map Information
Center, etc.)
1357 Broadway
Denver, CO 80203
(303) 573-5152

Henderson Museum
University of Colorado
Boulder, CO 80309
(303) 492-6165

Jefferson County Open Space
  Department
1801 19th St.
Golden, CO 80401
(303) 277 8332

Colorado Springs Parks and
  Recreation Department
1400 Glen Ave.
Colorado Springs, CO 80905
(303) 578-6640

Denver Museum of Natural
History
City Park, Mountview Blvd.
  & Colorado Blvd.
Denver, CO 80206
(303) 370-6363

Fort Collins Parks and
  Recreation Department
145 E. Mountain
Fort Collins, CO 80521
(303) 484-4220

Historic Denver, Inc.
Denver Union Station
1701 Wynkoop, Suite 200
Denver, CO 80202
(303) 534-1858

Pueblo Department of Parks
  and Recreation
City Park and 860 Goodnight Ave.
Pueblo, CO 81005
(303) 566-1745

Appendix V

Finding Maps

Maps published by the United States Geological Survey (USGS) and National Forest Service Maps are recommended as supplements to those in this guide.

The USGS maps are detailed 7.5 and 15 minute quads and are available from many outlets throughout the state. (See the list at the end of this section.) These topographic maps are by far the most detailed maps available and should always be taken on more difficult hikes, particularly if you are hiking in a little-used area or off trail.

The Forest Service publishes maps for each of the eleven national forests and two national grasslands in Colorado. The Bureau of Land Management publishes maps, as well. They provide a general view of the area in which you'll be hiking and also show most well-marked hiking trails. These maps are available at national forest and ranger districts, BLM offices, and at many of the outlets selling USGS maps.

The National Park Service has maps—generally as part of a brochure—for each of the parks. Stop in at a ranger staion on the way to the trailhead or call or write the regional office (see Federal Land Management Agencies, Appendix II).

The Colorado Division of Parks and Outdoor Recreation offers brochures—and sometimes maps within them—on each of the state parks (see State Land Management Agencies, Appendix III).

Many Front Range cities offer maps of their trail systems along with other information on their parks and recreation resources (see Front Range Resources Section, Appendix IV).

Local outlets in Colorado for USGS topographic maps are listed below. In addition, all topographic maps for the state may be purchased over the counter or by mail order from:

Branch of Distribution
U.S. Geological Survey
Federal Center
Denver, Colorado 80225

Alamosa:
    Alamosa Sporting Goods
    The Bookmark

Allenspark:
    Allenspark General Store

Arvada:
    Bookland, Inc.

Aspen:
    Aspen Kayak School
    Carl's Pharmacy
    Fothergill's Outdoor Sportsman
    Ute Mountaineer

Bayfield:
    Ponderosa Shopping Center

Boulder:
    Colorado Book Store
    Colorado Whitewater Specialists
    Education Arts Intern'l.
    Holubar Mountaineering
    Mountain Sports
    Neptune Mountaineering
    Sport Chalet
    University Book Center

Breckenridge:
    Breckenridge Ski Shop
    Recreation Sports
    The Great Northern Book and Poster Co.
    The Paper Place
    The Ski Stop

Buena Vista:
  Sportman Center
  The Hi-Rocky Store
  Trailhead Ventures

Canon City:
  Claar's Photo Shop
  Kent Fisherman's High County
  Outfitter
  The Book Corral

Colorado Springs:
  A & E Rock Shop
  El Paso County Park &
  Recreation District
  Holubar Mountaineering
  Mountain Chalet
  The Ski Haus
  Western Sportsmen's Association

Cortez:
  Morrison Electric
  Quality Bookstore

Craig:
  G.I. Buffham

Creede:
  Ramble House
  San Juan Hiking Service &
  Supplies

Crested Butte:
  The Alpine

Cripple Creek:
  Golden Leaves

Deckers:
  Deckers Resort

Delta:
  Jeans Westerner

Denver:
  Eddie Bauer
  EMS Mountain Sports
  Forrest Mountain Shop
  Gart Brothers Sporting Good
  Holubar
  Holubar Mountaineering
  Merrick & Co.
  Sports International
  Telemark Ski & Mountaineering
  The Colorado Mountain Club
  The Pathfinder

The Wilderness Institute
The Wilderness Society
University of Denver Alpine Club

Dillon:
  Green Mountain Inn
  Hambleton, Inc.
  The Sporting House
  Wilderness Sports

Dolores:
  The Outfitter Sporting Good

Durango:
  Colorado Alpine Sports
  Durango Magazine Store
  L. Gardenswartz Sporting Goods
  Pine Needle Mountaineering
  Richeys
  Ubaldo's General Store

Eagle:
  Johnson, Kunkel & Assoc.
  Powers Elevation
  The Strawberry Patch

Englewood:
  Book House
  The Prospector Cashe

Estes Park:
  Colorado Mountain Sports
  Estes Park Hardware
  Olson's Gift Haven
  Outdoor World
  Rocky Mountain Nature
  Association

Evergreen:
  Canyon Sports & Trading Post
  Conifer Village Hardware
  The Sport Mine

Fairplay:
  Park County Historical Society

Fort Collins:
  Alpine Haus
  Holubar Mountaineering
  Jax Surplus
  The Campus Shop
  The Mountain Shop
  The Outpost

Frisco:
  All Seasons Sports

Quickie Mart
The Alpinner

Georgetown:
Wildcat Rock Shop

Glenwood Springs:
All Star Sports
KKBNA, Inc.
Spurr's Sport Shop
Summit Canyon Mountaineering
W-B Surplus and Sporting Goods
Wilderness Encounter

Golden:
Jeffco Blueprint & School
Supplies
The Wildcats

Granby:
Rocky Mountain Outfitter

Grand Junction:
Lindsay Graphic Supply
Plaza Engineering Supply
Quahada Engineering

Grand Lake:
R & R Recreation
Woodland

Greeley:
Alpine Haus
Colorado Mountain Sports
Sportworld, Inc.

Gunnison:
Alpine Mountaineer
Sam's Communications

Idaho Springs:
Ponderosa Sports
Yankee Hill Trading Co.

Ignacio:
Wiseman True Value Hardware

Keystone:
Pathfinder

Lake City:
McGil's General Store
Silver Spur
The Timberline Craftsman

Lakewood:
Christy Sports
Holubar Mountaineering
Mountain World

Laveta:
West Peak Mountaineering

Leadville:
Bill's Sport Shop
Cass's
Dutch Henri Mountain Sports
Leadville Surplus & Sporting
Goods
The Salt Box
Ye Olde Book & Card Shoppe

Longmont:
Spencer Sporting Goods
Sport Chalet

Loveland:
Brown's Corner
Loveland Realty
Loveland Sports Center
Rocky Mountain Pedals & Packs

Meeker:
Chuck Whitman & Associates
Merrick & Co.
The Gentry Motor Lodge
The Surveyors

Monte Vista:
Bill's Sporting Goods
Ridpath Office Supply
Wolf Creek Pass General Store

Montrose:
Adams Office Supply
Jeans Westerner Inc.

Monument:
The Country Gun Shoppe

Nederland:
Dot's Wanderbar

Ouray:
Bear Creek Store
Ouray Cottage Motel and Gift
Shop
The Cabin Fever Shop
Wilderness Hut

Pagosa Springs:
  Pagosa Hardware
  Pagosa Springs Trading Post
  Rocky Mountain Gifts
  The Feed Store

Poncha Springs:
  The Sports Mine
  Village Store

Pueblo:
  Mountain Chalet
  Pueblo Blueprint Company
  Pueblo Tent & Awing Co.
  Rocky Mountain Hiker

Red Feather Lakes:
  Red Feather Trading Post

Salida:
  Mountain Maps
  Tuttle's Trading Post

Sapinero'
  Sapinero Trading Post

Silverthorne:
  Sav-o-mat Sporting Goods

Silverton:
  The Prospect Hole
  Timberline Trading Co.

South Fork:
  Rainbow Lodge & Grocery

Steamboat Springs:
  Inside Edge Sports

Mountain Craft
Ski Haus International

Telluride:
  Olympic Sports
  Telluride Art Gallery
  Telluride Sports

Thornton:
  Treasure Hut

Vail:
  Christy Sports
  Gorsuch Limited
  University of Vail Book Store
  Vail Mountaineering

Walden:
  Sportsman's Supply

Ward:
  Old Depot Store

Westcliffe:
  Colorado Advertising

Westminster:
  Woods & Waters Sportsman's
  Club

Wheat Ridge:
  Cres Mountaineering

Winter Park:
  Vasquez Sports

Appendix VI

The Hiker's Checklist

Always check the checklist

Hikers can—and will, of course—take almost anything they choose into the backcountry. But without a complete checklist, it's remarkably easy to forget an essential item. The following list is "overly complete"—there are items on it hikers rarely use. Still, it's always good sense to take a final look at the checklist before loading the pack into the car. The extra minute is usually worth it.

Clothing

_____Shirt
_____Pants
_____Underwear (extras)
_____Windshirt
_____Vest
_____Belt and/or suspenders
_____Jacket or down parka
_____Turtleneck
_____Poncho or rain suit
_____Gloves
_____Hat
_____Bandana
_____Walking shorts
_____Sweater
_____Swimming suit
_____Balaclava or headband

Footwear

_____Boots
_____Socks (extras)
_____Boot wax
_____Moccasins or running shoes
    (for around camp)

Bedroom

_____Tent
_____Poles
_____Tent stakes
_____Cord/guy lines
_____Ground cloth
_____Sleeping bag
_____Sleeping pad or air mattress

Hauling

_____Backpack
_____Day or belt pack

Cooking

_____Matches (extras)
_____Matches (waterproof)
_____Waterproof match case
_____Stove

_____Fuel bottles (filled)
_____Funnel
_____Foam pad for stove
_____Cleaning wire for stove
_____Cleaning pad for pans
_____Cook kit
_____Pot Gripper
_____Spatula
_____Cup
_____Bowl/plate
_____Utensils
_____Dish rag
_____Dish towel
_____Plastic bottle

Food and drink

_____Cereal
_____Bread
_____Crackers
_____Cheese
_____Margarine
_____Powdered soups
_____Salt/pepper
_____Main course meals
_____Snacks
_____Hot chocolate
_____Tea
_____Powdered milk
_____Drink mixes

Photography

_____Camera
_____Film (extras)
_____Extra lenses
_____Filters
_____Close-up attachments
_____Tripod
_____Lens brush/paper
_____Light meter
_____Flash equipment

Fishing

_____License
_____Rods
_____Reels
_____Flies
_____Dry fly floater (silicone)
_____Lures
_____Leader
_____Extra line
_____Swivels
_____Hooks
_____Split shot/sinkers
_____Floats

Miscellaneous

_____Pocket or Swiss Army kı
_____Whetstone
_____Compass
_____Topo map(s)
_____Other maps
_____Sunglasses
_____Flashlight
_____Batteries (extra)
_____Bulbs
_____Candle lantern
_____First aid kit
_____Snakebite kit
_____Survival kit
_____Repair kit
_____Suntan lotion

_____Insect repellent
_____Zinc oxide (for sunburn)
_____Toilet paper
_____Space blanket
_____Binoculars
_____Nylon cord
_____Plastic bags
_____Rubber bands/ties
_____Whistle
_____Salt tablets
_____Emergency fishing gear
_____Wallet/I.D. cards
_____Dimes
_____Ripstop tape
_____Notebook & pencils
_____Field guides
_____Toothpaste
_____Dental floss
_____Mirror
_____Garbage bag
_____Book
_____Towel
_____Water purification tablets
_____Car key
_____Signal flare
_____Watch
_____Extra parts for stove, pack and tent
_____Solar still kit
_____Rubber tubing

About the Authors

Caryn Boddie is a freelance writer. Peter Boddie is a hydrologist. They live in Denver, Colorado, with their daughter, Crystal Rose. Both are avid hikers and have hiked all over Colorado, in many other states, and in Scotland.

The authors hiking in Scotland.